Dead Air

The Rise and Demise of Music Radio

Bill Young
Edited by Jan Reid

Dead Air was edited by Jan Reid -- http://janreid.net/ -- Jan has served as senior writer at Texas Monthly. He has published numerous books and contributed to Esquire, GQ, Slate, Men's Journal, Men's Health and New York Times — http://www.amazon.com/Jan-Reid/e/B001HCU8C0

Cover concept by Jesse Caesar and Dave Mahavier — Final book design by Brian Love
Book prep and layout by Robert West — Web design by Freddie Hinojosa & Butch Ewing
Initial proof-reading by Tim Manocheo — Final reading by Kendall Dunaway
— Video special projects by Scott Young —

Special thanks to Mike McBath, Steve Kelly, Sid Farbstein, Pam Berezenak, and the talented staff at Bill Young Productions© "I'm glad you guys are on my side!"

http://deadair-thebook.com/

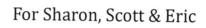
For Sharon, Scott & Eric

"Does anybody here remember radio? Anybody?"

Stan Freeberg

Chapter ONE
"IN THE BEGINNING"

It's early morning and the only sound, as I stare at a blank computer screen, comes from outside my window. The Purple Martin houses I installed for my wife a few weeks ago are finally attracting the early scouts that are just now arriving from South America. The male Martin performs aerial acrobatics hundreds of feet in the air while delivering his *'Dawnsong'* to celebrate the beginning of a season of avian copulation on a gargantuous scale.

Music is common to every part of our world. Martins and men enter and exit their life with music. It is the ultimate flow of language. Music science has demonstrated that after being introduced to a musical scale, a wrong note in the sequence will cause discomfort before a child's first birthday. Howard Gardner, renowned author and professor of Cognition and Education at Harvard, equates music intelligence to logical mathematical intelligence. Winter Wrens, Timber Wolves, Swamp Sparrows, and Humpback Whales all communicate with music. Music is hardwired into our brain and part of our genetic makeup.

I fell in love with music when I first discovered WLAC, a class-one, clear-channel, amplitude-modulated radio station, broadcasting with 50,000 watts of power from Nashville,

Tennessee. Clear channel was not a chain of radio stations back then, it was the language used to describe unique dial positions assigned by the Federal Communications Commission to only sixty-four select radio stations around the country. The original purpose of these *super-stations* was to provide coverage to areas of the U.S. where there were few if any stations at all. As a result, only three select stations in the country could broadcast from 1510 on the dial; one in Boston on the East Coast; one out Northwest in Seattle; and for those of us in the central part of the U.S. – where there were few if any stations at all.

~

It was 1955 and I had just discovered that Pat Boone's hit song 'Tutti Frutti' was the cleaned-up, sanitized, white boy's version and no comparison to the screaming, suggestive, wall-shakin' original by Little Richard. I was hooked forever!

WLAC was a parent's worst nightmare. The music was full of sexual innuendo and double-entendre' lyrics that only a very astute listener could understand, all performed by black singers. Not the Nat 'King' Cole kind of black singer, this was 'git-down, ever-thang that Uncle John needs' kind of black music.'

Every night at bedtime and much later than our parents realized, kids my age were discretely tuning the dial to 1510 and learning a whole new language. Chuck Berry, Fats Domino, Lightning Hopkins, Muddy Waters, Jimmy Reed, Etta James, and the chunky guitar sound of Bo Diddley were just some of the names that literally overnight—changed a generation.

While Nashville's WSM and its Saturday night Grand Ole' Opry was considered Mecca' for country stars, the cross-town WLAC was no less significant for white kids and black music. When the weather was right, WLAC's massive nighttime signal blanketed twenty-eight states and several foreign countries.

Because car radios had an antenna which improved reception,

I sat alone in our driveway at night in my self-customized four-door, bullet-nosed, stick-shift, fender-skirted, mean-green, fifty-three Studebaker Champion while listening to the distant drums of revolution, coming from a radio station over six hundred miles away from Lufkin, Texas. WLAC was connecting white kids to black music in a blend of culture much bigger and more complex than any of us understood.

While today's memory often fails to remember why I walked into a room, I can clearly recall - fifty years later - the names of the deejays; John R., Bill "Hoss" Allen, Herman Grizzard, and the raunchy master of double-entendre Gene Nobles along with his occasional cohort 'sterile Darrel the virgin's peril.' Even the sponsors became part of the legend - Randy's Record Shop, Ernie's Records, Royal Crown Pomade and, no joke --White Rose Petroleum Jelly.

Marlon Brando's 'The Wild One' in 1953 and James Dean's 1955 'Rebel Without a Cause' supplied the images that influenced the way we walked, talked and dressed, and prompted parents' groups to label all the changes happening as 'unclean' and 'satanic.'

It was 1957 - a magic time - in perfect sync with my raging hormones and it set in motion a passionate and rewarding lifelong fascination with music, and with music radio.

~

Prior to mid-century, music had been part of a community experience. We sang songs in church; in groups. The whole family gathered around the radio for *'Your Hit Parade'* - the popular countdown of the week's top songs. On Sunday nights, Ed Sullivan's *'Toast of the Town'* introduced the country to popular music stars as well as show tunes from Broadway. Music was part of a place and, because it was frequently performed before more than one person, it carried a level of social-connectivity.

3

As early as 1901, the Italian inventor Guglielmo Marconi had attempted to put a radio into a steam-powered automobile but since his radio took up most of the room in the car, the idea never quite caught on. Playing the radio while driving was a perfect idea however but it would be almost thirty years after Marconi's invention before it became a reality.

In 1929, Paul Gavin, after numerous failures in the storage battery business, became determined to put a workable automobile radio into production. There were a number of problems that needed to be solved; a suitable, sensitive receiver capable of working with the vehicle's inconsistent electrical supply and overcoming noise issues caused by ignition and tire-static. With help from inventor William Lear, Gavin finally developed a workable automobile radio and gave it the name 'Motorola.'

By the early fifties – new technical developments in totally separate fields came together to make music and radio more personal and changed the community that existed around it.

    * In radio--only half of the 2000 AM radio stations were affiliated with a network. That meant that many locally-owned stations were required to develop their own programming and for many of them, the solution available was cheap recorded music.

    * In records--RCA Victor developed a new seven-inch, forty-five revolutions per minute vinyl disc, and a ten disc automatic-change record player. Quickly, record labels started releasing music on 45's.

    * In jukeboxes--the larger hole in the center of the new 45's allowed multiple discs to be stacked on spindles for continuous play. Jukebox operators loaded the boxes with space-saving 45's and quadrupled the number of songs they could offer customers.

* In technology--the Texas Instrument's presentation at the 1954 Radio Engineers Convention in Dayton, Ohio stunned the audience by announcing the development of a silicon transistor. Small, portable transistor radios were soon available from T.I. and a previously unknown Japanese company named Sony.

~

Even before it became apparent to most of us, music and the technologies that changed the delivery of music was becoming more personal and portable. Radio — small, cheap and mobile offered music in places where televisions could not go. By the mid-fifties, it was common to see drivers, alone in their cars, singing along and moving to a tempo that was most likely being motivated by music on the radio.

The consumption of music had always been part of a public event; in church, a dance hall, a park on a summer afternoon or a small group of friends gathered around a radio - but overnight it seemed that music consumption became less connected and more personal. Dance partners no longer even danced together, instead moving to the beat by themselves. Dances like the Bop, Watusi and the Hully Gully--which included a still disconnected group--served to cement popular music as a uniquely personal experience.

In reality, music and the specific radio stations that delivered music, became a form of personal expression. Specific music artists became 'my' favorites, the clothes they wore and the way they talked became 'my' ways.' Even the selection of a particular radio station became part of 'my' image, with all of its cultural implications.

Music communicates in a language that zips right passed the brain and goes straight to the emotional level. Comments such as *"I don't like country"* or *"I don't like rap"* often says more about a person's self-image than it does about any deep-rooted musical bias.

In every era, pop culture is constantly re-inventing itself. Marketers, pollsters, broadcasters and new media companies spend an enormous amount of resources to understand and even take control of the many evolutions of mass culture.

~

Early in my career as a radio programmer, I began to see the audience as two distinct groups—actives and passives. An *active* was the trendsetter among his peers, the first to discover and then spread the word about new songs, clothes and trends. The *passive* listener comprised the majority, slower to change, but the group necessary to insure long-term financial success of new trends.

Actives wield enormous power, not only in their personal area of influence, but thanks to a world of rapid communication, in the larger universe of technology, language, fashion and music. An active would have been among the first to discover, and in-turn connect his peer group, to the Beatles or to Beavis & Butthead. Actives are an important audience and in many ways, they are the leaders of the universe.

As a radio program director, I knew that it was the active listener who would give my station credibility...but it was the passive universe where the larger, mass audience lived, the group big enough to drive ratings to the top. Passive listeners were loyal too, the ones who still loved Elvis even when he was releasing songs like *Kissin' Cousins* and *Do the Clam*. Passives develop long-term brand loyalty and are slower to change their hair styles, music tastes and favorite radio stations.

The problem is – actives don't stay in one place very long – they are always searching for what's next and they sometimes even get it wrong. San Francisco's 1967 Summer of Love had a huge influence on music and fashion, but most radio stations that committed their entire programming to the San Francisco sound fizzled out in a few months, same as they did with progressive-country, death-metal and techno-dance.

One thing dramatically clear in radio was that the program director, the owner or someone responsible for attracting the audience, had to think like an 'active'— but function like a 'passive.' I had to learn to walk that thin line between *"too cool for the room"* and *"too square to be rare."* It meant delivering the audience today's hottest new songs, while frantically searching for what would push it off the charts tomorrow.

~

What happened to change radio and perhaps all media? In a painful comparison, the dynamics that tracked the rise and demise of 'Top Forty' radio mirrored the career dynamics of its most celebrated personality. The Elvis Presley metamorphosis from the courteous, soft-spoken, hip-shaking' rebel from Tupelo to the overweight, zoned-out, dispassionate Las Vegas performer of twenty-two years later, closely tracks the changing cycles of popular music itself.

Near the end of the seventies, the evolution of music's public to private consumption came when Sony introduced the *'Walkman'*- a portable cassette player that effectively placed the music *'on'* a person's body. The availability of music was changing also.

In fact *'change for change's sake'* became the new addiction. We had a graphic portrait of how rapidly change would soon affect our lives in a 1984 Super Bowl half-time commercial created by Chiat/Day Advertising that introduced Apple's new Macintosh computer. The disturbing, Orwellian-type production, still considered an advertising masterpiece, showed big brother on a giant screen, lecturing a mass of matching drab-grey clad zombies. Just as the speaker yells *"We Shall Prevail,"* a young

7

woman racing toward the stage hurls a sledgehammer at the screen, exploding big brother's cultural strangle-hold into a bright-light hurricane of change. While the product changed the way people processed information—the commercial changed the way that advertisers marketed products.

Mobility, popular music, and the delivery of information had once been the exclusive advantage of radio. Today however, an angry crowd congregates on the streets in Tehran - an earthquake hits Haiti - or a friend shoots pictures at the Big Pink concert, and you download it to your cell phone seconds later. The process of acquiring music and information has become as important as the content. The definition of ownership, and particularly the transfer of that ownership, continues to keep attorneys busy, while Apple's successful iTunes store keeps creating new ways to market product. In early 2011, Apple celebrated its ten billionth App Store download. In the opinion of industry consultant Jerry Del Colliano, *"Apple may be the only communication company that understands today's audience."*

Radio ceased to be local and became a commodity run by Wall Street with decision-makers and even scripted deejays a thousand miles away from the markets they serve. Virtually no one spends time developing an audience anymore. Radio programming imploded into a variety of niches and quickly abandoned programming that was not immediately successful. The head-to-head competition between stations that once rewarded the audience with exciting options no longer exists. Richard W. Irwin, founder of reelradio.com, the web's largest collection of classic radio air checks wrote, *"the stations all belong to the man now, and the man could give a damn about radio, he just wants the profit...so what if you lose a point to your competitor? He's across the hall and you all go to the same Christmas Party."*

~

Music in the car has always been sacred ground for contemporary music stations. That changed when satellite radio suddenly offered hundreds of options with pristine clarity -- but suddenly, even those two options merged into one in 2008. By 2010, there was talk of automobiles that no longer came with a radio installed - not even a satellite radio because it "spoiled the aesthetics of the car's interior cockpit." Instead, they would be loaded with a hard drive--a huge drive--ready for the owner's own library that files the music into categories, and even—God forbid—allowed texting right there on the console.

~

Without the excitement generated by personalities such as 'the real' Don Steele or Barry Kaye, and the intense competition between broadcast entities owned by passionate owners, radio today—with few exceptions—is bland and boring. In a June 9, 2008 article in the New York Times' business section, writer Alex Mindlin reported that *"over the last 10 years, the average share of Americans listening to radio at any given time has shrunk about 14 percent, or 2.3 percentage points."*

For a time, it appeared that the music radio listener was moving to music videos on television. Don't get me wrong - I loved my MTV - but it quickly became clear that too much TV exposure burned out most of those artists. By 2009, the music channels rarely even played music videos anymore - instead airing shows like MTV's *Teen Mom* or CMT's *Mobile Home Disaster...*

Major concert tours became corporate-sponsored reruns of artists, many of whom are now eligible for Social Security. Ticket prices exploded so that an artist's most ardent fan had little chance of getting a seat down front. Instead of waiting all night in line, they now call a re-seller' (previously known as 'scalpers') rent a limo and take clients out for a big dinner before the concert. Few artists developed within the past few years will ever achieve the status of a Rolling Stones or U2 because there are simply too many actives with short-term attention-spans, and too few passives left around to make long-term commitments.

Arbitron, the radio industry's predominant rating's service, reports that today's radio audience is bigger than ever. But the basis for that claim depends upon a newly developed methodology that registers all the radio signals a person is exposed to throughout the broadcast day. This means if you are participating in the research and have lunch in a restaurant or walk through a shopping mall with radio stations playing in the background, you may be recorded as a listener to those stations. The idea for such a fuzzy connection is probably traceable to the mid-fifties when a water commissioner in Toledo, Ohio recorded a significant drop in water pressure during commercial breaks of the *I Love Lucy* television show. He originally envisioned patenting his new research method by naming it the *'flushometer'.*

~

The delivery of music content has also had a profound impact on its popularity. The world woke up one day to realize that the digital revolution had dramatically changed the recording industry. People stopped buying records anymore. They downloaded a digital music file, often swapping them with friends or people willing to share it on the internet. Instead of adapting to the new possibilities, the record industry fought it with lawsuits. As a result, only four major labels are still standing - EMI, Sony/BMG, Universal and Warner Music Group. Major artists, such as Madonna and Paul McCartney, fired their labels and signed direct deals with non-traditional retailers. Recorded music has become a marketing tool for live touring. Many hits are more focused on showcasing a new technology than creating a life-long favorite song. The touring concert business had its worst summer ever in 2010.

Albums are already a part of history and the CD boom is in major decline. According to media research company Enders Analysis, global music sales were predicted to fall to $23 billion in 2009 – half the peak of $45 million in 1997. Billboard Magazine's online Bulletin, dated June 24, 2010, bore the headline *"Album Sales Plummet to Lowest Total in Decades."* Another industry report revealed that forty percent of music purchased is older catalog items. An August 18, 2008 headline in Business Insider stated *"Wal-Mart Phasing Out Music Sales."* Since the song has become a grid of metatags, the record store no longer exists. People download just their favorite song--not the entire album.

Without each participant fulfilling their historic roles, there are less new artists that can break through the clutter. Would it even be possible for groups like Moody Blues or Genesis to get radio exposure on today's radio stations?

~

Top forty radio began because of what its owners did not have; a network to supply programming. Those stations had to experiment, to become local and had to attract listeners from their own community, and by so doing, discovered a need that resonated throughout the country, dramatically changing listener's habits one community at a time.

Just as music morphed from the old seventy-eights to a sequence of ones and zeros, change is inevitable. The story of Top 40 Radio is about more than just change in an industry however. It's about the young, passionate entrepreneurs who didn't know any better than to challenge the status quo. History is a legitimate study of how we got here - and how we will perhaps someday - get 'there.'

~

Hopefully, some things will never change; the magic to be found in the spoken word; the drama that exists in a simple

11

pause; and the amazing power of language—once heard on the radio from Stan Freeberg, Gene Shepherd, Garrison Keillor, and Paul Harvey.

Chapter TWO
"PRAISE THE LORD AND
PASS THE AMMUNITION"

War in Europe dominated the headlines on the day I was born, halfway around the world in Celeste, Texas. Nazi Germany, under Adolph Hitler, had already occupied much of Europe from Norway to Greece, while Russia's Joseph Stalin occupied the Baltic States. Britain and France had both declared war against Germany on September third and after approving a non-aggression pact between Russia and Germany, the Soviets attacked Finland on November 29, 1939.

The United States was still in the midst of the Great Depression. Life had been tough enough already since the 1929 crash of Wall Street. Fifteen million Americans were out of work, the country's gross national product had decreased by half, and now, reports of war loomed large on the world stage.

The American Dream had become a nightmare.

~

My father, William Redick Young, was born in 1917 in Honey Grove, a cotton farming community in Northeast Texas. Dad's parents later moved to a small, rented farm a few miles north of Tipton, Oklahoma.

This was a land of extremes with violent spring and early summer storms that spawned killer tornadoes, frequently sending the family to the dark, back-yard cellars that served the dual function of an underground shelter and a place to store home-canned food in a safe, dark place, free from the extreme summer heat. In 1934, the area set a new record high temperature of one hundred twenty degrees.

Summer brought the dust storms. Decades of overexpansion, poor land management and droughts from Oklahoma to the Great Plains states had stripped the native grasslands that held soil and moisture in place. The country's increasing demand for grain forced the elimination of timber which had once slowed the winds from the North Country. With turbulent clouds of dust up to two miles high and as much as a hundred miles wide, the sixty mile-per-hour winds propelled walls of valuable farmland. The dust buried homes and fences, choked farm animals and caused pneumonia and death to humans - mostly children. With cloth wedged into every crack of the doors and windows, the indoor temperatures could soar.

By late fall, frequent blue northers led by ominous walls of clouds roared in from Canada with screaming winds, and covered the area with weeks of snow and ice. In just a matter of hours, a cold front on 11/11/11 (November 11th, 1911) saw the area's temperature plunge from a record high 88° to a record low 14°. Some areas experienced tornados on Saturday and a blizzard on Sunday!

WKY in Oklahoma City became the first radio station west of the Mississippi on March 16, 1922 but since most people in rural areas did not yet own a radio receiver, weather warnings were limited to observations passed down a telegraph line, or for most - a trained eye on the sky.

On weekdays, dad walked two miles to a one-room schoolhouse

taught by a single teacher, then rushed home to hours of farm chores before he could begin his studies in the light of a kerosene lantern. He made an early decision that education would be the only way out of the challenging life his family had to endure. Surviving the devastating drought that hit Oklahoma in the early thirties sent dad south to East Texas State Teacher's College in Commerce, where his uncle Frank Young was the Dean of Men. Mowing lawns, painting houses, taking on a variety of odd jobs and sticking around for summer school allowed dad to hack out a Bachelor's degree and eventually, a teaching job at a one-room schoolhouse in nearby Tidwell, just north of Greenville, Texas.

Along the way, Dad met a young lady who became his lifelong partner. Jewel Maurine Beane was the ninth of ten children who survived from the marriage of Rufus Pittman and Cora Goode Beane. Originally from Alabama, the Beane's were cotton farmers who settled in the black-land prairie region of northeast Texas, a six-million acre region that runs roughly from the Red River in North Texas to San Antonio.

With the coming of the railroad, the tall grass native to the area gave way to the national need for cotton. The land was divided into small farms under cultivation. Like many others, the Beane family worked the land, planted and harvested the crop, sold it to the local cotton gin and gave an equal portion of the profits to the landowner, a process known as *"sharecropping."*

As the youngest girl in a family of ten, Mom had to wait her turn for the hand-me-downs that economic realities demanded. At the age of four, she and older brother Von Rhea contracted, but survived, Poliomyelitis, a contagious and devastating disease that killed thousands of children in the first half of the twentieth-century. After graduation from high school, mom enrolled in East Texas State. It was there that my parents met. Shortly after dad's graduation, Bill and Maurine became 'man and wife.' A year and a half later, I became their first-born.

~

Early radio broadcasts began as an extension of vaudeville with music and comedy acts. Radio news scarcely existed before 1937, but the words *"this is London"* changed things. Edward R. Murrow personalized World War II by describing his own feelings - *"my knees should have been strong enough to support me, but they weren't."* Reporting from bombing missions over Germany, standing on rooftops during bombing raids on London, or back in studios in New York, radio reporters like Murrow, Gabriel Heatter, Eric Sevareid, and H.V. Kaltenborn sent realistic and often dramatic word pictures back home each night and made the radio an important connection to the dangerous new world. Radio even became a weapon itself when the Soviet Union is believed to have transmitted over 600,000 watts of radio power to jam the transmissions from Radio Free Europe and BBC. For the first time in history, the sounds of war from the other side of the world were being delivered to living rooms in America and the impact of that immediacy was profound.

At 2:26 p.m. on Sunday, December 7th, 1941, WOR Radio, the Mutual Broadcast Network station in New York City, interrupted its coverage of a New York Giants - Brooklyn Dodgers football game with a surprise bulletin. It was morning in Hawaii and the US Naval Base at Pearl Harbor was under attack by the Japanese Air Force, setting off a new war front. The immediacy of radio coverage dramatically altered the speed-up of information after the bombing of Pearl Harbor.

~

Although teachers were exempt from the draft, Dad's career was put on hold in 1943 when he took a job working on the mile-long assembly line at Fort Worth's Consolidated Aircraft Corporation's manufacturing plant, one of the facilities building the giant B-24 Liberator bombers. For wages of seventy cents an hour, workers like Dad filled a role as patriotic as those in uniform. The working conditions were less than ideal, but we could live off of his single income, which meant Mom was at home with my new sister Judy and me.

We moved into the company's 'Liberator Village' housing project, situated on a high bluff overlooking Convair's plant and the Tarrant Field Air Force Base. The original village was built with white asbestos siding and some houses had open sewers, but for most of the residents it also provided their first home with running water and electricity. The rent was thirty-four dollars a month with all utility bills paid.

War is a tough concept for a kid to understand, at least from a distance. After dinner, my parents would gather as close as possible to the radio, as if proximity somehow increased their understanding of the war reports. I stayed as far away from the radio as possible; torn between the safety of my parent's presence and the childlike denial of the sounds from the next room. As much as I tried, the sounds of war were inescapable. Fear was everywhere, there on the faces of my parents in the next room; there in the strange and confusing sounds of distant static and air-raid sirens phasing in and out with snippets of voices on the radio; and it was there every few minutes when another real-world B-24 raced down the runway a half-mile from home. The almost constant roar and vibration of lumbering bombers straining to clear the rooftops of our village shook the windows, and for brief moments, drowned out the sounds of war coming from the box in our living room. Inside my four-year-old brain – it was all a constant, confusing symphony of fear.

~

Eventually, Dad returned to teaching. He accepted his first administrative job as Principal of Hollister, Oklahoma public school in the summer of 1944. We moved into a frame house across the road from the schoolhouse and during the annual wheat harvest, moved to the back-room of the town's only part-time cafe where Mom prepared lunches for the area's transient farm laborers.

Spring and early summer nights often required a rush to a neighbor's underground cellar as violent storms and tornadoes, with monsoon-like spring rains, pushed through the area known as *tornado alley*. Early warnings of storms came from the radio with afternoon forecasts from nearby KSWP in Lawton or KWFT in Wichita Falls, Texas. By nightfall, the radio signals were weak and distant with lots of static, particularly as the storms drew closer. If the storm came through after the radio station's sign-off, the intensity and frequency of dead air static still told us if the storm was getting closer or moving away. A *'hissy'* whistling sound warned us that lightening activity was nearby.

Mom, my sister, and I would huddle in the crowded cellars -- often with nearby neighbors -- while Dad and the other men held the cover door to prevent it from blowing open. Occasionally they would open it just enough to see if the storm was passing. After the storm, the increase of humidity and the decrease in temperature often set off a phenomenon called *'Tropospheric Ducting',* allowing a radio listener to tune into distant radio signals.

By summer, music on the radio merged with the addictive humming sound of a single oscillating table-top fan, the only defense against oppressive one-hundred plus temperatures from mid-afternoon into the evening. Having been born and raised in this part of the country, you would think I would have become accustomed to the heat. I never did.

~

Radio had other uses also, some not so beneficial. The

Japanese military used radio as a weapon of war. Tokyo Rose, the name given to Iva Toguri and a number of other English-speaking female broadcasters, beamed Japanese propaganda to Allied forces positioned near the enemy mainland. Rose's broadcasts attempted to discourage U.S. soldiers and sailors and even identified some of them by name and broadcast their unit's actual positions.

After demands for a Japanese surrender and dropping millions of leaflets with a warning "to the Japanese people", an executive order by President Harry S. Truman authorized the use of a nuclear bomb on the Japanese city of Hiroshima and then three days later, on Nagasaki. About an hour before the first 'atomic' bomb was dropped; radio stations in Japan issued an alert to the southern part of Japan and then signed off the air.

Those two bombs killed as many as 222,000 people, most of them civilians. At least half of them died later, after suffering from radiation poisoning, cancers and leukemia. On August 15th, six days after the final bombing, the Emperor of Japan used radio to announce that Japanese forces would not continue fighting.

~

After the end of wars in Europe and Japan, when troops started returning home from combat, the US experienced an unusual spike in birth rates. From 1946 to 1964, seventy-six million American children were born. By 1953, the country's population had grown to one hundred and fifty million people. In spite of the rapid growth however, we still knew all of our neighbors.

World War II had set off other unexpected changes in Americans' lives. The U.S. dollar became the international currency. Having actually energized the economy, the war created a virtual monopoly of American manufactured and agricultural exports that lasted well into the fifties. Many top scholars, scientists, and economists with names like Einstein and Von Braun, migrated to the U.S. from Europe.

During the war, women replaced men in traditional factories and industries and proved that they could perform most of the same jobs as their male counterparts. While many of them were required to give up their jobs to the returning men, these women had tasted independence and would soon demand a significant role in the work force. Separation of troops along ethnic lines contributed to the rise of the Civil Rights movement. The Supreme Court decreed that blacks had the right to vote.

~

Radio - the same vehicle that had brought frightening news from the war front and early reports of storms headed our way now became the primary entertainment source for the Young family. Radio introduced the country to Jackie Robinson - who broke Major League Baseball's color line and Joe Louis - whose defeats of Italian boxer Primo Carnera and Germany's Max Schmeling made him one of the most beloved American sports figures of all time. Bob Hope, Fred Allen, Charlie McCarthy, Groucho Marx, Bob & Ray and Fibber McGee & Molly kept us entertained with outrageously funny radio shows. Each program was live and new and the word "re-run" had not even been invented yet.

Even brands became famous because of their sponsorship of the most popular shows: Campbell's Soup sponsored Orson Wells' Mercury Theatre; Lum & Abner, by Quaker Oats; Bob Hope by Pepsodent Toothpaste; Your Hit Parade - presented by Lucky Strike; and Glenn Miller's Band - sponsored by Chesterfield Cigarettes. Many times, the performers themselves delivered the commercials.

~

Finally, the war was over -- the country was on the verge of the most dramatic growth period of all time -- and radio, the same box that had been the source of war news and storm warnings was about to become something very magical.

Chapter THREE
"HAPPY DAYS ARE HERE AGAIN"

Many believe World War II effectively ended the Great Depression. American industries stopped producing guns and tanks and began offering products that made peacetime life more pleasant. Millions moved out of big cities to new housing developments in what came to be known as the suburbs. Growing numbers of Americans started moving west. Population numbers soared with new births. Some immigrants came from Northern and Western Europe, but explosive numbers of immigrants started pouring into the U.S. from Latin America, Asia and Eastern Europe. Life expectancy increased from forty-seven to well past sixty years of age. There were Scout troops for the boys and Scout troops for the girls.

Radio and the developing medium of television increasingly became the way Americans stayed in touch with the world. Newspapers began a long, slow decline in circulation. Baseball was the national pastime, even though no major-league professional teams actually existed west of the Mississippi River.

> "Hello ever-body, ever-where, this is the Old Scotchman, Gordon McLendon, from high atop the press box with Liberty' Broadcasting's Game of the day"

The Western Union ticker tape machine sat silent for minutes at a time, then spat out cryptic single-word descriptions of action taking place in a major-league baseball park hundreds of miles away...

DIMAGGIO...STRIKE ... FOUL BALL ...DOUBLE

From a makeshift studio in Dallas, Texas, a former Yale graduate and interpreter for the U.S. Navy sat in an almost empty room, across the desk from an audio engineer. Using a mallet striking a grapefruit to emulate the sound of the bat hitting a baseball –four disc turntables for crowd effects – and relying on his imagination, Gordon McLendon brought professional baseball game broadcasts to fans in the western part of the U.S. He filled the silence between transmissions with descriptions of an event more exciting than reality.

> "that foul ball just missed a lady in a big fancy hat just a few rows back of the Dodger's dugout ... (bkg: *"Hot dogs, get your hotdogs"*) Nobody out – Slaughter up for the Card's, steps back into the batter's box, runner at first, pitcher starts his stretch, here's the pitch and it's--outside, ball two ... boy that was close."

Absolutely nothing was missing, even the stadium's public address announcements sounded authentic, delivered by a voice from down the hall in the reverberant, tile-walled men's restroom. By adding sportscasters Dizzy Dean and Lindsey Nelson, Gordon McLendon built a network second only to the giant Mutual Broadcasting System and delivered baseball, whose major league teams existed in the eastern half of the country, to the rest of the U.S.?

McLendon's Liberty Network was not the first to recreate baseball games; that began in the 1920s. Ronald Reagan described games from ticker-tape in Des Moines in 1932, Red Barber did it in '38 and there were others. McLendon just did it better, even sending engineers to all the different major-league parks to record the unique sound of the each home team's organist playing the National Anthem. Western Union's cost for the information feeds was as low as $25 a game and Liberty paid the league $1000 a year for the rights. McLendon then used his power of language and adherence to every detail to make his 'recreated' play-by-play games more exciting than most live-action broadcasts.

"Programs, get your programs right here."

By summer 1949, I was about to enter the fourth grade when Dad accepted the school Superintendent's position in the small community of Miller Grove, just a few miles south of Cumby in northeast Texas.

We lived in a four-room wood-framed house provided by the school district, just across the road from the schoolhouse. There was no air conditioning, so the windows stayed open from spring to early autumn. Phone service meant turning a crank one long and two short turns and then waiting for Maude Wise, the local telephone operator, to stop her peach-canning or sewing chores to walk to the system, put the headset on and after a discussion of the weather or the latest local news, connected you to the rest of the world.

Our house had a large wrap-around porch, a chicken house, and the community's first television set. The porch had a swing—a two-seater that squeaked; the chickens were Leghorns— nervous and noisy; and the TV was a Hoffman—with an Easy-Vision© green screen.

Even though dad's salary was just over $100 dollars a week, we purchased our first television set in late 1949, a year after WBAP-

TV in Fort Worth signed on as Texas' first television station. The Young family and a growing number of friends that frequently stopped by to 'just say hello', quickly fell in love this new magic gadget called television. Classic radio shows I Love Lucy, Amos and Andy, The Lone Ranger and Dragnet quickly became favorite TV programs at the Young house.

Some of those radio shows successfully made the move to television. Jack Benny's subtle facial expressions and his mastery of comedic timing played well in the new visual domain. Lucille Ball and Red Skelton also mastered the new medium to build enormous audiences. Radio's popular game show - The *Sixty Four Dollar Question* became TV's even more popular *Sixty-Four Thousand Dollar Question.*

In spite of the gee-whiz newness of television, I quickly realized that the TV versions of my favorite radio shows did not quite measure up to the pictures I had visualized in my mind. On the radio; the Lone Ranger was tall and strong – but on television; he was short and wore tight pants. Joe Friday looked like a pip-squeak and Roy Rogers' *Happy Trails* were actually just dusty old trails.

After beginnings that simply recreated popular radio shows with pictures, television shows soon began introducing new stars and new programs. Some of those initial efforts were outstanding; Gunsmoke, The Rifleman and General Electric Theatre (hosted by Ronald Reagan) became popular shows of the early to mid fifties.

~

Steve Allen began his radio career as an announcer at KOY in Phoenix and after time in the Army, returned to build successes at KFAC - Los Angeles. He moved on to Mutual Network and CBS Radio where he was heard by a national audience for the first time. Moving to WNBC-TV in New York, Allen created a local late night variety television show that became so popular that it was moved to the full network in 1954. The Tonight Show, with various hosts over the years, is still on the air.

In 1956, NBC offered Steve Allen an hour-long Sunday night prime-time comedy program that went head-to-head against the most popular franchise on television, the Ed Sullivan Show on CBS. Allen's show featured a brilliant group of comedic performers that included the jittery Don Knotts, Bill Dana-aka 'Jose Jimenez', Louis Ney as Gordon Hathaway, Foster Brooks 'the Drunk', the forgetful Tom Poston and later introduced Jonathan Winters and Tim Conway. The show created a cult following among my high school friends. The quirky show also inspired a new generation of entertainers such as Steve Martin, David Letterman and Robin Williams.

Meanwhile, the more traditional Ed Sullivan, whose variety show 'Toast of the Town' featured everything from Broadway performers to a children show's puppet mouse named Topo Gigio, began feeling the heat from Allen's increasingly popular show. Sullivan booked three different appearances by the hot new singer from Tupelo, Mississippi named Elvis Presley. CBS censors would only allow cameras to show the singer above the waist. Later, Sullivan was the first to introduce the Beatles to America's television audience.

~

American's had been reading for decades about the civil rights struggle, but seeing prejudice was very different from just hearing about prejudice. Television cameras were there when Birmingham officials used fire hoses and police dogs to disperse young black demonstrators. Cameras also showed us the first two black students' as they enrolled at the University of Alabama. We saw the massacre at Kent State and the first person to set foot on the moon. The historical impact of these events became even more profound because we watched them happen. Almost overnight, the speedup of information began changing the world.

~

Television found--or may in fact have created--a willing, addiction-prone audience. The rapid desensitization of violence in the age of television news wove back and forth between reality and fantasy—helicopters chasing a runaway driver in afternoon traffic; blood splatters on the screen in violent video games; the frame-by-frame playbacks of the assassination of a President; the hot new reality cop show or the latest car bombing in Pakistan. From 1959's *The Untouchables*, with machine guns blaring, to the modern day CSI, with grisly crime scenes and themes of incest and sadomasochism, the thin line between fact and fantasy has becoming increasingly blurred.

Many parents found it easy to park a kid on a couch in front of a television screen, prompting James P. Steyer, a professor at Stanford, to later write 'The Other Parent.' A child could sit for hours, glued to a TV screen, and never be required to think or be challenged. Some cartoons are considered quite violent and children often act out what they see.

A 2006 American Medical Association study revealed that children typically witness 32,000 murders and another 40,000 attempted murders by the time they reach the age of eighteen.

As if that was not enough bad news, the targeted advertising for most of these shows was crammed full of refined sugar-laden food advertising, which some experts believe hastened the appearance of adult-onset diabetes among children as young as twelve years of age.

~

Television's impact on radio listening was profound. By the late fifties, fifty million families owned a television and the three major networks; NBC (National Broadcasting Company), CBS (Columbia Broadcasting System) and ABC (American Broadcasting Corporation) claimed 90% of the total viewing audience.

Meanwhile, radio's revenues fell in half!

Chapter FOUR
"MY GENERATION"

In 1954, Dad's career as a school administrator took us further south to Hudson High School just west of Lufkin, Texas on State Highway 94. It was there I entered high school and came to the realization that I knew more than my parents.

Hudson was not exactly a thriving municipality; it consisted of a few classroom structures, a pre-fabricated Quonset-Hut gymnasium, and a two-pump service station across the highway from the school. A weekday drive down State Highway 94 was usually a calm, picturesque ride through giant, native Longleaf Pine forests. But on weekends, once you crossed the Neches River Bridge, things changed dramatically and business was popping!

Counties like Angelina were labeled *dry* counties because one could not lawfully sell or purchase beer or liquor. Some private clubs did exist in dry counties that were allowed to store member's bottles and gave the restaurant a way to charge a membership fee, but most people just made the short drive and crossed the bridge to the thriving package-store industry in Apple Springs, Texas.

State Highway 94 on Friday and Saturday nights was a strange place to be. We frequently had cars stopped in our front yard when a passenger urgently needed a place to relieve themselves or shed large portions of their digestive tract. There were also lots of sirens from Texas Highway Patrolmen, ambulances and wreckers speeding by each weekend.

Neither of my parents consumed alcohol, ever -- to illustrate how sheltered life was, I never saw anyone even open a can of beer until I went away to college, as a first-year ministerial student at Baylor University of all places.

Smoking however, was cool and acceptable in the fifties and even our pastor enjoyed after-dinner conversation with my dad, both breaking out their pipes and a can of Prince Albert when the ladies *retired to the kitchen chores.*

Hudson High was quite tolerant of male student and teacher smoking. In fact it provided a designated smoking area behind the Agriculture building. It was a twenty year depository of foul-smelling cigarette butts mixed with slugs of used chewing tobacco and who knows what else. My choice was Winston's.

~

It was the early stage of an explosive growth period as I neared my sixteenth birthday and I could swear that I grew from five-ten to six feet-two inches tall after Thanksgiving dinner, even though my weight stayed at a hundred fifty-five pounds. In my eleventh grade class picture, I looked like a long green-bean and all my friends wanted to know what the weather was like *'up there.'* I hated everything about my reflection in the mirror and tried all the new haircuts, like the *ducktail* -- later made famous by "Kookie", the character created by Edd Byrnes on the Sunset Strip TV show. Finally, I just cut it all off in a *'flat-top.'*

Lots of my time was spent in my room with the door closed – studying some – but mostly listening to music on the radio, which was always to loud for everyone else in the house.

My running buds were Jim Bob and Royce and sometimes, a girl named Patsy who was just as tough as the rest of us. We spent those years obsessively searching for the same things: the next hot date, the coolest new song, and the answer to how we were going to spend the rest of our lives.

~

Each October, Hudson High School loaded a bus full of high school students for the three hour drive - each way - to see Big Tex' in Big D on public school weekend at the huge State Fair of Texas. With a giant midway, Elsie the Cow, miles of junk food (including a hairy looking new treat called 'cotton candy') and free brochures on everything from new cars to color televisions, the State Fair was a day full of discovery.

For me, that first Dallas trip in the fall of 1955 also meant discovery of an exciting new kind of radio, KLIF - the Mighty 11-90 in Dallas. The music was just right, nothing but one great song after another. There were long musical jingles, singing the praises of the station. Plus there were exciting contests and terrific disc jockeys -- Bruce Hayes, Kenny Sargent, and Don Keys.

By this time, I never went anywhere without my prized Regency TR-1 transistor radio, a Christmas gift from my parents. The radio stayed on KLIF for hours that October day on the long ride to and from Dallas.

Mr. Tim Harvey, Hudson High School's principal and speech teacher, was our official chaperone on that trip to the State Fair. Mr. Harvey also served as the school's speech teacher, an area for which he became a major influence in my life. When he saw how much I loved radio, he casually mentioned that he had worked his way through college as a deejay himself. I could only dream of such a job.

Being the son of a school superintendent is not all it's cracked-up to be. When I did things that normal, bone-headed high school kids naturally do, most of my teachers would sternly remind me of how I had to set an example, being the son of Superintendent Young and all. Then I was reminded again when I arrived home that night. I hated hearing that speech. The last thing I wanted to be was a 'role model.' Mr. Harvey never reminded me.

In addition to his teaching responsibilities, Mr. Harvey also served as coach of Hudson's Drama/Debate/Speech teams. He drove our group all over East Texas to area and regional competitions. He took us to Austin where I won first place in the state's Class-A *Declamation* (oration) competition, even received a congratulations letter from Senator Lyndon Johnson to prove it. Later, Mr. Harvey taught me how to be a successful debater and 'one act play' actor, which brought awards and scholarship opportunities.

~

One of the KLIF deejays I heard on those annual trips to the State Fair was Art Nelson. Later, on my very first radio show, I tried my best to sound just like Art. He had a deep, resonate voice and the unique ability to clip his words in a gentle yet powerful way. (Art's career after KLIF included KFWB, KMPC, Los Angeles and later at WLS, Chicago.)

What I did not know at the time, was the influence this radio station in Dallas was having on the entire radio industry. Turns out, it was owned by the same person I had listened to years earlier on those Liberty Network baseball games—the Old Scotchman, Gordon McLendon.

Mr. Harvey recognized my fascination with radio and also knew that my tuition and living expenses at college were going to be a major financial hill for my family to climb. He offered – if I was so inclined – to go with me to visit the Lufkin radio stations to explore a weekend job possibility.

A week later, in November, 1956, Mr. Harvey and I met with

Darrel Yates, the owner/manager of KRBA, at their studios on Lufkin's 'Cotton Square'. Yates had owned the local 250-watt station from its inception in 1938. He was a crusty character with fiery red hair, an even redder face, and an intimidating presence. I was shaking.

KRBA had no jobs for someone without experience, but Yates said I could hang around afternoons and deliver school reports from Hudson High, information I am certain the more sophisticated Lufkin High School student body audience would find immensely exciting. A couple of months later, the night deejay had to take a week off for surgery and it became my moment.

~

That first radio show was a disaster. The afternoon disc jockey had left a stack of 45's and said it should last until sign-off at eleven p.m. He assumed of course that I would have something clever, or informative to actually say between songs which would consume a certain percentage of that time.

It's not easy to be cool and clever and capable of conversation when your heart is pounding like a sledge hammer, your mouth as dry as an Oklahoma dust storm, your hands sweating profusely and your lungs squashed into a state of hyper-ventilation. I was speechless that night, mumbling the time, the temperature, and the station's call letters and with nothing else clever to say, I just played the records. Unfortunately, the stack of forty-fives proved insufficient and disappeared by nine-thirty. Not knowing what to do otherwise, I simply signed the station off the air immediately–an hour and a half too soon. All you could hear on KRBA the rest of the evening was the crackling static sounds of *dead air*. It was not a great debut.

By the end of the week however, I was in my element, so much so that Richman Lewin, the manager of KTRE – the really big radio and TV station in town – called Mr. Harvey at school and asked if he could talk to me. After just one week on the radio, I was being recruited...and apparently, I had an agent!

~

There is no teacher better than experience. The owners of KTRE gave me time to develop, overlooking my enormous share of mistakes. Mispronouncing the name of the station's biggest client; hitting *rewind* on the tape machine instead of *forward* -- resulting in the Mayor's austere comments sounding like Woody Woodpecker's laugh in reverse; oh, and leaving the microphone switch *on* while arguing with my sister on the telephone, these were just some of the things that thankfully, never became part of my résumé.

Working beside East Texas radio personalities Hank Huggins, Boyd Porter, Royce Christenson and Hampton Keithly, whose morning *'Hamp and Eggs'* was the most listened-to show in the area, was great training for a kid just north of sixteen. That year at KTRE gave me confidence in front of a microphone. Within reason, I was allowed to choose my own music, but with frequent half-hour network shows and when celebrity speakers such as Ronald Reagan came to town, my nightly rock and roll show was frequently pre-empted. Fact is, my radio show was probably the best kept secret in town anyway.

The people who worked at KTRE were very supportive and the women in the front office immediately began trying to play cupid by introducing me to the only other high school employee on staff, a very attractive young lady from the larger Lufkin High School named Billie Sue Berkley.

~

Work until eleven o'clock every Friday and Saturday night made any social life difficult, except for meeting my best friends - Jim Bob and Royce at Read's Drive Inn after work and cruising up and down Lufkin's main drag.

Timberland Drive was the epicenter of teenage social life in Lufkin, Texas, circa 1956. The mile or so between the Panther Drive-In Theatre and the Dun Wandrin' Motel was crammed with a combination of kids, cars, and rock-and-roll on Friday and Saturday nights. The process was repeated weekly; cruisin' the drag with loud mufflers and even louder radios in cars full of guys - looking for girls doing the same thing. On Friday night, teens took total ownership of this public space.

Finally, there was a local runoff election on a certain Friday night and the radio station simulcast the vote count from KTRE-TV, negating the need for an announcer back at the radio studios. I called into the office and asked Billie Sue if she was up for a movie and maybe a burger after the show. *"Sure"*, she said, *"I'm working till 6:30 anyway so why don't you pick me up here at the studio."*

We had a great time. Billie Sue had a beautiful smile, loved to laugh and I instantly knew my friends and parents would love her also. Best of all, dating a Lufkin High School girl would improve my coolness factor at Hudson High because, well, she was a city girl and it was a well-known fact that city girls rarely dated *"hicks -- from the sticks."*

To be honest, even as a senior, I was not very comfortable around girls. Things were fine when I was in a group setting, but put me in a room with just one attractive female and I suddenly morphed into a bumbling idiot.

Somehow, Billie Sue and I connected. The last half of my senior year was the first time I had felt that close to another person. Billie Sue was a world of fun and my friends and parents instantly accepted her. We had creatively worked around our school and work schedules with late dates on Friday and Saturday nights. I would pick her up at eleven-fifteen after signing off the air and we would cruise around the drag for an hour or so, grab a malt at Read's, then go sit in front of her house or one of the back roads west of Lufkin and tune into music on the radio from WLAC.

~

My senior year, with a leadership role at school, successful wins in speech competitions, popularity with my peers (*because I played special songs for them on the radio*), and a fulfilling new friendship with Billie Sue -- all changed the fears of the future. The self-imposed isolation, alone in my room, had been replaced with a connection to friends and people who made me visualize new possibilities for my life.

As the end of our high school careers loomed closer however, I dreaded the loss of my first real relationship, but I still needed to focus on entering college. I visited the two Waco, Texas radio stations a week after graduation, knowing I would need to have a job by autumn to support room, meals and the tuition at Baylor University. KWTX had no openings, but after hearing my audition tape, WACO Radio instantly offered me a job. The only stipulation, according to the Program Director Art Holt, was that I had to report for work within two weeks. I was not prepared for the loss of that summer, but I needed the job and turned in my resignation to KTRE the next morning.

~

What I had hoped would be the summer of my life rapidly deteriorated into panicked packing, apartment hunting, and spending what short time I had with the people who had become important parts of my life. Baylor was just over two hours northwest of Lufkin and Billie Sue was headed another two hours in the opposite direction to Beaumont's Lamar Tech. We both knew that maintaining our relationship was going to be difficult, and though we planned all kinds of ways to spend time together, we knew down deep how unrealistic it would be.

The last summer evenings of '57 were bittersweet. Those weeks filled a book full of memories -- the way Billy Sue tossed her hair off to the side of her face, her soft laughter, the strange electricity I felt when she touched my hand, the tranquil summer symphony of cicadas and barred owls, reverberating through miles of dense forests along the back-roads west of Lufkin.

The music from the radio flowed through the windows and merged with the sounds of the night while WLAC's John R' scored those last few summer nights with songs like 'Sincerely' by the Moonglows ...

"Sincerely, oh-oh yes, sincerely –
'Cause I love you so dearly –
Please say you'll be mine..."

(C) 2002 Geffen Records

Chapter FIVE
"WE DON'T NEED NO EDUCATION"

WACO Radio's studios were huge and very modern. The station had built its own building after the original downtown studios in the Amicable Life Building (the first skyscraper in Texas) were destroyed in the deadly tornado that hit Waco on May 11, 1953, claiming one hundred and fourteen lives.

My first day at WACO was spent in the office of the co-owner and manager of the station, R.E. Lee Glasgow - nicknamed 'Sunshine.' Glasgow was a powerful and intimidating personality; a gruff military-styled voice and totally bald with a red face that turned even redder when he was agitated - which happened frequently. Receiving a call from his secretary Jody informing you that *"Mr. Glasgow needs to see you"* would strike fear into grown men and for a kid fresh out of high school, it was sheer terror.

The first meeting began with a bold declaration; *"Billy is a kid's name. From now on you are Bill Young on this radio station."* He then embarked on a lengthy lecture, full of homespun sage advice; *"Most people get caught up in the difficulty of making a decision. Hell boy - make yourself a damn list of your options and unless one side of the deal is immediately obvious, then flip a coin.*

Success is not about always making right decisions—it's about making the dad-gum decisions that you do make -- work."

~

The Program Director at WACO was Art Holt - a bright, energetic young man and recent graduate from the University of Texas. My original offer from Art came in a formal letter dated June 26, 1957, which offered *"$1.25 an hour for 40 hours weekly, sufficient to cover all expenses of your schooling."* I would soon learn that *'sufficient'* was a fancy word for *'poverty level.'* By the time I arrived in Waco to go to work, Art had traded positions with his college roommate, Homer Odem. Homer had previously been the Sales Manager at WACO, but he and Art simply swapped jobs.

My shift reflected my lowly status. I drove the WACO News Cruiser during the late afternoon and evening, racing around town to every fender-bender and traffic-jam. Later, I read the ten p.m. news before becoming a deejay until midnight. On Sundays, I had to sign the station on the air by 5:30 a.m. - the first six and a half hours simply running the control board for a bloc of local ministers. After a two-hour lunch break, it was back on the air with music until 6 p.m.

I had major trouble during this period of life waking up each morning - even with an alarm - so I rigged a complex configuration of the loudest clock radios, all set to go off simultaneously. On one particular Sunday morning however, the whole darned system failed. My roommate, Jerry Dickerson, woke me in a panic at 7:05 a.m. Out the door in a daze, I was even more shocked to discover that WACO was still silent - nothing but the crackling, static of dead air. I knew that on Monday -- I would have to face Glasgow.

Sure enough, when I arrived for work the next afternoon, a fire-breathing Lee Glasgow stormed into the studio and growled *"what happened yesterday?"* I told him that *"all of my clock radios were set to WACO and WACO failed to wake me."* After a moment of blank contemplation, you could see his face became redder, his breath louder and his eyes had this wild, frantic 'rolling around the room' intensity. Instead of an explosion however, he finally closed his eyes, shook his head in frustration and simply walked away.

~

The early evening deejay at WACO was Lanny Lipford, a native of Bonham, Texas. Lanny had it all; smart, funny, quick, great character voices, impeccable timing, and for a novice still short of my eighteenth birthday--a tremendous role model.

Lan always seemed to have girlfriend problems while in Waco. In fact, when I arrived at work one Friday evening, he was in a panic and pleaded to borrow my car because, well, the tires on his car were in bad shape etc. -- and he was about to lose his love of the moment, a young lady who lived in Abilene, two hours west of Waco. He simply had to borrow my car - right then! While not particularly comfortable, this was Lanny and at this point in my life, LAN was the MAN.

About nine-thirty Saturday morning, I woke to see Lanny and my roommate standing at the foot of my bed. I muttered a slightly coherent *'Hey man, see you made it.'* He answered, *'Yes I did—but your car did not.'* On the drive back to Waco, he rolled my beloved Studebaker. His injuries were minor and we would remain friends, but the call to my Dad was a difficult. I had moist eyes as I read the last rites to my smashed-up green glob of metal that afternoon.

Lanny eventually moved to Seattle and, using the air-name Lan Roberts, became the northwest's most successful morning deejay. KJR program manager Pat O'Day described him as the *"greatest morning personality in the city's history."* I learned much from Lan; how much you could actually say in seven seconds;

how to intuitively nail the correct inflection; how to back-time a record intro to the vocal; never to loan your car; and how to look cool while smoking. On December 30, 2005 - back home in Bonham, Texas - Lanny Lipford died after a long bout with lung cancer and emphysema.

~

I knew that unlimited financial support from Dad's school-salary coupled with my meager 'low-man' salary was not going to support much more than meals, class needs and gasoline to get to work. Even dating was virtually impossible because of my limited income and late-night work schedule. My roommate and I had been close friends back home in Lufkin and spent many hours cruising the streets back home, but our schedules now prevented any conversation other than passing each other on the staircase. All those stories of college parties and football and girls was, in my perspective, a mere fantasy.

Even my studies became huge mountains and my grades reflected the lack of focus. Class time always wound up with thoughts of some new intro line I was going to use that night on the air, or why my life was in such a state of confusion. On one hand, I had a life-long commitment to a higher calling but my immediate focus was on how I was going to introduce the new song from the Everly Brothers that night.

Dating was virtually out of the question with classes each afternoon until 2:30, then to work by 4 p.m until midnight. Study was relegated to late nights and frequently got shoved aside for an attempt at sleep. Even meals were usually a cheeseburger on the run. Last time I visited my parents, mom kept telling me how much weight I was losing and dad wanted to talk about why my grades were falling behind. In early high school, I was glued to the radio whenever Baylor played a big game, and now, even though the games were close by...I had lost interest.

It's midnight in Waco, just signed off the air—
       I'm hungry, alone 'n tired of this chair,
Phones stopped ringing but my head's still spinning
       from speakers with music too loud
Took a booth on the side, but as hard as I tried
       I could still feel the stares, hear the jokes...
Look at that hair, at's at kid on the air...
       sure looks funny, he ain't like most folks...

She said, 'my name's Hazel,
       what's your pleasure' she smiled?
Just crackers 'n thousand island
       and I'll check out the menu a while.
She said, 'get real', you could use a good meal.
       Bet you're not even eighteen.
Let me know when you're ready,
       bet ya got you a steady, least I did when I was a teen.

I ordered Chocolate Pie @ the Elite Downtown,
       but Hazel brought me 'chicken fried'
This ain't right, sh'said you played Elvis tonight --
       skinny kid like him, my-my
I don't have that money, she said don't be so funny
       with a wink and a hint of a frown.
Just be a good man, gotta get you a plan
       and don't forget Hazel at the Elite Downtown.

Friends don't come easy
       when you're a long way from home...
With the days gettin' shorter
       and the hours too long,
Never knew her mother but once had a lover,
       n' she hummed are you lonesome tonight,
Dreams big as mountains, nights full of tears ..
       hours of talking, relivin' the years.

I watched her drive slow by my house one day
       but I never asked her why
But all these years later I still think of Hazel
       when I smell the smell of chocolate pie.

In a life lived too fast and loves that don't last,
    she was more than a hello 'n goodbye
Taught me love w'out strings, wealth w'out things,
    and sometimes its ok to cry.

I ordered Chocolate Pie @ the Elite Downtown,
    but Hazel brought me 'chicken fried'...
"this ain't right", sh' said "Elvis came here one night,
    up here from Fort Hood, my my
He sat right over there, you know they cut all his hair,
    had me so shook up I could die...
Sho'nuff a good man calls his mom when he can
    'n signed 'love to Hazel' at the Elite Downtown

Don't know what happened or what she became -
    sad though it is, never knew her full name
After years of a lifetime, focused on fame,
    I still think of Hazel and her take on the game.
In a world full of anger in ample supply...
    she picked up the bill and just wrote "PIE."

I miss Chocolate Pie @ the Elite Downtown,
    but mostly I miss Hazel ...
Miss the way she would flirt, the curve of her skirt,
    and the sound of her laugh "my my."
I hope there's still Hazels, whose people appraisals
    build longer than five-minute friends
Share their smiles and their hurtin', love deeper than flirtin'
    and know the real value of Pi.

Chocolate Pie @ the Elite Downtown,
    but Hazel brought me 'chicken fried'...
's alright she sighed, you played my favorite tonight...
    I love 'at kid Elvis, my-my
She cried for "old shep" and laughed for 'shook up'
    as she danced with a smile in her eye!
You just chow down, get rid of that frown
    & thank God you know Hazel at the Elite Downtown.

©Bill Young 11.17.2004

43

In the summer of 1958, my parents left Lufkin when Dad accepted a new position as School Superintendent in the Northeast Texas community of Talco, which touts itself as the Asphalt Capital of the World. By the end of my freshman year, I made the decision to return to Lufkin and go back to work full-time at KTRE. I would travel to nearby Nacogdoches, Texas each morning for classes at Stephen F. Austin State College and spend afternoons on the air at KTRE.

~

Leaving Baylor, the largest Baptist-supported University, meant a decision of sorts about the big, unresolved issue in my life. At an early age, I had walked forward in the Happy Hour Church and declared to the twenty or so faithful present that my life would be devoted to the ministry. My year at Baylor convinced me that the ministry is not where I was meant to be.

A visit with an older—wiser minister suggested that I might be attempting to fulfill the dreams of my parents. In an industry that would soon make headlines for sex, drugs and rock 'n roll and a world becoming crazier by the day, I realized that my challenge was to simply live my beliefs. The incongruity between my faith and my love of rock music was only a problem if I let it be a problem. The challenge was to live my beliefs ... regardless of where my career led me. Music is an important part of our lives and thankfully, it speaks many languages. By the 90's, Christian rock songs frequently showed up in the Top 100.

I was headed home although it was no longer a home. My family had moved away, my friends were building careers and families and I had struck out in the big college world — but radio was about to change my life.

Chapter SIX
"I WANT TO GO HOME"

I returned to KTRE in June 1958. A new program director, Mark Blinoff, had moved to Texas from California and accepted his first programming position at KTRE. Mark became one of my first mentors in the business and also my neighbor in one of Lufkin's few apartment complexes.

After morning classes at Stephen F. Austin State College in nearby Nacogdoches, Texas, I rushed back to Lufkin each weekday for my three p.m. music show and at five o'clock, became part of the afternoon news block.

Mark, who used the air name Mark Kennedy, would deliver the national news and I followed with state and local information at five-fifteen. The booth announcer who delivered all the commercials was Hank Huggins, a colorful character with ten times more years in the business than Mark and I combined!

> *'Hi Hank, how are you this afternoon?'*
> *'Well Bill, I seem to be lost in the twilight of a very mediocre career.'*

Hank Huggins was a crusty sort of fellow who had worked at a long list of different radio stations throughout the South. Late in his career, it appeared he had found a home for himself at KTRE.

Hank did it all: sold advertising during the day, ran the control board and delivered commercials for the five o'clock news, then drove ten miles north of town where he would don coat and tie before delivering the local weather on KTRE's television news block. On Saturday afternoons, the Hank & Juanita Huggins Band performed live on the Saturday *Kay-Tree TV Jamboree* and often at family reunions and school barbeques in the area.

For reasons only Hank understood, his greatest joy in life seemed to be testing less experienced announcer's ability to keep a straight face while delivering serious information, such as a live newscast. Early stage actors called uncontrolled laughter *'breaking face'* while British actors call it *'corpsing.'* In Lufkin, it was called simply *'losing it.'* England's Benny Hill and Carol Burnett show's Tim Conway became famous for their ability to send fellow actors into fits of uncontrollable laughter.

Since the local news was sponsored by the area's largest funeral home, much of the news involved reading local obituaries and enumerating the deceased's many accomplishments. Because of the serious nature of such, Hank's pet project became not only insensitive but actually jeopardizing the sponsorship - and some of our jobs.

Mind you, uncontrolled laughter can be serious stuff. There are many stories in history of *'fatal hilarity'* which is death resulting from the effects of uncontrolled laughter. In 1989, Danish audiologist Ole Bentzen died while watching the movie *A Fish Called Wanda*. Greek philosopher Chrysippus died of laughter in the third century B.C. after giving wine to his donkey. Guess you had to be there to see the humor in that one.

Since Hank ran the audio board for both newscasts, he introduced each program and then read the sponsor's interspersed commercials. Oh, and each day Hank would push Mark and I to the absolute precipice of self-control.

*"Its 5 p.m. - time to giggle through the world news,
then at 5:15, we'll guffaw through the local news."*

There were very few days that Hank did not send one or both of us into a meltdown of composure. Mark and I began receiving daily memos about how the news was a serious matter and should be delivered in a professional manner. Increasingly, Station Manager Richman Lewin's interoffice directives became more intense and finally became an ultimatum. We both assured him repeatedly, in our most sincere voices that we understood the sensitivity and he could rest assured that *"blah blah blah."*

But Lewin had obviously not sent the memo to Hank!

Hank was only beginning; he had many more diabolic ways to test our limits. If the truth be known, Hank probably did not care if our jobs were in jeopardy anyway. *'Real Radio Men'* had to learn to perform, regardless of the situation.

My first defensive measure meant avoiding any visual contact with Hank whatsoever. I tried everything, once locking the studio door and sitting on the floor under the news-desk so I would not have to look at him. It did not work –

"now with the local news, here is Bill Young ... somewhere around here."

That's all it took! Believe me, I was trying everything. Using techniques learned in my high school drama class, I would *'get into character'* by focusing on the saddest, most depressing scenario imaginable. Unfortunately, even my worst life experiences were no match for Hank's madness. In the midst of my self-induced gloom – just as I would begin reading the most serious news story of the day - Hank would walk into the studio, sit down immediately across the desk, take a giant puff of his cigarette and somehow use his tongue to flip it back inside his mouth while picking up a coffee cup and pretending to take a big swallow – then flip the cigarette back out and blow smoke rings in my face, all while breaking into a devious smile and sometimes, even removing his two front teeth. No matter how hard I tried, Hank always found the right button.

The local funeral home sponsor was getting fed up with the context in which his most serious public service image was being presented. The salesman on the account was a short-term employee named Frank, a quiet man who kept to himself and was not often seen at the studios in the afternoon. Everyone on staff was aware of the news problem but no one had to deal with the sponsor's mounting disgust or suffer cancellations like the salesman assigned to the account, and that was Frank.

~

On one of the occasional days when Mark took the day off, Hank had to read the local news himself. Recognizing the opportunity, Frank took matters into his own hands and decided, once and for all, to show Hank that his conduct worked both ways. The studios were located upstairs, above the local J.C. Penny store. Frank discreetly entered the building one afternoon about five, knowing that Betty Mae Corwin, the office manger, was usually gone for the day by this time. He climbed the long stairs and walked back to the dark, empty, announcer's booth on the right side of the main control room - separated by a large glass window. Enough light bled from the control room to wash the desk in a soft, dramatic glow. Frank quietly placed a waste basket on top of the desk, climbed up on the desk opposite Hank (whose head was buried in a stack of news copy), dropped his trousers and sat down on the basket.

On this particular afternoon, Betty Mae left work a bit later than usual and had stopped by the powder room to touch up her makeup, unaware of Frank's entrance. Repeating her daily exit ritual, she walked down the hall toward the studio to let Hank know she was leaving. A soft knock on the glass caused Hank to swing left to see a sudden look of horror on Betty's face, who had just spotted Frank in all his wonder. Hank swung to the right in sync with Frank's perfect reverse-somersault with a half-twist off the table, flashing Betty Mae, Hank -- and through the magic of radio, the entire Lufkin listening audience.

There was a long period of dead air on KTRE that afternoon before Hank – once again the consummate professional - resumed the 5 o'clock news. The local funeral home cancelled all future sponsorship. Frank moved on to a new position in New Mexico. Mark Blinoff and I kept our jobs at KTRE, simply because there were no responses to the immediate search for replacements. Hank began sleeping through our newscasts.

Note: The previous described event of Mark Blinoff's checkered past obviously did not hinder his prestigious growth within the industry. He later became the highly acclaimed Program Director of KMPC, Los Angeles and in the '70s, left radio to become VP/ General Manager of Merve Griffin Productions. Later in life, Mark became an elementary school teacher.

~

In our part of the world, many my age had already chosen their mate by the end of high school. Only a few of us had hopes of a life bigger than just getting married and finding a good-paying job we could stay with for a lifetime. Already a couple of years behind most of my friends, who were already building their families, I popped the question to a very attractive newcomer to Texas from Los Angeles. Pat Snodgrass became my wife a few months later. I immediately started to take a more serious look at my future. The first step was to improve my salary status so I placed a call to the only other radio station that knew I existed. WACO in Waco needed an afternoon deejay to replace Lanny Roberts and someone to take over the role of Production Director. I said *"sure"*, took the offer of $125 per week and then started calling friends in the industry to find out what a *'production'* director actually directed.

While there were many *'firsts'* that started popping up in my life, it was my second go-round at WACO -- this time, my role included an official title. Since all the local commercials at KTRE were presented live, I had absolutely no idea what I had been hired to do. My friend Mark Blinoff had to explain to me what a *'production director'* actually produced.

~

At KTRE, the announcer on duty read the commercials *live* because there was no alternate studio to pre-record anything. The only pre-produced ads to appear on the station were those supplied by national advertisers. Lack of knowledge was never much of a deterrent however as I said *'yes'* to new challenges and then figured out the *'how'* part. A repeating pattern which became both a blessing and a curse in later life revealed itself; I had a tough time ever saying *"no."* I accepted WACO's offer and bluffed my way through the first few weeks.

~

I may have been a bit slow out of the gate in the marriage game, but I was a blazing study in my new radio production role. The work was challenging, matching the right music and sound elements to advertising scripts, and then master them onto twelve inch blank discs for on-the-air use. I loved the privacy of the production room and the luxury of time to work on voice delivery, music edits, drama, timing and all the other neat things I discovered in this new world of composing sound. The sales staff was very complimentary and, in his strange way of expressing it, so was the owner-manager Lee Glasgow.

Every local commercial on WACO had previously been created

on a quarter-inch, full-track Scully 280 tape recorder. The station had a small library of 'royalty-free' stock production music used for commercial backgrounds and soon I was actually turning out some pretty decent sounding radio ads. Since the endless-loop cartridge tape machine had not yet come to Waco, each commercial had to be transcribed to acetate discs on a large cutting lathe. This was very unforgiving; any mistake and you simply had to start over. Most of my first commercial discs had multiple X's drawn in white grease-pen through the many unusable tracks.

For me, production was always more challenging than being a deejay on-the-air because every project was different and started with a blank page. Unlike the redundancy of on-the-air work in a tight format, I had control of the project from start to finish. With only a *fact sheet* from the sales department, the script could be written and edited on-the-fly. Instead of an assembly line process, every element—script, voice, attitude, music, sound effects, processing—all of it was under the control of the producer.

WACO's production studio also had a four-track, half-inch Scully. Multi-track recording was new technology in commercial studios and previous production directors at WACO simply did not take the time to learn how to use it. It was my first experience also but I experimented with various configurations. AM radio was broadcast in mono only, so track-one could be used for music, track-two for sound effects or music changes, and I could utilize tracks three and four in a way not used before, at least not in our part of the world.

Two-voice commercials were all the rage with separate announcers alternating copy lines, giving the commercial a higher intensity level. Unfortunately, there were no extra voices around most hours, so I simply became my own second voice, bouncing alternate copy lines between tracks three and four. The technique served dual purposes; it allowed the increased energy inherent in two voice commercials that were too lengthy for one person to read in the allotted time, and it also gave me the breath capacity I needed for a full sixty-second, high-energy commercial. With the four-track recorder, I could read a line; stop the machine; rewind; switch tracks; then record the next line. By altering the intensity of my voice on some lines, even stacking two reads in unison, I had accidentally discovered a process that allowed me to harness enough breath control needed to create spots far more energetic than before. I would then mix all tracks down to the single track recorder while adding a level of audio compression and reverb before its final transfer to disk.

For all of my life, the simple act of breathing had been an issue. As a child, I had recurring bouts of intense coughing and wheezing. Doctors said I was sensitive to allergies and seasonal bugs, but it didn't stop me from attempting everything my friends were doing. I competed in sports in junior and high school, but could never quite stay up with my teammates, prompting the coaches to accuse me of not 'digging in.' By the mid-fifties, my friends and I discovered James Dean with a pack of cigarettes folded into his tee shirt, and the cool way the smoke framed Marlon Brando's pouty--bad-boy appearance in "The Wild One." I bought into the lie. It would be thirty years before a savvy doctor diagnosed a rare, genetic form of lung disease called 'Alpha One Antitrypsin Deficiency' that made smoking particularly destructive to my lungs.

~

WACO was the top station in town, I loved all the new things I was learning and the marriage was still in the honeymoon phase, but balancing the budget for two on my salary was becoming increasingly difficult, a fact my new wife occasionally pointed out to me.

Chapter SEVEN
"HAZY SHADE OF WINTER"

There were not many radio jobs around for production directors in the late fifties. Most local commercials were still delivered live by the announcer on the air. My growth in the business had to be as a more visible disc jockey, but I always found ways to spend some extra time in the production studio after the air shift.

By late 1959, I was anxious to get a major-market career going and sent out a number of audition tapes of my work to larger stations. The only offer came from Steve Shepherd, the station manager at KOIL in Omaha, Nebraska, to be the new morning drive disc jockey on the market's number one radio station. KOIL was the flagship operation for the Star Stations, owned by a man named Don Burden. His station was already showing up on a number of big-name deejay's resumes.

Omaha was the place where Todd Storz, owner of KOWH in the early fifties, is credited with introducing the first version of a programming concept that became known as *Top 40*. KOWH was enormously successful and influential, but it was a daytime-only station, meaning it had to sign off the air at local sunset.

Across town, Burden's KOIL built its own version of Top 40 and with 'round the clock' programming, eventually toppled

KOWH's dominance.

I was hired to replace Bobby Dale, who had just left to become the new morning show host on KDWB in Minneapolis. The programming genius of Crowell-Collier's chain of stations, Chuck Blore (a former McLendon programmer), would later bring Dale to the group's KEWB in San Francisco and KFWB in Los Angeles. Replacing Bobby Dale was going to be a challenge and quite candidly, I was not yet ready for morning prime-time at such an influential station. But I took the offer anyway.

~

I had never driven a car in snow before, so traveling to Omaha during the second week of January, 1960 was a frightening experience. From mid-Kansas north, my car was 'slippin' 'n 'slidin' all over the highway. I quickly learned that fast acceleration and quick braking do not work so well on ice. When Pat and I arrived, there were twenty-seven inches of snow on the yard of the basement apartment we rented in north Omaha.

We were able to pick up the KOIL radio signal about the time we crossed the Kansas/Nebraska state line. I was beginning to get really nervous for two disconnected reasons. First of course were the steep hills that were covered with ice, but the other issue was equally bothersome.

Every commercial break on KOIL had an announcement that said, *"Starting Monday, KOIL goes Western."* What was I getting into? Had I just driven eight hundred and fifty life-threatening miles from central Texas, across Oklahoma and Kansas, through ice and storm, only to find that this career changing station was switching the music format to country? The huge popularity of country music radio was still decades away. The future superstar George Strait was only seven years old, and Tim McGraw would not even be born for another seven years. I could just picture myself starting each day with Ferlin Husky and Kitty Wells. Not that I had anything against country music mind you, but you would have thought they might at least have had the decency to clue me in to the change.

As soon as we arrived in Omaha, I stopped by the KOIL studios at Aquila Court to confront manager Steve Shepherd in person. That's when I was told that my new on-the-air name was to be Bill 'Western'. I made a mental note to remember that marginally brilliant promotion idea.

~

KOIL was the entre' to the Big Time and listed on the resumes of many great talents. The Mighty 1290 appears in the early careers of Gary Owens of *Laugh In*, WFIL and KFRC's Dr. Don Rose, the future Kris Erik Stevens, Gary Gears, even WCW Wrestling announcer "Mean Gene" Okerlund. Fred Winston once shared the KOIL microphone before his long career in Chicago. Newsman Bob Benson became ABC Radio's news director. Jimmy O'Neill of TV's *Shindig* was a KOIL Good Guy, as was Roger W. Morgan and KHJ-Los Angeles's Real Don Steele. KOIL deejay Mike McCormick went on to become Program Director at WLS in Chicago. Even the man often credited with inventing the Top 40 programming format, Bill Stewart, was briefly the National Program Director of the Star Stations – the owners of KOIL.

This was going to be the start of something really big. KOIL had great deejays at the time - Sandy Jackson and Bob Wilson were outstanding talents - but Steve Brown would be the one person who changed my career. Steve was the only other person on staff my age and he had tremendous influence on my understanding of the 'production' side of radio. Just a month before I arrived, Steve joined the station as a night deejay and production director and was then quickly appointed National Program Director for the group. It was Brown's deep resonant voice that was featured on most KOIL promotional announcements.

Of all Steve's many talents, it was his unique creativity in the production room that taught me how to 'see' sound— a way to visualize voice and effects just as if they were musical notes, capable of all the varying appassionato (passion) and capriccioso (volatility). In Steve's hands, a simple music background suddenly became a scored soundtrack. He would take ordinary sounds that we are exposed to every day, and condense them, enlarge them and alter them to become huge production elements.

I would often hang around the KOIL studios at night just to watch Steve work his magic. On one occasion, he needed a powerful impact sound as the opening for a station promo but none of the typical sound library's tympanis or explosions worked to his satisfaction. Steve then wrapped splicing tape around the Ampex's capstan spindle, which effectively increased the tape speed well past its maximum fifteen inches per second speed. He then opened the return potentiometer for the tape recorder to just under feedback level and dropped the stylus onto the turntable, running at 78 rpm. The explosive impact shook the walls of the studio. In another experiment, Steve added tape slap-back echo from a second recording machine to a previously recorded voice being played backwards. By then reversing the newly recorded tape, the gushing attack of each word became a strange other-world sound. Before that moment, I had been limited by sounds and effects that pre-existed in prepackaged libraries. What I learned altered (no actually it destroyed) all the previous limits I had been taught. Long before the appearance of black boxes, such as Eventide's 1974 introduced H910 Harmonizer, Steve Brown was creating his own sounds by pushing existing technology to the limits. He crashed through every boundary - voice, music and effects - even subtle timing tweaks such as introducing a momentary pause in the middle of a production, just before all hell broke loose. The impact of watching all this combined to inspire more than a career. Pushing sound to the limits became a passion. Steve Brown's imagination was boundless, with no rules - and I watched in wonder.

The experience also taught me that a consistent, unique sound of a radio station could actually be created right there in the production room. Lots of stations played the same music and ran similar types of promotions, but with a different disc jockey interpreting all that content every three hours, a station ran the risk of being inconsistent. While music and deejays would— and should—remain the focus of the listener, it was the environment that surrounded all these elements that differentiated one station from another. I began to imagine an entirely different kind of radio station, and I wanted to prove it.

~

Omaha was a miserable three months for Pat--stuck in one small room with twenty-seven inches of snow on the ground outside. Plus, she had just told me that we were expecting. Although my ego was shattered, I was actually relieved when Steve Shepherd told me that they needed a change on the morning show. Pat and I both wanted our child to grow up near our families and I needed a place to practice all that I had learned. I placed a call to a small-market station back in East Texas that quite a few radio people were talking about—KDOK in Tyler, Texas.

The snow was melting on the morning we left Omaha and while driving out of our neighborhood. Omaha became just a brief line-item on my resume, but what I learned there was significant and had a profound influence on my career.

It was becoming apparent to both of us that marriage was not as easy as we had anticipated, but with recent news that our first child was on the way, Pat and I were excited to be headed home – closer to our families and a renewed effort to put the relationship back on track.

Chapter EIGHT
"RAMBLIN' ROSE"

Tyler, Texas was a beautiful city in 1960 and remains so today. The *Rose Capital of the World* boasted an inordinate amount of millionaires for a city of only fifty thousand residents. The soil and climate made the area a fertile center for agriculture - first cotton, then peaches and finally - roses. First grown in the 1920s, more than half of the U.S. supply of rose bushes would eventually be grown within ten miles of the city. In 1930, the nearby East Texas oil fields set off a huge economic boom. Many of the oil companies and field developers built their homes and established offices in Tyler on picturesque, brick-lined streets.

After the cold, lonely existence we had in Omaha, connection to family was important and Tyler's location was perfect. Our parents and childhood friends lived just over an hour's drive away and my favorite uncle and his family lived close-by in Tyler. Just as important was the impact the city had on my confidence. I was treated like a big city celebrity when I walked into the KDOK studios for the first time.

K-DOK was a daytime-only station. It signed on the air at 6 a.m. each morning and, depending upon local sunset each month, signed off at varying times. That same *ionosphere* issue that allowed radio stations from Nashville and Del Rio to be heard hundreds of miles away when I was a kid, also meant that many local stations around the country, such as KDOK, would have to either sign off the air at local sundown, reduce power, or 'directional-ize' their transmitter's signal coverage array. Otherwise, they would be blasted away by a more powerful distant station's nighttime signal on that same frequency.

The station was owned by the Adams family - no relation to the Addams family of mid-sixties television fame. Dana and Mary and their three sons were delightful, caring owners whose station was a family business and a true labor of love. The Program Director was Jim Brand, a bright fellow who was full of enthusiasm. For the first time in my brief career, I felt like I had found a place to call home. When Jim left the station to become Program Director of KOKE in Austin, I was offered the position and moved to the important morning drive spot on the air. Finally, I was in a situation that allowed me to experiment with all that I had learned.

~

Our son, Scott was born December 13, 1960 after twenty-one hours in the labor room. In spite of the hours of stress for Pat during delivery, bringing Scott into our home for the first time was a defining moment. He was a beautiful child and revitalized our home. Holding my son in my arms for the first time was, as it is for most new parents, an awesome and life-defining moment.

Scott quickly made it clear however, that life in the Young household would no longer exist as before. He was a terror when it came to falling asleep. He would rock back and forth in his bed for hours, making sleep difficult when I had to show up at the radio station by five-thirty each weekday morning. Eventually, Scott won the battle and pushed the bed's structural integrity past its limits. He landed wide-eyed on the mattress at 2:30 one morning with each side of the bed spread out in four opposite directions. Not a good way to wake up!

Signing on the station each weekday morning after long nights of baby eruptions 'till the wee hours of the morning' became the new reality in my life. Though otherwise healthy, our son had two episodes of what were labeled fever convulsions that - while frightening to watch - prompted doctors to reassure us that these things were fairly common and could be controlled with medication. Unfortunately, the medication made him hyperactive, particularly at bedtime. Sleep most nights came in brief and sporadic waves.

~

Programming a radio station became a significant turn in my career. With no real ratings war to contend with at that moment (it would be years before that developed in Tyler), I could concentrate on honing some 'people' skills and experiment with programming ideas.

KLIF, the powerhouse Dallas station owned by Gordon McLendon, the same baseball voice that I had listened as a boy, was within listening range. I was not above borrowing a funny joke from Jack Parr on last night's Tonight show or a perfectly timed intro to the newest Bobby Rydell song that I had just heard on KLIF. At least I plagiarized from the best which, I suggest, denoted a certain level of good judgment on my part.

But KLIF and other McLendon stations were not above listening to Tyler radio either. In fact, the McLendon stations hired numerous KDOK employees over the years - Rusty Reynolds, Art Nelson, Michael Spears, Jimmy Rabbitt, Steve Lundy, Randy Robins, John Bass, Jim Brand, Tim Tyler, Mike and Ron Selden and others – eventually including me.

John Bass, KDOK's News Director, was a Tyler native who was a music graduate of Southern Methodist University and a frequent soloist on Sunday mornings in Tyler's austere First Methodist Church choir. John's ambition was to become the world's next Wagnerian tenor. Having not, for the moment at least, achieved such a lofty calling, John became a radio newsman on KDOK. His big powerful voice shook radio speakers throughout East Texas every morning and was almost enough to keep me awake and rockin' on KDOK. The station had enough in the budget to hire one more fulltime deejay at $100 a week and a part-timer, usually a beginner in the business, for about $5 an hour.

Jack Foshee was a high school student who walked up to me at a High School Senior Sock Hop on the city's downtown square one Friday evening and asked - *"what do I have to do to become a deejay?"* Hearing his deep, resonant voice, I quickly responded --*"hoss, you just found the right way!"* We changed his air name to Steve Lundy.

Randy Robins, another native of Tyler, worked weekdays on KDOK and joined me for a brief but non-spectacular attempt to build a two-man morning show. Randy achieved later success in Dallas at KLIF, KFJZ in Ft. Worth, WQXI in Atlanta and WFIL in Philadelphia.

In spite of the low salaries, the daytime-only status and the market size, little KDOK became a nationally recognized radio proving ground. Many of its deejays would later become celebrated names in the industry. In the 1977 textbook *This Business of Radio Programming* ©, Dr. C. R. Hall wrote –

> *"Kaydock, as it was known, was a Top 40 station where a very "young" Bill Young was programming a day-timer that was sounding better than anything anywhere in the Midwest. It was a natural training school for the next generation of big time - big city radio stars."*

I never felt the call to be a teacher, but from the day I was born, I was surrounded by them. My Dad, his brother Bob, my Mom and her sister Clara, Uncles Von Rae and Edward Beane, great-uncle Dr. Frank Young, and cousin Bobby Young —all teachers. It was indeed the family business. Finally, it appeared those genes were beginning to kick in.

Since the station did not have the resources to hire experienced, trained deejays, a beginner's talent had to be developed. First, I encouraged each of them to find role models. The phrase *"good artist's copy—great artist's steal"* is a reality not often discussed, but a significant part of the careers of many beginning artists. The late Silvia Plath, a Pulitzer Prize winning poet and novelist, freely admitted that she learned to write by imitating great writers. The National Gallery of Art in Landover has a *'copyist'* program that has existed since 1941. By copying respected artists' actual paintings, thousands of beginning art students are exposed to time-tested discipline, technique and eventually— the thinking process available to them. Ray Charles, Elvis Presley and Aretha Franklin have all had enormous influence on singers who followed. Eventually, a true artist finds their own style.

I met regularly with beginning deejays to critique recorded tapes of their shows. At times, we would also study a stack of air checks of other successful deejays. We re-wound, discussed, argued, and dissected tapes containing the work of such masters as Dan Ingram, then at KBOX, later at WABC - Art Nelson at KLIF, KFWB and WLS and eventually we would add names like Rick Shaw from WQAM – George Michael at WFIL or KHJ's Real Don Steele and Robert W. Morgan. We listened, rewound, and rehearsed timings and all the subtle nuances that made each of them unique. By studying and even emulating the masters' talents and feeling their intensity - each of these deejays eventually found their own voice.

KDOK was a comfortable place to be. I had creative freedom, supportive employers, a growing reputation, a beautiful wife, a home with a new son, my first garden, and no real worry about ratings ... yet.

~

After three years of no direct competition, a full-time station in Tyler put together the right team and challenged KDOK's dominance. KGKB was a two hundred and fifty watt local frequency at 1490 - down on the less desirable right side of the radio dial. Stations on the left side of the AM spectrum usually had more coverage because of less interference from other stations, but it got a bit crowded down on the right side of the dial where most local stations were located. Then KGKB Program Director Eddie Payne and deejay Paul Williams were good air-talents themselves, but they scared the hell out us when they hired John Paul, known on the air as *Long John Silver* - the *"Bluebeard"* from the powerful WNOE in New Orleans.

Bluebeard was a rapid-fire, high-energy deejay who already had strong name recognition in Tyler since WNOE's powerful nighttime signal blanketed a large area of the southland. We were in shock that such a big name personality would show up at a 250 watt radio station in Tyler, Texas. Apparently, Bluebeard needed to quickly establish residency outside of Louisiana after filing for divorce and, according to PD Eddie Payne, accepted the job for just sixty dollars a week. Fortunately, Beard did not stay around Tyler long enough to inflict any long-term damage to KDOK.

The same FCC regulatory body that required KDOK to sign off at local sunset also forced certain stations–like KGKB–to drastically reduce or re-configure their transmitting coverage at night. This made KGKB's nighttime signal very weak and full of static in important growth areas outside the city's Loop

323. Payne came up with a clever but caustic line that reminded listeners of KDOK's daytime-only status, *"You're listening to KGKB...we don't run down at sundown!"* The slogan cut deep, but it also described the daytime-only status of KZEY, the ethnic-soul station in the market. The best response to KGKB's new slogan came when one of the Crazy K-ZEY deejays, who responded on the air, *"we may run down at sundown but at least we don't poop at the loop!"*

~

I hired Eddie Payne a few weeks later and he took over mid-days at KDOK. His style was unique and conversational with a subtle, naughty bad-boy edge. After a year on the air, Eddie received a major market job offer. My friend from Baylor days – John Borders – had left KBOX in Dallas to become Program Director at McLendon's cross-town KLIF. He called one afternoon and asked if I objected to his talking to Eddie about a move to KLIF to replace super-jock Russ Knight. I thanked him for the considerate call, told him I was proud for Eddie and to proceed with his discussions. Eddie moved to KLIF, assumed the air name Jimmy Rabbitt, and embarked on an enormously successful career that would eventually take him to top positions in Los Angeles and an ABC-FM network radio show.

~

Gordon McLendon's Texas-Triangle of stations in Dallas, San Antonio and Houston made him the major kingpen in Texas radio. While his KTSA in San Antonio had its battles with KONO and KILT in Houston was still in a dog-fight with KNUZ, Dallas' KLIF dominated much of north, east and central Texas from their first move to Top 40. KLIF seemed invincible, but a July, 1958 story buried in the business section of the Dallas Morning News was about to have a significant impact on Dallas radio and a new generation of radio programmers.

Dallas Radio Station Sold

St.Louis, Mo. (UPI)—
The Balaban group of radio and television stations Monday announced the purchase of radio station KGKO in Dallas.

KGKO, with the horrid dial position of fourteen-eighty on the AM dial and coverage that hardly reached much of the Dallas audience, was purchased by the Balaban group of stations, based in St. Louis. The company changed the call letters to KBOX and went head to head against KLIF, McLendon's fifty-thousand watt powerhouse. KBOX took the top-40 concept McLendon had introduced to Dallas and turned it—and the city—upside down!

Starting out in July 1958 with a measly 'two' share in the Hooper ratings, K-BOX began to build a passionate audience with a highly-produced, high-energy sound. By the spring of 1960, KBOX' audience had grown to a twenty-six share, just two points behind KLIF. KBOX' success also attracted the attention of radio program directors from around the country. Some checked into Dallas hotels with taping equipment in tow for days at a time, just to document every subtlety of what was being billed as *"the most exciting station in the nation!"* I was one of those who made the pilgrimage.

K-BOX's initial success was credited to the program/production genius of Bob Whitney. In Whitney's online biographical blog site, he tells the story of how he landed the influential position in Dallas. He was flying to Houston for an interview after receiving an offer to become KILT/Houston's new morning deejay. Bob had to change planes at Dallas' Love Field. Stan Kaplan, then Sales Manager for the St. Louis based Balaban group (owners of KBOX), paged him in the terminal before he boarded the flight and convinced him that, since Houston was too hot and full of mosquitoes, he should just stay right there in Dallas to become Program Director of KBOX. The sound and excitement he created at KBOX still remains one of legendary proportions. Future Program Directors Chuck Benson and later, Chuck Dunaway would see the station achieve even more growth.

Years earlier, WLAC had first introduced my generation to ethnic cool, but now, KBOX cranked up the energy with raw, bigger than life excitement. In a word, KBOX was an 'original.' Every thing on the air was a huge production, almost as if it had been spliced together in the production room. Everything was fast, everything was exciting and everything was big. The deejays sounded younger, the technical sound was brighter, and they detonated key words with a massive Fisher Space Expander *'boom-box'* reverb chamber. Weather forecasts sent the deejay into a filtered 'weather tower' but then, there were the newscasts –– yes, even the newscasts were different!

News was a mandatory part of a station's FCC programming commitment, but for a music station, news had the potential to drive younger listeners away. News was *'talk'* and too much *'talk'* stopped the flow of music. It also meant that listeners searching the dial for music would not be stopping on your radio station. To capture this listener, many stations experimented with placement of certain elements as a way of counter-programming to their competition's weaknesses. Since KLIF delivered its news on the top of the hour, KBOX's positioned it's newscasts at five minutes *'before'* the top of each hour so that it could be back to playing music, just as KLIF was beginning their top of the hour newscast...

> *"Dateline DALLAS"* (filtered newsman's voice - immediately followed by a series of rapid-fire beeps and bongs that sets the stage for the headline) *"ESCAPE FROM THE COUNTY JAIL."*

A dramatic three to four note musical stinger underscores the importance of the news story. The machine-gun delivery by the KBOX newsman continues with the busy newsroom background sounds of teletypes, beeps and phones. Some called it *"news you could dance to."*

An important element of the KBOX sound was a unit called the Mackenzie Repeater and it was probably the reason why it was so difficult to duplicate KBOX elsewhere. The ten-stack, random-access, tape-player was developed in 1955 by Louis G. MacKenzie. It was originally built for Disneyland to play random sounds during some of its rides. It was also used by television game shows to add laugh tracks and applause. The Mackenzie utilized quarter-inch magnetic tape in continuous loops. The instant start/stop capability, key to the KBOX newscasts, was accomplished by placing adhesive foil strips on the tape itself, allowing a sensor to read the beginning and end of each element. There was room for twenty different individual sounds - lasting from one second to fourteen minutes long! The unit was so significant in its contribution to the sound of KBOX that even after the introduction of cartridge machines; KBOX continued to utilize its Mackenzie.

~

The deejay lineup read like a who's-who list of the best...

6-9 a.m.—Morning drive with super-jock 'Big Daddy' Dan Ingram, who came to Dallas from New Haven. Ingram spent twenty-one years as the top-rated afternoon drive deejay at WABC.

9-12 a.m.—Hosted by my Baylor friend, John Borders, known on the air as Johnny Dark. John later moved to KLIF as program director and played an important role in my own career.

12-3 p.m.—Patrick "Aloysius" Hughes, a Tyler, Texas native, who built a long career at Kent Burkhart's WQXI and became a successful concert promoter.

3-6 p.m.—Program Director Chuck Benson, who became a national commercial voiceover. Chuck was replaced as program director by another Chuck, with the surname Dunaway.

6-10 p.m.—Bill Holley *"The Night Creature."* KBOX's coverage was very weak at night and only covered parts of the city, yet the *"Creetch"* still became one of the area's most popular radio stars.

~

Eventual Program Director Chuck Dunaway tells of a fourteen year old eighth grader named Charlie Van Dyke who hung around the KBOX studios most afternoons. Charlie was just a kid with a surprisingly mature voice. Officially, he was called KBOX's "eighth-grade high school correspondent." Chuck says his mom would call every afternoon when it was time for Charlie to come home. With little actual experience, Charlie was told he was 'too young' to work at KBOX, so he went elsewhere. While still a teenager, he became the top-rated afternoon drive disc jockey at McLendon's KLIF. Charlie's remarkable career both on/and off the air, eventually took him to top stations; in Windsor at CKLW, WLS-Chicago, RKO's KHJ-Los Angeles, KFRC-San Francisco and WRKO in Boston. Charlie Van Dyke has also become the most successful TV voiceover talent in the country.

KBOX validated—in a very dramatic fashion—the lessons I had first learned while sitting in an Omaha production studio watching Steve Brown do his magic. It was the locked-in, produced elements and hot-clock consistency that was the thread that defined a station's sound. The contest promos, the top of the hour ID's, the news openings, the *Pick Hit of the*

Week intro—all created in the production room—surrounded the deejays in a huge, adrenalin-pumping environment. Having originally focused just on a deejay's talent, I came to realize that when those super-jocks left for greener pastures, the sound of the station changed. Talent matters, but the audience deserves to always–regardless of the hour–hear the station they chose. KBOX taught me the importance of consistency.

~

Tyler, Texas was not exactly considered a major market for the concert touring industry. In fact, in my five and a half years in the city, we only ran commercial ads for one single Tyler area event, but that's all it took for me.

Chuck Berry, nearing the end of a string of hits during the mid-fifties, was booked to come to Tyler in 1958 by Pat Hughes, a Tyler native and one of those deejays at KBOX. I had built a friendship with *Aloysius* (as he called himself on the air) and he phoned me to see if we would run commercials for the event on KDOK in return for receiving sponsorship billing. Once he said that 'he' would be the voice of the commercials, we jumped at the chance to have just a taste of the KBOX sound on KDOK.

Such sponsorship arrangements with concert producers were common practice since it gave the radio station exclusive promotional ownership of the event, while giving the promoter a top station to promote the event.

Chuck Berry was booked to play a city-owned venue near downtown that could host about two hundred people for a dance/concert. The show was a total sellout of mostly students from Tyler Junior College. The event was exciting although I became worried about possible negative reaction from graphic lyrics in the live versions of many of Chuck's hits.

Suggestive lyrics did not begin with rock music – in fact, Louis Armstrong's recording of the 1930's – *Body and Soul*, from the

Broadway revue *Three's a Crowd*, was banned from radio play. Rosemary Clooney's hit song *Mambo Italiano* and even Cole Porter's *Love for Sale* were all banned from radio. By the early sixties, double-entendre' song lyrics seemed to be a precursor to success for some artists. If you listened really closely; maybe even changed the speed or played the record backwards, you might hear really shocking things. The Kingsmen's controversial 'Louie Louie' survived for years with an incoherent vocal that was supposedly chocked full of smutty lyrics.

Some of Chuck Berry's *revised* lyrics were blatantly sexual however and not at all difficult to understand:

> *"We did it in the kitchen, we did it in the hall ...*
> *I got some on my finger and I smeared it on the wall ...*
> *And we rolled - reelin' and a rockin"*

I knew that by Monday morning, after the Adams family arrived at the studio to find a stack of complaints, my judgment would be under review.

But nada - not one single complaint!

~

Ultimately the most memorable thing about that concert was Pat Hughes' commercial. It was big and full of super high-energy, more so than any produced radio ad I had heard before. That one commercial merged with the no-limits manipulation of sound that I had learned from Steve Brown in Omaha and inspired a career path that would eventually allow my work, and the work of those I –in turn– influenced, to be heard for the next fifty years and counting!

Chapter NINE
"THE SOUND OF SILENCE"

In most ways, November 22, 1963 started out as a normal Friday. A light rain fell that morning but the weather was clearing when I signed off the air at 10 a.m. I started pulling together a mountain of commercial scripts to record before the weekend. John Bass' top news story of the morning had included President John F. Kennedy's remarks at a breakfast meeting in Fort Worth. The president and his popular wife Jackie's visit to Texas was scheduled to conclude ninety miles away in Dallas after a noon speech at the World Trade Center. A full-page advertisement in that day's Dallas Morning News asked why Kennedy had allowed *"thousands of Cubans to be jailed and wheat sold to those who were killing American's in Vietnam."* The president was quoted that morning as telling his wife *"we're heading into nut country today."*

The political climate in Dallas and nearby Tyler in the early sixties spawned a number of politically active groups, including the ultra-conservative John Birch Society. Texas native General Edwin A. Walker, a commander of troops in Germany and Korea, had become a controversial and outspoken anti-communist. Walker was accused of distributing right-wing John Birch literature to his troops and initiating an anti-communist indoctrination program called 'Pro-Blue.' After being relieved of his command, General Walker resigned the Army in November, 1961 and became an outspoken organizer of protests against what he termed *"definitely pink"* political figures. According to the Warren Commission Report, an attempted assassination of Walker was believed to have been made by Lee Harvey Oswald seven months prior to Kennedy's visit to Dallas.

Earlier that morning from Love Field, KLIF News Director Joe Long reported live, awaiting the arrival of Air Force One. In his remarks, Long said *"the President is entering the heart of a real political tempest today."* Prior to the visit, Dallas city officials voiced concern about the negative way the city was being perceived in national press. Local television editorials were touting Kennedy's visit as an opportunity to show the world that Dallas was a modern, thriving city on the move. KRLD radio posted reporter Bob Huffaker downtown at Main & Akard to describe the President's motorcade. It was an enthusiastic broadcast, with horns and cheers from thousands of office workers on lunch break. After the motorcade passed his location, Bob's effusive comments about the crowd's response set a different tone to the President's arrival. He then sent the broadcast back the KRLD studios and a *"return to its regularly scheduled broadcast – Back to the Bible."*

Back in Tyler, KDOK's John Bass had just delivered the 12:30 half-hour headlines and I was in the next-door production studio working on scripts for commercials that needed to be produced that afternoon. John suggested we grab a quick lunch on the first floor of the People's Bank Building, where the KDOK studios were located. Manager Dana Adams usually had lunch with a client, so Mary Lou Elrod, the receptionist and Roby Morgan, the engineer joined us downstairs for a quick lunch. Eddie Payne was the deejay on the air and said that he would cover the phone while the rest of us headed downstairs. Less than a minute after we left, the Associated Press teletype machine started ringing, non-stop - a rare ten–bell signal indicating that a major news story was being transmitted. Most of us had never heard this sound before. Eddie started calling for help, but there was no one left in the offices. He rushed to the teletype just as the Associated Press machine printed the first bulletin:

"DALLAS AP - President Kennedy was shot today as his motorcade left downtown Dallas. Mrs. Kennedy jumped up and grabbed Mr. Kennedy. She cried, 'Oh, no' as the motorcade sped on." (Associated Press)

Nine stories below, John, Robey, Mary Lou and I had just stepped off the elevator on the ground floor and immediately heard Eddie's bulletin on the deli's radio. We quickly ran back to the elevators, now full of lunch crowd workers and stopping on every floor. We ran for the stairs.

At KLIF in Dallas, a news alert sounder had interrupted the Chiffon's hit *"I Have a Boyfriend"* at 12:39 p.m. during the Rex Jones Show on KLIF and newsman Gary DeLaune delivered the first bulletin, *"This KLIF Bulletin from Dallas - three shots reportedly were fired at the motorcade of President Kennedy today near the downtown section. KLIF News is checking out the report, we will have further reports, stay tuned."* The music resumed.

Radio stations around the country reacted quickly. In Cincinnati, WLW stopped music at 1:36:50 EST --*"We'll have to stand by here just a moment, there may be something...yes, there is, there's a bulletin just handed me from Dallas, Texas..."*

ABC Radio News headquarters in New York broke into Doris Day's *'Hooray for Hollywood'* at the same time -- *"Here is a special bulletin from Dallas, Texas. Three shots were fired at President*

Kennedy's motorcade today in downtown Dallas, Texas..."

~

As best our small staff could do with limited resources, we reported the events taking place that afternoon just ninety-five miles away at Dallas' Parkland Hospital. Some of the staff crowded around the only television set in the office, watching KRLD TV, the CBS outlet in Dallas. The station's Eddie Barker had been awaiting the President's arrival at the Dallas Trade Center. Since the Center was just across the freeway from Parkland Hospital, Barker appeared frequently in Walter Cronkite's network bulletins from CBS studios in New York. Our own AP wire and monitoring Dallas television stations continuously fed breaking information - some of it unconfirmed.

In Dallas, KLIF's Gordon McLendon rushed back to the studios from the Trade Center where he had been awaiting the President's arrival and joined News Director Joe Long who was calling in all of their local resources for information. At 1:38 p.m., just as McLendon started speaking on the microphone, the AP teletype machine again sounded ten bells in the background. You could hear the hesitations in McLendon's voice as he ad-libbed, waiting for the completion of the latest Associated Press bulletin -

> Gordon McLendon: *"The President is clearly, gravely ... critically, and perhaps fatally wounded. There are ... strong indications that he may already have expired, although that is not official - we repeat - not official. But...the extent...of the injuries to Governor Connally is, uh...uh, a closely shrouded secret at the moment..."*
>
> KLIF News Director Joe Long interrupted, almost whispering to McLendon: *"President Kennedy is dead, Gordon. This is official word."*

Gordon McLendon: *"Ladies and gentlemen, the President is dead. The President, ladies and gentlemen, is dead at Parkland Hospital in Dallas."*

By mid-afternoon, President Kennedy's casket was loaded onto Air Force One while Vice President Lyndon Johnson was quickly sworn in as the new President. Lee Harvey Oswald, an employee of the School Book Depository - a building next to the President's motorcade - was arrested eighty minutes later after killing a Dallas Police officer in the nearby Oak Cliff area of Dallas. News of the suspect's history competed with the planning of a state funeral in Washington on weekend newscasts.

~

It was difficult to decide what direction our programming should take that weekend. I knew that a significant number of Tyler residents would be tuned to Dallas TV stations with much larger news departments––yet it seemed inappropriate to resume normal pop music broadcasting. Because our weekend staff included a number of part-timers with little experience, I spent many hours on the air that weekend.

On Sunday morning, November 24th at 11:25 a.m., during KDOK's broadcast of the Sunday morning services from Tyler's Marvin United Methodist Church, the Associated Press wire again pre-signaled a major news story––just as a call from my wife alerted me to turn on the television.

While being transferred from the Dallas Police headquarters to a different interrogation office, local strip-club manager Jack Ruby walked into the loading ramp at Police Headquarters and in front of numerous police officers and a bank of photographers -- shot and killed the assassination's prime suspect, Lee Harvey Oswald. Alone in the studios that morning, I stood in front of the television monitor in total disbelief, confused and saddened by the events and wondering how I should handle this latest development.

My decision as to whether to interrupt the live church broadcast was difficult, just as many other decisions had been that weekend. I made the snap judgment that ample numbers of news services were adequately covering the breaking news and listeners to a church service had made that choice consciously - perhaps even as a needed escape from the week's violent news. I waited until the end of the broadcast before airing the story. It was weeks before radio stations in the area would comfortably resume typical programming.

Chapter TEN
"THE LAST ROSE OF SUMMER"

More and more of my time was being spent in the production studio, recording commercials and station promotions for KDOK itself, but also filling requests to produce similar promos for other stations. With the help of KDOK's big-voiced morning newsman, John Bass, we started marketing recorded ID's and Promos for other stations under the name 'Dynamic Promotions'. We were soon represented by one of the well-known Dallas jingle houses and the work load increased.

For the next few years, life settled into a predictable, but physically challenging period. We purchased a small home on a large lot in the northern part of Tyler. Even though I had hated work in the garden as a teen, I suddenly discovered the rewards of planting and watching vegetables grow.

Our son, Scott, brought a new level of joy into our lives, but signing the station on the air at six every morning after frequent baby eruptions during the night; assuming a full workday of programming responsibilities with only one other full-time staff member; then returning to the studio until late most nights to fill Dynamic Production's orders, was beginning to take a major toll on me, physically and emotionally.

In the midst of a visit to our family doctor's office with a case of the flu, everything in my life suddenly crashed around me. The room was spinning, I was gasping for air, could not swallow, and my hands were shaking uncontrollably. After I calmed down, the doctor described it as a *panic attack*, but at that moment it felt like the world was coming to an end. In anticipation of a repeat, the days following the episode did not get much better.

The Doctor prescribed the medication Meprobamate, marketed under the brand name *Miltown* - the first blockbuster psychotropic drug in American history. The literature, that would years later be required for such prescriptions, labeled it as *"a tranquilizer used in the treatment of anxiety disorders and for short-term relief of the symptoms of anxiety."* The small print, not usually given to patients then, also mentioned that *Miltown "could be habit-forming."* Perhaps I should have asked about reactions or the doctor should have mentioned the long-term issue or monitored my prescriptions, but neither of us took the responsibility. Looking back on the events of that period, I suspect that I became dependent upon *Miltown*. By 1967, Meprobamate was placed under abuse control amendments to the FDC Act, and limits were placed on prescription duration and refills.

After close to a year of living in a foggy disconnect with life - I awoke one morning to the same problems, the same fears and the same ineffective pill box waiting to mask reality. In a moment of frustration and certainly not the physician's recommendation - I flushed the remaining pills down the drain and made the decision to face the world just as it existed. I loved my work but I wanted to love my life again also. I resigned my job at KDOK and accepted the Program Director's position back at WACO, my third go-round at the station. Even though our marriage was at its lowest point, Pat made the decision to make the move to Waco also.

Small market radio in Tyler, Texas had provided my career with five and a half years of relatively pressure-free experience, wonderful people to work with, developing raw talent and a bit of recognition in some influential circles — but it was time to face the personal issues in my life as well.

Chapter ELEVEN
"CROSS THE BRAZOS AT WACO"

For the third time in my eight-year radio career, I was headed back to Waco -- the Texas town that got lost somewhere between Dallas/Fort Worth and Austin. Waco rarely made front page news except for a killer tornado that virtually destroyed its downtown in 1953, and forty years later when the self-proclaimed prophet David Koresh and seventy-six of his Branch Davidians' died in flames after a fifty-one day standoff in nearby Mount Carmel. The city and its surrounding area served as home of the Baylor Bears, the Texas Rangers Museum, George W's nearby Texas White House and home for Ted Nugent, the Motor City madman.

At least this time at WACO, I had a management level title – Program Director. Winning back the top ratings for the station would, in my opinion, actually be quite simple if I could convince the owner to make some difficult decisions.

The station had all the right elements in place, a long history of quality programming, locally known personalities, a great news department, Paul Harvey (the very popular ABC Radio news commentator), and the best call letters in the country -- in fact the only radio station whose call letters spelled out the name of its home town. The problem was simple, WACO was too successful. It aired far too many commercials to sustain high average quarter hour audiences. The competition was killing us with the amount of positive program elements each hour.

The pricing of commercial time is much more sophisticated in today's radio. Using computerized research information, a station can adjust its rates almost daily based on a variety of factors, such as availability of air time, ratings changes, etc. Fixed position ads - those that are guaranteed to run at a specific time - are sold at a higher premium than the ROS (run of schedule) ads, which can be slotted anywhere within a specific day part. ROS spots are less expensive, but an advertiser may miss the maximum audience available during peak listening periods, such as morning rush hour. As demand increases- rates also increase, and in fact, the lower-priced availabilities may even be eliminated if enough fixed position ads are sold.

In 1964, convincing a sales staff, whose personal income was dependent upon their sales' commissions, to sell less ads would usually require them to call advertisers to discuss those horrible double-R words...Raising Rates! Making those calls to clients was uncomfortable for most sales personnel and in this case, meant they would have to convince the client to *"ignore those last ratings when we got our butts kicked, because we are now raising your rates so we can run fewer commercials and then yes, if the ratings do go up we will probably be raising your rates again!"* I could understand the problem, but that's why they called them *'sales-people.'*

Owner/Manager Lee Glasgow assured me he would do what it took to win back the ratings and he was true to his word. WACO's numbers bounced back stronger than before and – voila - there was even more revenue coming in!

We made a down payment on a new home in a development of flat pasture land near Lake Waco. The three-bedroom home came with a brand new Chinese Tallow tree in the front yard. Tallow trees were the rage among the get-in and get-out quick developers because of their rapid growth habit. Years later, the imported tree would prove to be a major invasive problem, aggressively taking over large areas of the South. But at that moment, we had a nice little shade tree in the front yard and that's all we needed to know. Scott was nearing three years of age and had a small back yard to play in. Pat took a job as bridal consultant at Goldstein-Miguel, the upscale women's clothing store in the nearby Lake Air shopping mall.

My salary had grown to $175 a week and we purchased, on credit, a bright new '65 Plymouth Fury. Life seemed to be settling into a comfortable routine.

WACO was sounding better than ever. I hired a young weekend deejay from Denver named Lee Randall to take over nights and soon, the younger demographics, so important to Top-40 radio's success, returned to WACO.

During my stay in Waco, I met one of my radio idols. Paul Harvey, the ABC radio news commentator, came to town to speak to a large meeting and originated his noon broadcast from the WACO studios. Listening to Paul Harvey on the air was an education for many of us in the industry, but watching him on the air was a special gift. Harvey's timing was always precise and his pauses often appeared to be an 'opinion' of a particular story. Many of those pauses, that I had always considered to be masterful strokes of drama, actually occurred while he was re-arranging the order of his stack of self-written stories.

One of the most unique qualities of Harvey was his ability to transition from serious news to commercials. While I cannot imagine a Walter Cronkite or Edward R. Murrow interrupting a newscast to deliver a commercial, Harvey did it flawlessly. In fact, his audience not only accepted the incongruity, they placed tremendous trust in his recommendations. Paul Harvey only promoted products he and his wife used, he wrote his own advertising copy and he required at least a one year commitment from each advertiser -- once thanking a sponsor for *'putting their money where his mouth is.'*

Mr. Harvey was a delightful gentleman who started each day of his seven decade career at 3:30 a.m., rewriting each news story on his standard typewriter. My lasting impression was of his smile and the courteous way he made each fan feel special, even those that probably interrupted his work just to shake his hand. Paul Harvey died in Phoenix on February 28th, 2009 at the age of ninety.

~

It was a year or so later and 'the call' came into the studio during the noon news. *"Johnny is on the phone,"* the secretary said. John Borders was, by that time, the Program Director at KLIF, the powerhouse Gordon McLendon station in Dallas. I had first met John years before during my first job as night deejay at WACO. When I left WACO to return home to Lufkin, I recommended Johnny to be my replacement. His time at WACO served as the launching pad for his own radio career as deejay, program director and eventually, a successful owner of radio stations. I answered the call from my friend.

> BY: *"Hey John, what's up?"*
> JB: *"Young, how would you like to be the program-director of KILT?"*
> BY: *"What? Johnny -- you gotta be kidding!"*

In 1957, my senior year at Hudson High School, I had been elected President of the student body and, along with the other officers and chaperons, headed to Galveston's Jack Tar Hotel for the annual Texas Student Council Convention. KILT, owned by Gordon McLendon, had just become the top rated station in nearby Houston after one of its deejays sat on a flag pole for thirty days until the station became number one in the Hooper Ratings. KILT completed McLendon's Texas Triangle of stations that already included KLIF in Dallas and KTSA in San Antonio. These were all adrenaline-pumping stations with great talent, but, for me, there was a certain *funky* quality about KILT that did not exist in the others. It was more soulful, gutsier and more in-sync with my student body presidential tastes. I could not turn the radio off of KILT that weekend.

~

> JB: *"You're going to get a call this afternoon from Bob White, the current program director at KILT and he's going to ask you to submit a tape for the new deejay opening in the noon to three slot."'*
> BY: *"Uh Johnny, you know I don't want to be a jock anymore, I love programming."*
> JB: *"I know, I know-- Young, just listen, send him the tape and don't ask questions!"*
> BY: *"OK... whatever you say."*

Just as predicted, I received the call from Program Director Bob White a half hour later. He was a pleasant fellow who said the station was losing Bob Presley, the noon-three deejay, and my name came up as a possible replacement. I sent the tape.

~

Two days later, Bob called again and offered me the position. I verbally danced around for a moment, finally telling him that I was not sure I wanted to get out of programming.

> BY: (to self) *"Dammit Borders, what are you doing to me?"*

Twenty minutes later, John called with instructions to phone Bill Weaver, the General Manager of KILT, at his home that evening. I wrote down the number and felt a momentary twinge of guilt, knowing I just had fallen into a very uncomfortable situation, but then again, the possibility of being Program Director of a Gordon McLendon radio station! I made the call.

~

On Sunday morning, I arrived at Weaver's home in Valley Lodge, west of Houston. Bill had been a top executive with the McLendons from their first radio station in Palestine, Texas. His role with the company had been similar to a management gadfly, having managed KLIF, KTSA, company properties in Chicago and Milwaukee, McLendon's venture into international waters with Radio Nord (a pirate ship broadcasting off the coast of Sweden) and since the company's acquisition of KILT, the station's only General Manager.

Weaver was a tough, no-bull military man, having served under Generals George Patton and Mark Clark during WWII. His service time included six Battle Stars and a Bronze Star for Heroic Achievement in combat. Smart too, graduated Magna Cum Laude from the University of Texas after his military career. Bill appeared intimidating at first, but he had done his homework on my career and I told him I would let him know about the offer by the following Friday.

My enthusiasm lasted for about five minutes after my wife and I started the drive home to Waco. Pat did not mince words--*"I'm not moving."* Growing up in a strict Southern Baptist home, I had been taught that marriage could not be *'torn asunder.'* There was already enough trauma in my life with a tenuous marriage and a four year old fighting various health issues. I wanted this job, but I was not prepared to abandon my responsibility as a parent.

On Tuesday afternoon, I made a tough call and declined the

offer at KILT. Weaver said he would hold the job open until the weekend. I thanked him, but said it was highly unlikely.

My parents always talked of a master plan in life, but at the moment, I felt very confused. My one chance of fulfilling a lifetime dream had just dissolved. I had one close confidante at the radio station, Lee Randall - the nighttime deejay. Upon hearing the news, Lee appeared to be even more upset than I about the decision. He had some harsh words about the reasoning for my decision, but I assured him that family was more important and there would be other opportunities.

It was a tough couple of days on the air. All of us in the business for any length of time understand the importance of always sounding 'up', even when the world is falling-in around us. The audience had their own set of problems; our job was to be consistent. Some, such as Chuck Dunaway, were always capable of being professional, regardless of issues that might be out-of-whack at that moment in his life.

Lee seemed to be more disappointed about the decision than I -- in fact he was royally pissed! I learned weeks later that he left the studio after our conversation; drove to the fancy clothing store where my wife worked; stormed inside and publically suggested she was about to destroy a world-class opportunity.

That night at home, Pat said she had changed her mind about the move. I was in shock. Friday morning, I made the call to Weaver, telling him that I had changed my mind and decided to take the position. He informed me that, *"just minutes before"*, he had hired someone from San Antonio, but then he hesitated and asked if he could call me back. The phone rang in two minutes and Weaver said, *"I un-hired him, how quick can you get here?"*

~

Conflicting waves of emotions rushed to the surface. Psychologist Robert Plutchik proposed that there is a basic set of emotions that all people experience. His emotion wheel demonstrates the relationship between opposites––Joy/Sadness – Anticipation/Surprise – Anger/Fear - Confidence/Insecurity. My emotions were spinning out of control.

~

Weaver mentioned that he wanted to hold off making an announcement until Monday and I assured him that I could wait to make it public on my end. I hung up the phone but within minutes, Chuck Dunaway--then afternoon-drive deejay at KILT--called to congratulate me. Ten minutes later, then Houston record promoter Bill Ham phoned after hearing the news. Before evening, I was taking calls from radio and music names I had only read about. So much for secrets in the big city!

Chapter TWELVE
"FROM THE BEGINNING"

Pat and I drove to Houston in late January to look for a new home. Some friends in-the-know suggested we begin our search among the new developments in the southwest area of the city. It was a slow process because of our not knowing the city well and fighting more traffic than I had ever encountered. It would take two exhausting days to find the right house, a newly constructed three bedroom in the Sharpstown area. We submitted a deposit and headed back to Waco. A tough call a few days later informed me that our stellar credit rating would not qualify us for the house, so we found ourselves back at ground zero. It was back to Houston for a repeat the following weekend.

During those drives to and from Houston, I listened to all the local stations, familiarizing myself with KILT and the competition. In my initial meeting with Bill Weaver, he talked of how, with exception of consistent winning afternoon drive-time ratings from Chuck Dunaway, the overall numbers kept bouncing back and forth between KILT and its primary competitor, KNUZ.

In the late fifties, Weaver had attempted to hire KNUZ deejay Paul Berlin, the most popular personality in the city. Rumor had it that the week-long bidding war between the two stations was fierce before Berlin decided to stay at KNUZ. The station's other personalities; Arch Yancy and Joe Ford were also formidable competitors.

~

One thing of concern as I listened to KILT was that I did not recognize much of the music being played. Back at WACO, we adhered to a playlist that reflected the Billboard Top 100 weekly list of national hits, but with the exception of Nancy Sinatra's *'These Boots are Made for Walking'* -- which was number one on Billboard that week -- I was un-familiar with most of the music being played on KILT. I made a note to check out the reasoning as soon as I landed on site.

It happens in our industry, effort and success are often disconnected. Many talented people eventually leave radio for careers with a more predictable effort-to-reward ratio. Some in our line of work achieve superstar status in markets of millions, while others become big fish in small ponds. Many just give up and get a real job while a few find their voice in ways they never imagined when starting out.

After a move to Sacramento, California, an up-state Pennsylvania deejay using the air-name Jeff Christie became the successful talk show host Rush Limbaugh, while a naughty, raucous Morning Zoo deejay in Corpus Christi, Texas morphed into the teary values champion Glenn Beck. Both of them took the precursors of controversial talk radio – Joe Pine at WILM in Wilmington, Delaware in the early 50s, and the early 80's Morton Downey, Jr. at KFBK in Sacramento -- and turned political talk radio into enormous franchises.

~

I had no history with Houston and I also knew that no one would be given unlimited time to connect with the audience. Big city radio's primary objective was profit. I had to get this station moving quickly. The last days in Waco involved a crash study about Houston.

Beginning its existence as a small backwater settlement, *Houston Town*, as it was originally named, was founded in 1836 by two real estate investors, John and Augustus Allen. After the civil war, immigrants, including newly freed slaves and displaced Mexicans, started flooding the city.

Oil exploded out of previously considered wasteland at Spindletop in nearby Beaumont on January 10, 1901, the single find tripled the entire oil production capability of the United States. By 1913, Houston had everything the oil industry needed; access to the Gulf for shipping; a growing labor force; and no shortage of lawyers, all of whom claimed expertise in the intricate issues unique to the oil business. On November 10th, 1914, President Woodrow Wilson sealed the deal of the area's bright future when he officially opened the Port of Houston, a fifty-mile long dredged shipping channel through the shallow Galveston Bay to the Gulf of Mexico.

Texas oil millionaires fought hard to demand and maintain tax concessions. The most important of these was the oil depletion allowance, allowing oil producers to deduct 19% off the cost of their original investment -- a tax break unprecedented in American business. The emergence of powerful politicians, John Nance Garner and Sam Rayburn in the House and Lyndon Johnson in the Senate, insured that the special tax breaks would remain in place for decades.

By mid-century, a new generation of visionary with far more ambition than the Allen brothers ever dreamed, began building a massive infrastructure. World class medical facilities evolved on land contributed by petroleum philanthropists. Names like Cullen, Fondren, and Menil started showing up on hospitals, museums and universities. Baylor College of Medicine and UT

Health Science Center quickly earned world-wide respect as major research centers and MD Anderson was on the path to become the most respected cancer center in the world.

Rice Institute, University of Houston, Texas Southern University, and St. Thomas became respected educational centers, and just down the road in Kemah, the LBJ Space Center became home to the Astronauts and the US Space Program.

But nothing compared to the huge dreams of 'the judge'. Initially billed as the Eighth Wonder of the World, the Houston Astrodome - the singular vision of Roy Hofheinz, a flamboyant former radio station owner, Harris County judge and Houston Mayor - defied the skeptics. 'The Dome' became the first fully air-conditioned baseball park with a roof over the top. The Astrodome had everything...even rain delays when the air conditioning system occasionally created condensation on the inside of the dome's roof.

Texas experienced explosive growth during the Fifties and Sixties at a rate faster than anywhere else in the country. During that period, Houston's population increased by 17%, while the rest of the country grew at 13%. By the end of the sixties, Texas would account for six percent of the total U.S. population. Most of that growth occurred near Dallas-Ft Worth and Houston.

~

The radio rating services referred to a surveyed area as the MSA—'Metropolitan Survey Area' (a radio or television region in which that specific population receives the same programming.) A look at a detailed map of the Houston MSA of that period showed explosive growth throughout the area, but particularly in areas that I considered to be KILT's best potential for audience growth; to the north, toward Dallas -- west toward Austin/San Antonio -- and to the Southwest along US Highway 59 toward Mexico.

Developing a new strategy for KILT involved knowledge about each area's changing demographics, the various cultures and the ongoing development in each area. It also meant simply stopping at the neighborhood 7-11 or local record shops, talking to the audience and connecting with listeners. Certainly we would attempt to reach listeners wherever they lived, but those three area developments were full of new Houston residents with no previous loyalties. Specifically, they had no long-term history with KNUZ, our primary competitor, and their limited coverage weaknesses played well for KILT's future.

~

Back in Waco, we accepted the first bid for our starter home and its increasingly intrusive tallow tree. The previous two weeks had been too busy to focus on what was in store for the Young family, but now - after loading the Plymouth and a rented trailer with perfect Jed Clampett approved packing skills - all the flashbacks of Waco and Tyler and Omaha and Lufkin faded in the rear-view mirror. The drive south plunged us headlong into a new set of dreams and fears. I had once been labeled by a coworker as *'a big fish in a little pond'* but it was time to dive into a very big ocean and face the sharks!

~

I reported for work at KILT on February 15, 1966. The first day on the job was mostly a blur, meeting people I would have to re-introduce myself to later and confronting the uncomfortable transition of offices with the previous Program Director Bob White, who would remain on the air for the time being. Bob was gracious and helpful, even though I could empathize with his feelings. I moved into the noon to three spot on the station the first week.

Most of that week was spent in informal one-on-one meetings with the program staff; getting to know each employee, understanding their jobs, and hearing their comments about the station's strengths and weaknesses. At Weaver's suggestion, I called a meeting of the entire Program, Promotion and News staffs for Sunday evening to discuss the new agenda.

It was also a week when it seemed every record label executive in the country left messages. This level of attention was new to me but I knew that the effusive compliments had more to do with KILT's importance in selling records than any real accomplishment on my part. Record promoters were experts at inflating a program or music director's ego. I quickly realized that I might need to check my ego at the door each day.

~

The most popular music artists usually received automatic addition status on top station's playlists. New releases by unproven artists however needed to get exposure somewhere. Touring as the opening act for a known performer was a career starter for some as were magazine ads and TV appearances. However it might come to be, wide radio exposure was critical at some point if a new song was to become a hit!

In 1966, that exposure took place at a handful of breakout areas around the country. The ratings charts--Billboard, Cash Box and the published *tip sheets,* would pick up radio adds and sales reports directly from labels. Sales information from key retail outlets, juke box play and reports of requests and chart growth at influential radio stations were thrown into the mix and if all systems were positive, the record label would quickly spread the word around the country, rushing stock to retailers in those markets with radio support. If the station was a *reporting station* to one of the industry *'tip sheets'* the word spread rapidly. A successful launch could set in motion a massive amount of radio additions which, in turn, activated the industry's distribution network to supply ample product to retail outlets.

The unique history and diversity of the Houston music scene made it one of the country's most important breakout and talent-laden markets.

Pioneer black record store owner and entrepreneur Don Robey founded the Peacock recording label in Houston in 1949 with releases by Clarence "Gatemouth" Brown, Memphis Slim, Floyd Dixon and "Big Mama" Thornton - who in 1953 recorded the original version of *"you ain't nothin' but a hound dog."* Taking on a group of partners, Robey launched Duke Records in 1952 with hits by Johnny Ace, Joe Hinton, Bobby "Blue" Bland and Junior Parker.

The Daily Brothers - owners of the largest record distributorship in the area - teamed with producer Jack Starnes to form Starday Records with country artists Dottie West, Red Sovine and Roger Miller.

Nearby Rosenberg artist B.J. Thomas and his band - The Triumphs - released a cover of Hank William's *'I'm So Lonesome I Could Cry,'* in 1966. The million-seller launched a long, successful career with *'Hooked on a Feeling'* and *'Rain Drops Keep Falling On My Head'* -- both of which became #1 hits.

Down the road in Winnie, Texas - and eventually at Sugar Hill Studios in Houston - the son of a sharecropper family from Louisiana, Huey Meaux - the "Crazy Cajun" - began producing an impressive string of national hits with George Jones, J.P. Richardson- *"The Big Bopper",* Sunny and the Sunliners, Little Willie John, Jivin' Gene, Roy Head, Rod Bernard, Barbara Lynn and later, Doug Kershaw, Doug Sahm's Sir Douglas Quintet, Mickey Gilley, Ronnie Milsap, Archie Bell & the Drells, Johnny & Edgar Winter, Freddy Fender and a host of others!

Local oilman Richard Ames, his brother Steve, and manager Bob Cope built a popular teen club--the Catacombs, and their own record label to support releases by a stable of bands that included Neal Ford and The Fanatic's, Dueces Wild, Magic Ring and Movin' Sidewalks (with a young guitarist and lead singer named Billy Gibbons).

Houston Post writer Scott Holtzmann and wife Vivian produced an LP by local band 'Fever Tree' featuring vocalist Dennis Keller, and recorded the hit "San Francisco Girls"

International Artists, founded in 1965, was the first label to introduce psychedelic rock bands to the area--13th Floor Elevators, Bubble Puppy, Rory Ericson and Krayola.

~

New music breakout stations received a lot of recognition within the industry, but more important, KILT's priority needed to be its local listeners. Having big names in the music business as neighbors was not reason enough to spend valuable program time in uncharted waters. New releases carry an inherent level of uncertainty since many listeners only want to hear their favorite songs. Unfamiliar music—sometimes even by established artists—needed time to reach the mass audience. The KILT I envisioned had to use every second of program-time focused on delivering the largest audience. The safest route, of course, would be to always wait for new music to be proven elsewhere. On the other hand, when you did take ownership of a giant hit song first - you could win big with the more 'active' listener. These were the ones that would spread the word about a station to their friends. We had to find that delicate balance.

A perfect example of the rewards for being on the leading edge of trends came when KNUZ deejay Arch Yancey first introduced his listeners to a group from England named simply 'Beatles.' Arch first played their initial US release at a local record hop. By being the first, KNUZ rode the wave of Beatlemania to top ratings. KNUZ deejay Buddy Macgregor later flew to London to interview the group. By 1965 however, when the Fab Four came to the states for their second tour, it was KILT's Bill Weaver who personally flew to New York with a blank check from Gordon McLendon in hand, and convinced Beatles' manager Brian Epstein to add two additional performances at Houston's Sam Houston Coliseum to their second US tour.. The coup trumped KNUZ's advantage and gave new ownership of the Beatles to KILT.

By the time I arrived at KILT in early 1966, the station was still in a dog fight with KNUZ. Winning meant addressing every facet of the station's programming, including the selection of music. That much scrutiny however would put me on a possible collision course with KILT's music director Chuck Dunaway, the top rated deejay on the station and the only previous friend I had in the building.

~

Bill Weaver suggested that I meet with the entire program staff to discuss the station's new direction. On Sunday evening, February 20th, 1966 - I faced the staff for the first time. Two members of the news department were not present. Dan Lovett was in Viet Nam, interviewing soldiers and sending reports back home to the stations while the News Director, Richard Dobbin, simply boycotted the meeting.

Dobbin was a unique character whose sensational morning newscasts had become the talk of the town. On the week before our meeting, Richard returned from a week in Las Vegas as guest of the Houston Oilers. A call to Weaver from the team's PR Director however, complained that Richard's bar bill had set an outrageous high for the annual event. With the additional news that Dobbin had boycotted the meeting, Weaver picked up the phone, called the News Director and before I even had a chance to meet Richard, summarily fired him.

Chapter THIRTEEN
"YOU TURN ME ON I'M A RADIO"

An old radio mantra says—as goes the morning, so goes the rest of the day! For decades, that axiom underlined the importance of strong ratings in the morning, usually the most lucrative advertising slot on any radio station. According to Arbitron's rating service, today's audience reaches more than two hundred and twenty million Americans. That's ninety-four percent of everyone twelve and older. Eighty percent of adults listen to radio in their cars and that most concentrated use occurs during the morning-drive period between seven and nine a.m.

When I arrived at KILT, the station was in the midst of a decades-long war with KNUZ, particularly in the important morning drive period. A year earlier, Don Keyes, the McLendon Station's national program director had put ads in trade publications, looking for British deejays. The intent was to take advantage of Ian Fleming's *James Bond* craze and the audience's fascination with everything British.

Alex Bennett was on the air at the time in Carmel, California, just south of San Francisco. Faking his best British accent, Alex sent an audition tape to Don and fooled everyone enough to land the important morning drive position at KILT. Bennett changed his air name to Bond -- James Bond -- and went head to head against the most popular disc jockey in the city. In 1966, in spite of KNUZ' inferior signal, Paul Berlin was the still the personality to beat in Houston Radio.

In reality, Houston's rapid growth and the increasing ADI (area of dominant influence) actually favored KILT's signal, louder and more powerful with less interference in the new growth areas of the city. It was only a matter of time before the area's expansion would exceed KNUZ' local coverage capability.

~

There were two incidents that occurred quickly that I believe contributed to a turnaround in KILT's morning show ratings.

The first came within my first two weeks on the job. In the initial Sunday night staff meeting, I suggested that we needed to become more 'visible' to our audience. That meant getting outside the studios, showing up and participating in places where the audience could get to know us on a personal level. On a morning a week or so later, I received a call from one of the large high schools in the area asking if we could provide a deejay for their pep rally that afternoon before the big game with a cross-town rival. Even though it was late notice, I welcomed the opportunity to have one of our personalities before a large group of active radio listeners. KNUZ' popularity over the years had been aided, in large part, by staying personally involved in these kinds of events. KILT needed that audience to change their listening habits which meant we needed to become more involved.

When Alex Bennett signed off that morning, I gave him the assignment of showing up that afternoon at the school's rally. Alex responded immediately - *"I was hired by Don Keyes and told I did not have to do this kind of thing."*

Uh-oh, this response presented an immediate challenge to my effort to turn things around. I suspect my surprise was obvious but I told Alex I had not been informed of any such agreement and asked him to wait around a few minutes as I needed to get a ruling from Weaver.

When I first visited Bill Weaver's home before the job offer, he said that he was pleased with the progress of his morning, afternoon, and night-time ratings, but needed help in mid-days and weekends. Recalling my impressions of the earlier success of KBOX, I told him of my firm belief in creating a *total station'* sound with consistencies in all day-parts and I could not accept the job without authority over all areas of programming. After discussion, Weaver said he would support that, but this confrontation with Bennett was about to become a quicker test of that commitment than I wanted.

I ran downstairs to the manager's office to get a quick ruling. *'Everything ok,'* Weaver asked? I told him that his fair-haired morning man had just refused an assignment. Before I even explained, Bill said *"look, we agreed, you manage the upstairs and I run the downstairs - fire them all if you have to."* I took his response with an even quicker *"thank you sir"* and ran back upstairs to find Alex standing in the hallway. As he followed me into the office, I asked if he still felt the same way about the assignment; *'yes'* he said. I reached for the phone and dialed Sue Reid, the company's office manager, and asked her to get a one month severance check ready for Alex Bennett who would be down in a few minutes to pick it up.

Without looking, I could sense movement on the couch to my right as our very own Agent 007 nervously cleared his throat. *"Can you do that"* he asked. *"You bet I can"* I answered, *"and you can check that with Weaver or call the home office if you like. We are building a new radio station here and I intend to do that with people who will do what it takes to win."*

Alex's demeanor changed immediately as he asked if we could

talk about it. Our Agent 007 was the star cheerleader at the high school pep-rally that afternoon.

~

A week or so later, the second significant change took place. I came to the conclusion that the British accent was phony and *un-relatable* for the biggest audience in Texas. Alex gladly dropped the accent but kept the *'Bond'* name. In the real world, the constant attention Alex was committing to being a character, interfered with his own extraordinary talent — a caustic, spontaneous humor that would eventually lead us to drop even the James Bond name and move him to a late night *'in your face'* style talk show under the name, Alex Bennett. The show was a smash and built the groundwork for what would later take Alex to a similar show on New York City's WPLJ and host of PBS' *Comedy Tonight*.

Finally, with a newly energized morning show, we started seeing consistent winning numbers in this important day part. Alex's competition -- Paul Berlin -- remains one of Houston's treasures and a respected friend, but his days of winning mass audience ratings came to an end.

~

If you grew up in Texas and you loved radio, you knew the name Chuck Dunaway. With time spent on the air in Dallas, Houston, Fort Worth, Austin and Corpus Christi - Chuck probably holds the record as the *'Big Tex'* of Texas Radio.

Chucky Wucky - as one of his singing jingles called him - was arguably the most exciting radio disc jockey in America. He has been recognized multiple times by Radio Halls of Fame in Texas, Ohio, The Radio/TV Hall of Fame, listed in Who's Who in America, Who's Who in the Media, Who's Who in the South & Southwest, included in the official publication of Radio's 75th Anniversary, and there is even more. Chuck's resume boasts stops at some of the most respected radio stations in the country, including WABC in New York City. Chuck built a massive audience at two different radio stations in Cleveland, the place where Alan Freed coined the term 'rock and roll' in 1954.

With all Chuck had accomplished by the time I arrived at KILT, I admit to feeling intimidated. I worried that my limited small town experience would prohibit me from gaining the respect of industry heavyweights like Chuck and merge all these diverse egos into one cohesive station sound. One radio insider predicted that these guys would slice me for lunch before the end of the first week.

In reality, Chuck quickly became an influential force in pulling the staff together to accomplish everything I sought to achieve -- except when it came to the music on KILT.

~

Since music was such an important programming element, I had always been in charge of that area as Program Director in Tyler and Waco. But Chuck held the title of 'Music Director' at KILT and it was a role he took very seriously. Complicating any change was the fact that Chuck was also the top-rated disc jockey on the station. If I made music changes without Chuck's involvement - I could easily win that battle, but lose the bigger war!

In my opinion, KILT's playlist was out of sync with the national hit charts. I could imagine kids watching Dick Clark's *American Bandstand* each afternoon, but only hearing one of those songs on KILT -- Nancy Sinatra's *'These Boots Were Made For Walkin.'* That bothered me -- a lot.

A blockbuster hit was validated when it gained total momentum, showing up at many different places at the same time; on the juke box at the bowling alley, on radio stations we listened to when we travel out of town, on the eight-track in the car next to you at the stop light, on Dick Clark's American Bandstand each afternoon, or the song your little sister keeps humming at the dinner table.

Every successful trend, including new hit songs, is dependent upon *'momentum'*. Unless the song was performed by a major *'must-add'* artist, being the first station to play a new release might bring lots of recognition from music press but it was an unfamiliar song to the mass audience. It meant your station had to go it alone at first and since nobody had a one hundred percent batting average, that strategy appeared to me to be very dangerous. Even though stations that were early in adding new music were popular with the labels and the local record reps, it meant you could be out of sync with the most important person in your universe -- your listener.

It was going to be a balancing act to get the music more in sync with the rest of the country without alienating the most important personality we had on the station.

~

Early in the spring of 1966, KILT announced that we were bringing the Rolling Stones to Houston. Within days, I received a call from a local public relations representative asking if we would put one of the local bands he represented on stage as the opening act for the Stones. Opening for a major act has historically been a significant breakout moment for many artists.

Since the concert was still three months away, I told him that we would not be making that decision for some time yet but thanked him for his offer. Two weeks later, same man—same request, followed shortly by yet another call from Mr. P.R. Man. This time he sounded even more urgent. I firmly reiterated that we would not be making the opening act decision until a few weeks before the Stones appearance and I knew how to reach him if we were interested.

It wasn't long before Mr. PR man called again and asked if he could take me to lunch. I immediately interrupted--telling him that there was no need to rehash the issue but he insisted that lunch was not about that subject at all. Seems he also represented a local company that was going to run an advertising campaign on KILT and he needed to discuss a joint promotion.

Mr. Man picked me up at noon and we had a quick lunch at one of the nearby restaurants. There was no mention of the concert over lunch but on the way back to the studios he asked, *you have a son don't you?'* Having opened a subject that was very close to me, I naively started telling him about my son Scott, but he quickly interrupted, *'I'm going to open a bank account in Scott's name this afternoon for $500.'* I turned to him with a surprised look and he immediately added *'what the hell, lets make it a thousand.'*

'Stop the car!' I yelled as I made a loud exit. The sight of two men in a shouting-match in the middle of Montrose began attracting a symphony of horns from the lunch crowd traffic.

"Come on man, I'm not going to tell anyone!"
I yelled back --
"I am going to tell, in fact, I'm gonna' tell everyone!"

Back at the studio, I fired off interoffice memos to all the management team - Gordon McLendon and Don Keyes in Dallas, to Bill Weaver at KILT and I kept a copy for my own files.

As I sat in my office, still shaken from the episode, I realized that the manager of the group that Mr. PR Man wanted to put on stage with the Stones was also the manager of two other local bands, both with records prominently featured on KILT's current playlist.

I immediately placed a call to Mr. PR man's boss and informed him that, while I could not prove that he was responsible for the offer, I could absolutely assure him that his band would not be opening for the Rolling Stones. I also made a note to monitor more closely the actual sales reports of his artist's records on future playlists.

~

Record promotion representatives seemed to visit the studios at all hours of the day. Occasionally, I would walk into the main control room and find a record promoter in conversation with the deejay in the midst of their air-shift. While most label representatives were gentlemen and business-like, a couple of them did not inspire much trust. One particular local rep seemed to drop in frequently during the evenings. After a national deejay convention in 1968, that same promotion man and his boss were convicted of the *Mann Act*, also known as the *White Slave Traffic Act* (which banned the interstate transport of females across state lines for immoral purposes).

The company set a once-a-week-only music meeting that limited record promoter's free access to the studio area. New releases at other times during the week could be left at the reception's desk downstairs. We also set limits on other contacts as well as limits on lunches and promotional gifts.

It was the mid-sixties and an entirely new street language, developed by the drug culture, was becoming commonplace in music lyrics. From the Beatles psychedelic/LSD-coded *'Lucy in the Sky with Diamonds'* to Peter, Paul and Mary's child-like *'Puff the Magic Dragon'*, music lyrics had the potential to influence youthful choices. Rumors circulating through the office led me to issue a *'no drugs tolerance'* and *'no visitor's policy.'* In part, the memo said *"what you choose to do on your own time is your business, but you will not break the law in this building."*

In spite of my concern, music continued to release cleverly hidden and at times overt references to drugs, and a new wave of rock stars made it sound like the *'in thing'* to do.

~

I was surprised to find that KILT had no 'hot-clock' in place. For those not aware, the *'hot clock'* is a breakdown of each hour into program segments. The clock could insure that the current methodologies of the rating services matched the preferred choices of the listeners available in that day-part. For instance, a well-designed clock might require the top of each hour to begin with a song that came from the A-list, containing the hottest hits of the day. These would be followed by a classic hit, then a recurrent (recent hit), and followed by another 'A' cut. If there were five A-level hits in rotation for instance, the placement of those important titles could have enormous impact on ratings.

Assume that most of the downtown offices closed their doors at 6 p.m. each weekday and a normal walk to the parking garage might take ten minutes. A well-designed clock would insure that at 6:10 p.m., just as thousands of office workers would be turning on their car radios, KILT would have the strongest possible musical selection on the air. At other times, when a blue-collar factory along the ship-channel shutdown for the day, that might mean Roger Miller's *'King of the Road'*. For the end of a school day, it might be the new release from The Monkees. Listeners tuning their car radio dials were more likely to stop at 6-10 on the dial if we were playing a song that was important to them.

Knowledge of each community's unique timetable became very important in winning ratings. The largest percentage of a station's entire cumulative audience might actually only listen during one or two quarter hours each day so it was important to maximize every minute. A sold-out Houston Oiler football game in the Astrodome would mean thousands of people stuck in their cars on the freeway for as much as two hours before kickoff. To me, that could mean up to eight quarter hours of listening for each separate person in that car.

Even placement of potential negatives became part of the strategy; things like commercials and for some listeners, newscasts. Music sweeps of two, three or more songs, strategically placed back-to-back, were popular ways of accomplishing this. For instance, if we could keep you tuned in for a continuous twenty minutes (:00 - :20 minutes past the hour) then you had, in ratings' speak, listened for an entire half hour. By moving newscasts to twenty minutes after and before each hour, consultant Bill Drake had designed a 'hot clock' that gave his stations credit for a full hour of listening.

This same principal exists in today's television when the first thirty-five minutes of an hour-long drama might have little or no commercial interruptions, but the last two quarter hours --after the audience is hooked into the storyline--are loaded with commercials.

It was also important for the listener to know when and to whom they were listening. Placement of the call letters became important in order to take ownership of a listener when they filled out a rating's diary or responded to a random survey call. Since many people frequently turned the dial and stopped only when they heard a favorite song, the first thing out of the deejay's mouth at the end of the record might be *"KILT - with the latest from Santana."* Apparently, these little things made a difference. By summer 1966, the ratings began showing consistent, number one ratings for all day parts.

Media consultant Kent Burkhart recalls conversations forty years ago with industry pioneers Todd Storz and Bill Stewart about the future of ratings. *"We believed that someday we would have real-time electronic measurement that was entered on a screen in the program director or general manager's offices that gave instantaneous ratings, actually measuring the popularity of a single record or the deejay's one-liner."*

The first stage of space-age surveys already exists and more sophisticated methodologies are on the way. Houston and Philadelphia became Abitron's first PPM (*Portable People Meter*) service in July 2007. The PPM methodology uses a passive audience measurement device, about the size of a small cell phone, to track consumer exposure to all media. The reports encompass a much larger definition of *'media'*, which now includes broadcast, cable, satellite, radio and television, terrestrial and online radio as well as cinema advertising and other types of place-based electronic media. Carried by willing and randomly-selected listeners through the day, the PPM device tracks when and where a person watches television, listens to radio, and how they interact with other forms of media. Simply walking into someone's office where a radio is being played can register you as a listener to that station. By measuring *exposure* instead of *recall*, it turns out that people were exposed to a lot more radio than the earlier methodology had indicated. The system came under fire however in 2010 because of the methodology's tendency to under-represent the listenership of minority-owned stations.

While ratings have always had major influence on radio sales, you can bet there are lots of programmers out there right now working on updated versions of the *hot clock* in order to influence these new wrinkles in ratings.

Chapter FOURTEEN
"GETTING TO KNOW YOU"

From the late fifties to the mid-sixties, Gordon McLendon's Texas Triangle stations had a massive statewide audience. Except for the brief success of KBOX, KLIF's ratings had dominated Dallas radio from 1954 until 1973. San Antonio's close local battle between KTSA and KONO made for great radio if you lived there - but outside the immediate area, KTSA's vast coverage and rapid-fire super-jocks like Ricci Ware gave it a huge audience throughout South Texas. In the early sixties, KILT - the final building block of McLendon's Texas Triangle stations - was locked in a fierce battle for number one with KNUZ and its popular deejays Paul Berlin, Arch Yancy, Joe Ford and Buddy McGregor.

KILT's evening deejay when I arrived in Houston was Russ Knight, *"The Weird Beard."* They say his best friend, Bill Drake, gave him the name back in Atlanta when Russ was having trouble growing a beard. Bill and Russ were both deejays at WAKE in Atlanta in 1960 and saw each other daily with back-to-back shifts. Russ decided to sport a beard, but it grew sporadically - in a scraggly, spotted sort of way. With daily jokes about his friend's appearance, Bill Drake started calling Russ the *"Weird Beard."*

The name stuck. Russ Knight once achieved the highest Hooper rating recorded by that time with a sixty-two percent share of the Dallas audience. He was featured on the cover of the popular "Cruisin" series of albums in 1962 & '63. Russ moved to KILT in 1965 and took over the important 6-10 p.m. show.

~

During the years prior to my arrival, KILT had dominated this time period with Jim Wood. Jim called himself the *Vanilla Gorilla* because he was white, but sounded black. In a unique twist, Jim was recognized in 1970, 1971 and 1972 as Billboard Magazine's top Soul Music personality in the country. But Jim's unpredictability often won him a reputation with management as being out-of-control. Much of Jim's delivery - and content - sounded like that from a *'dirty old man'* so the station was constantly fielding complaint calls from parents. Bill Weaver frequently fired, and then rehired, Jim after a promise to *cool it.*

Representatives from the Houston Police Department visited the KILT studios one morning after Jim, sometime around eleven p.m. the previous night, whispered to every kid in town to open their windows, put the radio on the sill and, on his signal, turn the radios to full volume. On cue, Jim yelled out, *"ATTENTION -- THIS IS THE POLICE, COME OUT WITH YOUR HANDS IN THE AIR!"* Thousands of bedside lamps switched on around the city at the same time, blowing out power in certain areas and the Houston Police Department's phone lines went crazy.

Russ Knight had the same edge and unpredictability as Jim Wood, but thankfully, his intellect kept him just south of a total meltdown. Russ was also, just plain smarter. He held a Master's degree in Journalism after acquiring a Drama degree from Dallas' Southern Methodist University. Russ knew exactly what he was doing and was already solidifying KILT's leadership at nights.

~

By summer, Bob White, the KILT program director I replaced, moved to sales, creating the first opportunity to begin building my own team. The first call was to that kid with the big voice from Tyler, Texas. Steve Lundy immediately resigned his job at ABC's WXYZ in Detroit to come home to Texas and KILT. Steve took over the noon to three spot and I moved to ten a.m. – noon.

Chapter FIFTEEN
"ROCK & ROLL MUSIC"

In 1965, the summer before I arrived at KILT, Manager Bill Weaver, with blank check in hand, flew to New York City to meet with Beatle's manager Brian Epstein at his suite in the Plaza Hotel, and convinced him to add two performances in Houston to the Beatles' 1965 American tour. Gordon McLendon had given Weaver a signed company check with instructions to let Epstein *"fill in the amount."* Signing the group was a major coup for KILT and it undercut KNUZ' claim of being the Houston headquarters for every-thing Beatles.

After an appearance at Atlanta Stadium, the group arrived at Hobby Airport at 2 a.m. on Thursday, August 19, 1965. Earlier that evening, KNUZ' Buddy McGregor had found out when the Beatles were to arrive and broadcast the information on the air. In spite of the early morning hour, long lines of cars blocked streets around Hobby. KNUZ broadcast live reports from the airport and quickly, an estimated four-thousand screaming fans rushed through the gates and surrounded the group's plane. The Beatles' welcome to Houston quickly turned into a dangerous nightmare; literally imprisoning the Fab-Four inside the aircraft.

Dickie Rosenfeld, then sales manager of KILT, paid someone in airport security to drive a hydraulic catering platform to the emergency exit of the plane. Screaming fans surrounded the scissor-lift with some even attempting to climb aboard. The group safely made it onto the platform, but manager Brian Epstein injured his back while making a last-minute jump over the cart's railing.

The group was taken to a secure location in another part of the air field where they, along with KILT newsman Dan Lovett, boarded two Brinks armored trucks for the trip downtown to the Sheraton-Lincoln Hotel. Avoiding another waiting crowd downtown, the group used the hotel's loading dock and freight elevator to reach their 10th floor rooms.

By 3:30 the next afternoon, the first Beatle's concert began to the screams of an almost sold-out Coliseum. KILT's Chuck Dunaway and Russ Knight were the emcees and primed the crowd for the event. The shows also featured opening acts Cannibal and the Headhunters, Brenda Holloway, Sound's Incorporated, King Curtis and his band and the Discotheque Dancers! Because the Coliseum had no secure dressing rooms, the group had to return to the Sheraton between performances in a chartered bus in order to change clothes. KILT hired one hundred and fifty off-duty Houston police officers to handle crowd security, but then had to add another fifty officers at the last minute.

The tickets read *'Radio Station KILT presents The Sixth Annual Back-To-School Show, starring The Beatles (in person).'* All tickets were general admission (no reserved seats) and sold for $5 each — yes, you read that correctly.

~

By the following summer, I had arrived at KILT and Bill Weaver booked two more major concert events for the Coliseum during summer 1966, The Rolling Stones on Monday, July 11th and then two weeks later, the Animals and Herman's Hermits. We announced the events early in the spring in order to take ownership of both major tours right from the start. Chuck Dunaway was the immediate choice to introduce the Stones, but I drew the two best assignments of all.

First, I created my first-ever concert commercial. Since hearing Pat Hughes' Chuck Berry commercial in Tyler, Texas radio six years earlier ... this had been my dream job; *"KILT PRESENTS THE ROLLING STONES – LIVE!"*

My second role was to hire the limos and meet the group's private jet at Hobby Airport; chauffeur them to the Rice Hotel; see that they did not trash the suite; sign the tab for their dinner in the room; get them to the Coliseum on time; then deliver them back to Hobby Airport late that night for their departure -- all while keeping the information confidential, even from our own staff.

~

The Rolling Stone's arrival was on-time and we traveled in two limousines to the Rice, Houston's famous downtown hotel, arriving about 2:30 p.m. I spent the next five hours with the group in their suite discussing everything from politics, family, books and music trends. Mick Jagger and Brian Jones were both very outspoken about British and American history. Mick in particular had strong feelings about U.S. politics and his opinions made for a stimulating afternoon of conversation. Bill Wyman mostly read but spent time talking about his children and said that leaving them was the toughest part of touring. Charlie Watts talked about the ups and downs of touring, while Keith Richards said little during the afternoon, mostly sitting on the couch dozing and watching TV.

After a surprisingly elegant sit-down dinner with Mick's very specific selection of the perfect wine, we left for the Coliseum in our two waiting limos. As I stood with them backstage while Chuck was on stage priming the crowd with the introduction, bassist Bill Wyman leaned over and asked *"Bill, do you think we should go out and throw cigarette butts at them to live up to our image?"* The agent who booked the show would tell me later that I had apparently caught them on a particularly good day since they had a few disruptive and highly publicized episodes in other cities. The Stone's performance in Houston was a total sellout.

After the concert, we quickly boarded the limousines and were out the big double-doors of the Coliseum within seconds. I was in the front seat of the lead limo with Mick, Brian and Keith in the backseat. They were still revved from the performance and swapping stories of unique quirks in the performance that only a member of the band would have noticed. Mick asked me to board the plane with them before they departed, where each member of the band signed a full group photo for me. I made the mistake of parading it around the studio on Monday morning and proudly placed the photo on my desk ... where it quickly, mysteriously, and permanently disappeared.

~

Two weeks later, KILT hosted the last of our summer '66 sellouts in the Coliseum with a double-bill; Herman's Hermits and the Animals. I was a major fan of the latter group and always believed that their version of 'House of the Rising Sun' was one of the most perfect rock radio songs of the sixties. For this event, we booked the bands into the famous Warwick, the extravagant hotel built by oil wildcatter Glenn McCarthy, whose personal life was said to have inspired the hit novel and movie "Giant."

In person, Eric Burden was quiet and reserved. His band rested in their rooms most of the afternoon. But in the suite down the hall, Peter Noone, the teenage lead singer of the Hermits was living the life of a fun-loving rock n' roll rascal. Girls were running, squealing, popping in and out of rooms and everywhere in the hallways plus a sizable contingent of fans with posters gathered outside the hotel. While much less organized, the sold-out concert came off without a hitch, but I breathed a sigh of relief that night as their plane lifted off the runway at Hobby.

KILT actually booked and produced its own concerts until the late sixties. The station manager would negotiate the terms of the booking and we would have exclusive promotional rights – i.e. *"KILT Presents--Jefferson Airplane."* Eventually, major concert promoters would take over the role of hiring the acts, booking the hall, arranging the ticket sales and produce the concerts. One local radio station was then chosen by the promoter to be the sponsoring station–in name only–in return for a special packaged advertising fee. After KILT began dominating Houston ratings, virtually all the promoters who came to Houston sought to strike their deal with The Big 6-10.

~

Since my early experience in Tyler radio, my ambition had been to produce commercials for concerts, just like those that I heard when Pat Hughes created spots for a Chuck Berry appearance. With two back-to-back mega-star shows to sell, I had been handed two dream projects and they were both sellouts. After these events, a few area promoters started talking about those commercials. Soon, I was being hired to create ads for almost every concert that came to town. I never considered myself a great disc jockey, in fact, I was probably average at best. But now -- alone in the production room -- I had finally found a way to run with the big dogs.

~

On an afternoon in early May, 1966, three months after my arrival at KILT, Bill Weaver called for a meeting of all department heads in his office; immediately. I could sense a different attitude that morning. Weaver's World War Two military leadership kicked in and the urgency of his call quickly started the rumor-mill churning. Never having seen this side of Bill, I was immediately intimidated as he started barking orders in military fashion.

"Gordon McLendon and Don Keys are coming in to monitor the station next Tuesday. They will stay at the Houston House. I'm not sure how long they will stay."

~

In most of their markets, the McLendon stations' maintained a full-time apartment for home office visits. The KILT location was on the ninth floor of the downtown Houston House high-rise. You could feel the sudden change of intensity in the building as Weaver started barking assignments;

"Sue (Reid-Office Mgr) book a barber for Gordon for ten Wednesday morning, be sure it's a good one, oh see that things are in order at the apartment and take a dozen writing pads over with you, you know what they need."

"Robert (Jones-Chief Engineer) check-out all the phones and radios in the apartment to be sure they're all working, buy extras if you need, oh and check the TV reception."

"Dickey (Rosenfeld-Sales Manager) be sure the apartment is stocked with Gordon's favorite bourbon and plenty of cokes and snacks."

"Harry (Rogers-Asst Sales Mgr) get a limo booked to meet 'em at Hobby, they have a 10 a.m. arrival … oh and go with the driver to be sure they don't have to wait."

"Bill (my palms were sweating) take a good look at everything you've got on the air right now. Keep it quiet to the jocks, Gordon wants to hear the station as it normally sounds ... just be sure it sounds great!"

There was no way of keeping a McLendon visit a secret. Within an hour, the news was all over the building.

While I was excited about meeting what I considered to be two of the most influential men in radio, I immediately became aware of the increased tension exhibited by those who had been through such visits before. According to rumors, McLendon had once written a ten-page detailed manifesto to all program directors, describing-in detail how each element of a McLendon station should sound. Unfortunately, no one had shown me that document. Gordon McLendon and Don Keyes would hear a very different KILT from the one I had inherited.

Stories had circulated for years in the radio rumor-mill of Gordon and his executives flying into an existing or newly-acquired station and immediately firing the entire staff. Whether such rumors were true or not, it certainly added an element of tension to the visit. Bob White, the previous program director, had been a great help to me for the first four months, but when the news broke that Gordon and Don were coming to town, Bob's normal nervous demeanor suddenly turned into panicked pacing of the hallway outside my office. *"They're going to kill us for the changes you've made. No one has taken this much liberty with McLendon programming before."* The air was thick with anticipation.

The monthly C.E. Hooper ratings had been increasing those first three months and for the first time, we were winning all day-parts, even mornings -- not by a comfortable margin yet, but the audience was clearly moving our way.

Experienced radio programmers intuitively know when a station has momentum, even before the release of the ratings. It's a sense that comes from experience and an innate understanding of the audience; some called it having a *'good ear'.* In spite of the concern going on around me, I was anxious to hear the big guns' response to the changes.

Guess I had expected a call from Don Keys when they arrived on Tuesday. We had spoken daily on the phone during my first three months, but now – nada – nothing, for two and a half agonizingly silent days. My initial confidence began fading by the hour.

One could have hoped for a formal staff meeting where first Gordon McLendon, one of the two legendary creators of Top-40 radio; and then Don Keyes, the technician that made KLIF come alive – would both stand before the entire KILT staff, and perhaps members of the national trade press, and use their immense language skills to announce to the company and the radio industry that the new KILT, under its new program director, was nothing short of brilliant and its ground-breaking new ideas would immediately become mandatory for the entire chain of McLendon stations, under Young's tutelage of course.' Perhaps a toast of Champagne and a significant bonus would have been a nice touch also.

But nothing; nada; only dead air from the Houston House!

~

On Thursday morning about eleven fifteen, I was preparing to go on the air when Bill Weaver called the control room. *"Need you to join Don Keys and me for lunch at Lee's Den on Main Street, get directions from Sue."*

After quickly finding someone to take over my air-shift, I walked into the crowded lunch spot and found Weaver in a booth over on the right side of the room. I walked to the table and was introduced for the first time to Don Keyes. My hands were sweating. I had listened to Don on KLIF from the time I was a senior in high school, and later, Don had become the first

Program Director of KILT in 1957... now I was sitting across the table from the man, knowing that my entire future was about to be revealed.

Don spoke first ... *"who's been punching buttons around here?"* Bill motioned toward me and Don's next words erased all the worry of that stressful week. *"We have owned this radio station for ten years and in just three months, you have accomplished what we had failed to do for all of those years!"*

It's amazing how much time I have wasted in my life, obsessed with worry. Don stayed in town through the weekend and we spent the next three evenings discussing McLendon history, theories and stories from the inside. Don, a natural storyteller, described the huge success, the enormous egos, and the traps that had destroyed the careers of many great talents. I was a sponge ... absorbing every word.

Don spoke of his own fear of inadequacy after replacing the company's first National Program Director, Bill Stewart - whose reputation had reached legendary status for his role in the initial growth of Top 40 radio. Fearing he could never fill Stewart's shoes, Don made the commitment to over-compensate by always being available, regardless of McLendon's agendas. He told of one Thanksgiving dinner with his family when the phone rang and Gordon said to meet him in one hour at Love Field so that they could fly to Chicago. In spite of the intrusion of the special family time, Don showed up, ready to leave on time.

That level of commitment would challenge my own status within the company before the end of my first year.

Chapter SIXTEEN
"WE CAN WORK IT OUT"

I'm often asked how it felt to be on the radio. It felt like work.

A three-minute song goes by very quickly while you are organizing the next stop-set with relevant comments, commercials, station promos and pre-selling what is coming up in order to influence the audience to stick around for another quarter hour. All of this occurred under a public microscope with the understanding that your work was being judged and compared to a constantly changing set of standards. Get it right and reap the rewards. Get it wrong and consider a career in Pickles Gap, Arkansas.

Some deejays I worked with did massive amounts of preparation, virtually scripting their entire show. Most however, started each day with no plans but stayed open to surprises - a quirky news story, a question from a caller, or simply a reflection of the deejay's imagination - anything that could be developed into an interesting theme.

One of Don's favorite stories was about how Gordon McLendon could energize a radio station. An example occurred after he and the local program director were called into Gordon's office and told that KLIF was *"becoming boring."* Not knowing exactly what

McLendon meant, Don defensively started listing the promotions that were going on at the station, only to be interrupted with *"you're missing the point Don, there is not enough happening to keep a listener glued to KLIF."*

McLendon then proceeded to demonstrate. He picked up the phone and dialed the control room hotline. The deejay on the air answered, and just hearing the voice on the other end say *"this is Gordon McLendon"* immediately increased his level of intensity.

> *Would you make an announcement on the air and ask the person who parked the '62 blue Chevrolet Bellaire out front of the KLIF studios this past weekend to please remove it as soon as possible, otherwise, we're going to have it towed.*

As soon as the record ended, the announcement was read on the air. Five minutes later, another call from McLendon –

> *"This is Gordon again - we need to cancel that request about the Blue Chevy since there are people now who appear to be searching the car."*

"Is it ok to say that sir?"

> *"Of course it is -- hmmm, it appears to be what looks like, uh hold on a minute"* - (off mike) - *"is that lingerie they are taking out of the trunk?"*

With each new call, McLendon's imagination turned a previously passive listener into a rapidly increasing number of listeners who started calling their friends - who in-turned called their friends - spreading the news about mysterious things happening on KLIF. Using the same imagination that allowed him to turn single words from a ticker tape into a complete baseball game description, McLendon had just demonstrated how to make a radio station come alive.

It was during the station's early development that KLIF ran an apology in Dallas' newspapers --

"KLIF wishes to offer this apology for the unfortunate language used in an interview during a live broadcast last friday night. In covering news from the scene, as we do, the remarks of a witness, who may be in a highly-charged emotional state, cannot be governed. However, in all humility, KLIF tenders this apology."

Another promotion credited to Bill Stewart, occurred during National Library Week when he recorded announcements to encourage people to *'visit their local library.'* The announcement reported that the station had placed $5, $10, $20 and $100 bills in certain books. All they had to do to win was visit the library and find the bills. The result was a loud, virtual trashing of the library while employees watched in horror!

It was abundantly clear that McLendon and his team of young-gun prodigies at KLIF knew how to electrify a radio station. It's a more serious world now and the audience less appreciative of such shenanigans, plus the Federal Communication Commission and local governments would correctly frown on a station for creating a panic situation.

After that first visit, Don and I spoke daily on the phone. He made frequent trips to Houston and each evening, he would share more fascinating stories about the beginnings of the McLendon dynasty and the people who made it happen. Don clearly deserves much of the credit for the attitude that made the McLendon stations so successful. His colorful stories and the joy he exhibited in the simple act of retelling them gave me a unique perspective of the company's willingness to stretch the limits.

Hooper had been broadcaster's most available ratings service since 1935, the 'Golden Age' of radio. Claude E. Hooper used a *telephone-coincidental* sampling methodology, making random calls taken from the local phone directory. Each respondent was asked what program they were listening to at that moment. Once ad agencies began demanding more information about a station's listeners and a higher confidence level in the data itself, more sophisticated services such as Pulse and Arbitron began offering demographic and later, *psychographic* information, both broken into specific day-parts. For Program Directors however, the Hooper met the need for a quick-read tracking of audience trends.

Hooper's influence faded during the latter part of the sixties and the new standard became Arbitron, known simply as the "A-R-B." Arbitron used a diary method to track a listener's choices. For the payment of one dollar, the participant agreed to record their radio listening in a pocket diary for a full week. ARB gained credibility with ad agencies by providing an increased amount of information, such as age demographics, and spawned developing technologies which made radio buys much easier for agency buyers.

~

By the end of summer, 1966, the Hooper, the Pulse, and the ARB ratings all agreed that KILT had reached a dominant role, in all day parts, in its long battle with KNUZ. That's why the entire staff was in shock the morning Bill Weaver, the only General Manager in KILT's history, announced his resignation.

Before radio, Bill served in the US Infantry under Generals George Patton in North Africa and Mark Clark in Germany and France. He was awarded six Battle Stars and the Bronze Star for "Heroic Achievement" in combat. After returning home, Weaver graduated magna cum laude from the University of

Texas before joining the McLendon's in their first radio venture in Palestine, Texas. Bill's military discipline was apparent at times in the autocratic way he appeared to manage issues and although many found him brash and intimidating, I appreciated his candor. Weaver spent nineteen years with the McLendon stations, serving as General Manager of KNET, their first station in Palestine, Texas, then at Dallas' KLIF, KTSA in San Antonio and new startups in Chicago, Milwaukee and Los Angeles before taking over the newly purchased KILT.

In 1960, Weaver took over additional responsibility for McLendon by becoming the overseer of Radio Nord, a fully-equipped floating "pirate radio" ship broadcasting pop music from international waters to listeners in Sweden, southern Finland and parts of Eastern Europe. The ship, owned by Gordon and his friend Clint Murchison Jr., had turned into a nightmare with constant political, Swedish management and technical problems associated with operating a radio station bobbing around in the Baltic Sea. The Swedish Parliament's continued pressure on the station's broadcasts combined with personnel and language issues, frequent storm surges, equipment failures and personnel issues finally forced a series of moves and re-registering of the ship to Spain, under the name 'Mi Amigo.' The ship finally limped its way into the Port of Galveston for needed repairs while Bill handled the negotiations to sell and transfer the ship to a British group, who renamed it Radio Atlanta. According to Bill's wife Beverly, *"Bill was so relieved when that nightmare ship finally sailed through the Houston Ship Channel."* During the last years of Bill's life, he wrote of the bizarre Radio Nord project in 'Triple/Double Cross', a book that centers on events leading up to the Kennedy Assassination.

Bill and Don Keyes built KTSA and then KILT from the start and it was assumed that Bill Weaver had found a permanent home in Houston, while Keyes moved on to the McLendon's home offices in Dallas to become National Program Director. Some suggest that Bill Weaver had a special confidence with B.R. McLendon, but a less cordial relationship with Gordon himself. Weaver could definitely be a rebel at times and was not shy about confronting the home office, particularly Gordon -- in fact he seemed to enjoy that process. The relationship also produced some interesting episodes.

~

McLendon was adept at choosing clever, community-connected call letters. KABL celebrated the Cable Cars of San Francisco, KLIF came from its first location in Dallas' Oak Cliff area, KILT referred to his *"Old Scotchman"* moniker, WYSL celebrated Buffalo's railroad hubs and steel mills, XETRA was McLendon's powerhouse Tijuana, Mexico *'all news'* station broadcasting toward Los Angeles, but KTSA was, well *'blah'*. Gordon felt it needed a more localized connection and memorable identity. McLendon believed he had found it by capitalizing on the strong presence of military personnel in the area. Lackland, Randolph, Fort Sam Houston and Brooks Air Force Bases were each large military facilities located in the San Antonio area and, other than the city's equally large Hispanic population, defined much of the dynamics of the city. In fact, San Antonio promoted itself as *"Military City, U.S.A."* McLendon applied for, and was granted, the new call letters KAKI, a reference to the servicemen's traditional *'khaki uniforms.'* Unveiled with billboards, flyers and typical McLendon flair and extravagance, the change provided Weaver one of his favorite and oft-repeated McLendon moments.

The same day that KTSA became KAKI, Weaver made a sales call to a Houston ad agency that had clients in San Antonio and they were all joking about the new San Antonio station's identity. Seems the pronunciation of KAKI in Spanish was very similar to 'caca'- the Spanish slang word for baby feces; translated into English as 'poopy.' Rather than notify Gordon discreetly, Bill enjoyed sending a TWX message to the openly visible receiving machine in the Dallas home office.

"Gordon, did you think to check what KAKI sounds like in Spanish?" The TWX machine went silent except for the humming sound of a small compressor. Bill paced back in forth in front of the machine, mentally visualizing the process taking place in the Dallas office. Finally, a cryptic response from McLendon came across the TWX: *"oh shit!"*

Thanks to a powerful and responsive FCC attorney, KAKI returned to being KTSA within twenty-four hours. A massive amount of Billboards, bumper stickers, letterheads, and business cards had to be destroyed, the old fashioned way. Bill Weaver loved each retelling of that story.

Chapter SEVENTEEN
"ROLLIN' ON THE RIVER"

Texas' two biggest cities have always been competitive and unique in every way. Dallas was Dom Pérignon and Neiman Marcus, while Houston was Lone Star Beer and Stelzig's Western Wear.

Positioned midway between the two Texas metropolises was Madisonville, and just to the southeast of Madisonville, the seven-hundred and ten mile long Trinity River meandered south to the Gulf of Mexico. The waterway was named in 1690 by Alonso De Leon, who called it "La Santisima Trinidad" (*the most Holy Trinity.*) Flowing from three principal branches in North Texas, they all merged into one frequently flooded and increasingly polluted river just a mile southwest of downtown Dallas and began its long journey to Trinity Bay on the northeast headwaters of the Houston Ship Channel.

In 1957, the Trinity River Authority prepared a master plan of lakes and dams that would control flooding and aid conservation along the Trinity. Multiple reservoirs were on the drawing board at Navarro Mills, Bardwell, Wallisville and a massive lake with a two and a half mile long dam to be constructed just west of Livingston at an eighty-four million dollar price tag. The Livingston Dam would permanently end the free flow of the

Trinity between Texas' most formidable and competitive cities.

With the impending permanent closure of the river's historic connection, the McLendon stations decided to turn back the clock one final time with "The Last Great Texas River Race."

In the summer of 1966, Chuck Dunaway and an un-named captain, who claimed expertise at operating and repairing outboard motors, boarded a twelve foot flat-bottom aluminum boat with a ten horsepower engine to carry the colors of the radio station I now proudly called home – KILT, the Big 6-10 in Houston.

A few yards away, in an identically equipped boat, was Eddie Payne, a former co-worker from KDOK, the little daytime radio station we had both once shared in Tyler. Eddie was now to be considered a turn-coat and unabashedly hiding behind the pseudonym – *'Jimmy Rabbit,'* a silly name he would shamelessly use for the rest of his otherwise, illustrious career.

All decorum and civility between the two sister-stations rapidly deteriorated into childish insults and name-calling. Never mind that both KILT and KLIF were sister-stations and owned by the same company - the Last Great Texas River Race was much bigger than personal rivalry; it would permanently establish the superiority of one Texas metropolis.

Sam Houston's historic Battle of San Jacinto was about Texas' Independence: the Cowboys vs. the Oilers was mere sport but it was left to the Great Texas River Race to determine, for all time, Texas' dominant city. The eyes of Texas were focused on the muddy waters of the Trinity and its two brave captains.

The weight on Chuck's shoulders was immense. There could be no draw - one winner only and one lonely loser. You could feel the pressure and intense competitive focus in Dunaway's eyes as he loaded the last case of Lone Star Beer onto the KILT craft.

~

The race began its long trek down the Trinity in Dallas at the I-30 Bridge, just south of downtown Dallas. Both stations were to broadcast play-by-play accounts of the competition at various stops throughout the day, but this all occurred prior to the development of cell phones. Realistically, we had to rely on occasional calls from the teams when a reporter from one of the stations would spot the two floating past a black-topped or dirt-road bridge near small Texas communities with names such as Hall's Bluff, Old Elwood, and Simmons Bottom.

Within the first few hours, Chuck began to have serious doubts about his boat captain's claimed maritime experience after guiding Chuck and Rabbit's trailing boat on a wrong turn into a small tributary. After hours of no contact, both stations had to report that the teams were apparently lost. As the evening sun set in the west, the screeching sounds of a distant bobcat layered on top of the constant roar of barred owls and bullfrogs and their only light source – flashlights - frequently revealed gators, coons and moccasins slivering along the overgrown shoreline. The sailors bravely lashed their crafts together and floated the dark waters while openly revealing secret admissions of life's sins, until the miraculous rediscovery of the main river channel. Chuck's Captain [sic] resigned the race after this experience with loud and colorful parting comments that reverberated through the dark and lonely river bottom.

Chuck was joined by KILT newsman Jim Carola, who acknowledged even less previous boating experience, for the remainder of the race. Chuck bravely assumed the role of Captain, Navigator, Mechanic and Cook in an inspiring demonstration of confidence; which frequently trumps talent.

By day three, the KLIF boat - Jimmy and his own colorful co-captain - began building a slight lead that would increase each day until the boats neared the waters of upper Trinity Bay.

When news stringers from each station or local newspapers would encounter either team, they reported a diminishing level of civility on the part of the participants.

Nearing the last leg of the race, the KLIF boat, through suspected trickery, was some twenty odd minutes in front of the KILT team.

The area where the mighty Trinity empties into the large Galveston Bay complex is known as Trinity Bay, near the small community of Anahuac. Outside the river channel, there is a wide, shallow estuary with numerous small islands. Large limbs and trees and an occasional refrigerator, deposited over the years by flooding and changing river currents, presented challenging obstructions. Depending upon the tide, one could easily become disoriented, lost or grounded. As the two boats neared Anahuac, the sun was setting and all parties agreed not to attempt to cross the larger body of water until the light of the following day.

Meanwhile, Chuck Dunaway noticed a small seaplane circling overhead. The pilot, who turned out to be a huge fan of Chuck's radio show, landed near one of the many small oxbow lakes that fed into the main river and offered to buy the Houston team's dinner. Back at the KILT studios, News Director Brad Messer had spent the afternoon studying aerial photos of the shallow waters of upper Trinity Bay and at last, had developed a plan. To help maneuver Chuck across the upper reaches of the bay, Brad would replace Jim Carola as navigator on the last leg of the race.

After Brad arrived in Anahuac and met Chuck's new-found friend, he devised an even more brilliant plan. Knowing that the Dallas boat would need guidance, he suggested that the pilot might offer his services to lead their team on a more scenic route to the finish line, which would include parts of the vast Galveston Bay. This diversion would, of course, allow Chuck and Brad to take a more direct path across the flatlands, shaving valuable time off their current position in the race. Appearing to all present to be a wonderful idea, a toast was raised to celebrate the strategy.

~

The morning's first light revealed a layer of haze over the surprisingly calm bay where the fresh water from the Trinity meets salt water from the Gulf, creating an abundant estuary – a literal factory of life. As small puffs of fog begin to dissipate, a shrimp boat drops its nets for the first drag of the morning, setting off a breathtaking display of aquatic life in its wake. Plovers and sandpiper and a host of shorebirds begin their daily symphony of song and dance amidst colorful water hyacinth. Seagulls, diving for breakfast, compete with Redfish and Speckled Trout, chasing shrimp to the surface and churned the water in a ritualistic orgy of feeding while egrets and blue herons by the hundreds fill the sky with color and majestic beauty.

Meanwhile, a small flat-bottomed aluminum boat with two trusting souls from Dallas chugged south into the wide waters of Galveston Bay, grateful for the last-minute offer of guidance from a kind soul in a seaplane. At the same time, two brilliant but devious sailors from Houston slipped westward, straight across the flatlands, singing loudly as they made their way on a direct path to the finish line; claiming a triumphant come-from-behind victory for Space City USA.

Chapter EIGHTEEN
"CH-CH-CHANGES"

Finally, things were beginning to settle down. Being the program director of a McLendon station was a thrill a minute and we were finally winning ratings in all day-parts, plus I enjoyed the people I worked with.

But change was in the wind.

In September, Bill Weaver - the only general manager in KILT's history and a major part of the McLendon team since its early beginnings, suddenly resigned.

Bill and his wife Beverly had purchased a home at Valley Lodge, a country community some forty-five miles to the west of the studios. Gordon Mclendon was not happy about his manager being that distance from the studios and was frequently vocal about his displeasure. Bill was fiercely independent, so with a long-standing and lucrative offer from the mammoth Cap-Cities chain of radio properties, he resigned and accepted management of WKBW in Buffalo, New York.

~

Each day, a package containing all the home office memorandums and paperwork arrived with the morning mail. It would be full of brown inner-company envelopes with the name of the past and current recipients written in longhand on the front. I would frequently get them from Don Keyes, but then came one from Gordon McLendon himself.

"Bill, as you know, Bill Weaver has decided to leave the McLendon Stations. I'm pleased with the progress the station has made since you arrived and do not want to see that direction change. Would you let me know, by return mail, your recommendation for the manager's position at KILT?"

What? I was stunned. To this point I had not met nor spoken to Gordon McLendon, yet here he was asking me to advise him on who should be my new boss. The truth is that I had rarely stepped outside the studios for the first few months and the only Houston radio people I knew were the ones I saw each day at KILT. I immediately called Don Keyes, assuming that McLendon's interoffice memo was misdirected. Don was equally surprised but said that Gordon always knew what he was doing so, *"just tell him what you think."*

The only Houston management level person with a title that I even knew by this time was Dickie Rosenfeld, the KILT Sales Manager. I returned the interoffice memo to McLendon with that suggestion but also mentioned that my knowledge of the market was still limited. Within a week, the announcement was made. Richard *"Dickie"* Rosenfeld became the new KILT General Manager.

~

In spite of the changes downstairs in the sales and management offices, the upstairs/programming group was becoming even more autonomous and Rosenfeld quickly assured me that he had no intention of becoming involved. With increased ad rates resulting from the ratings trends, all members of the sales staff wore smiles to work. Harry Rogers, a true gentleman, was appointed Sales Manager and other than my touching base with that part of the building each morning, nothing changed in the day to day programming operation.

My primary focus was the overall sound of KILT. Using what I had learned from Steve Brown's production magic in Omaha; from the influence of the produced sound of KBOX in Dallas; and creating all those promos in Waco and Tyler -- we began structuring an exciting environment 'between the music'.

KILT added a subtle but constant level of reverberation to everything on the air, sounding as if it was being broadcast from a giant cathedral. Because we were the only station in the market with that effect, a listener instantly came to identify KILT with BIG! In fact, we started calling ourselves *"The BIG 6-10."* We still had work to do on the technical facility itself, but the Houston ratings picture was already showing change.

With Chuck Dunaway's guidance, we developed a playlist with more emphasis on current hits, introduced an hourly hot-clock that matched audience flow and defined the rotation of music to fit the constantly changing audience flow. The deejays still had the ability to select music, but only from a controlled list and within the format's hourly parameters.

We also went to great lengths to understand the audience's movement at various times of the day; what time classes began and ended in the colleges and public schools; when the major industries started their work day; and we kept abreast of traffic counts on the freeways. We asked a lot of questions and experimented with a lot of 'mini' ideas.

By autumn, Houston's Hooper ratings confirmed the growth trends for KILT and my November 8th memorandum congratulated the staff for beating KNUZ in all day-parts for the first time. But as the saying goes, nothing stays the same.

Changes that were totally out of my control were just over the horizon.

~

In mid-November, Don Keyes, McLendon's long-time National Program Director and my primary mentor, resigned to finalize the purchase of his own radio station in Canton, Ohio.

Four days later, Bill Stewart, the mysterious programming guru, considered by many to have been an integral part of Top Forty's development, became my new boss. Bill had a reputation for making major changes.

I had heard that life was crazy in the big city.

On Sunday evening, November 20, 1966, just three days after Stewart returned to reclaim the position he had created years before, I spoke with Bill for the first time. The call came to my home at about 9 p.m. and we spent a few minutes in introductions and small talk. Then Bill came straight to the point - *"you've got good press here in Dallas and I want to switch you and John Borders. You will take over as program director here at KLIF and we'll move Borders down to Houston ... oh, and I'd like to have you here next week."*

Suddenly, the panic attacks were back.

~

In my early conversations with Don Keyes, he had told me how much more he was able to accomplish when he programmed KILT than he was ever able to complete at KLIF. According to Don, there were many layers of senior people in Dallas that often slowed down the process of getting things accomplished. Gordon was the boss, but his father, B.R. McLendon, had a sometimes volatile temper, colorful language and since Mr. Mac was in charge of the company's finances, he always took control when he entered a conversation. Layer in a *'national director'* of every facet of the operation, plus local manager Al Lurie, long-time home office fixtures Glenn Calison, Edd Routt, Mitch Lewis, Les Vaughn, Gordon's secretary Billie Odem, Dorothy Manning - the treasurer and queen mother of the company - and none of them shy about voicing opinions, meant KLIF appeared to be an impossible maze. One thing stood in my favor, the two UT grads that had originally hired me at WACO - Art Holt and Homer Odem - were now members of that McLendon home office management team and were supportive Dallas' inside cheerleaders of my work.

As impressive as KLIF could be to a resume, I knew that the autonomy available in Houston would not be duplicable in Dallas. The reality was that I simply felt more at home with what some described as Houston's *"blue-collar slobs"* than with Dallas' *"white-collar snobs."*

Long time KLIF morning personality and Program Director Ken Dowe is the person believed to have been best at confronting the maze of home-office issues. Ken virtually took ownership of the direction of KLIF for years before its sale in 1971. When McLendon sold KLIF AM to Fairchild Industries, the sales contract stated that he would not operate an AM radio station within 150 miles of Dallas for 10 years. Nothing was said however about McLendon's FM station in Dallas -- KNUS. With his son Bart as manager and Dowe as Program Director, they took the left-over talent that McLendon retained in the sale, hired a team of brilliant young guns, including Beau Weaver, Tommy Kramer, Christopher Haze, Michael Spears, Jon Rivers, Fred Kennedy and took KNUS to number one, beating KLIF in ratings for the first time. KLIF never recovered.

~

I started rattling off all the reasons I could think of to stop this train. *"Oh Bill, we just bought a new home and my son started a new school last week and I really haven't had time to accomplish*

all I want to with KILT and I hate to lose this momentum, and, and,"
(think fast Young) - but Stewart abruptly ended the conversation
himself. *"Well, we'll talk about it later."* Boom! Conversation over!
Bill Stewart never mentioned the move again but from the sound
of his voice, I sensed that he was not accustomed to a member of
his department questioning any change.

~

The interoffice communication came through as I arrived at the
studio a few weeks later. Bill Stewart was inviting all McLendon
Program Directors to Dallas for a weekend group meeting
beginning the following Thursday evening. We would also sit-
in during the Friday manager's meeting going on concurrently
at Gordon's Cielo Ranch -- an eighty-three acre estate on Lake
Lewisville, north of Dallas. Stewart would use the rest of our
time together to discuss policy and strategy. It was my first time
to meet both key figures in the evolution of Top 40 radio. I had
already been apprehensive about meeting Stewart and now I
would also meet Gordon McLendon himself.

When we arrived at Dallas' Adolphus Hotel, not far from the
KLIF studios, we were given the message to meet Mr. Stewart
in the hotel bar. Bill was a tall, distinguished looking man with
a soft, deep baritone voice and an extraordinary command
of language. Even though it had been years since he was on
the air, Bill's voice was instantly familiar although his quiet,
reserved distance was a bit intimidating. Most of the evening
was social with a lot of radio stories and sufficient amounts
of alcohol consumed by the group: as always, I abstained. The
only business discussed was when Stewart announced that he
wanted to move all station's two hourly newscasts to 20/20 -
twenty minutes past, and twenty minutes before each hour —
a concept first developed by radio consultant Bill Drake. KHJ,
the red-hot Drake station in Los Angeles introduced the 20/20

concept as a clever competitive move that took advantage of a unique part of the ARB methodology. After listening for just five continuous minutes in a given quarter hour, an individual would be counted as a full quarter hour listener. By playing music at the top of the hour, when most of the competition was broadcasting news, KHJ would theoretically attract a listener searching for music and hold onto them for a full twenty minutes before their own newscast, in effect giving them credit for two quarter hours. The process was repeated, in reverse, the next half hour. Other than that announcement, Bill Stewart remained very distant and watchful all evening, but I had the impression that he was making mental notes.

Bill asked me to join him for the forty-five minute cab ride to Gordon's Cielo Ranch the next morning. Cielo, the Spanish word for heaven, was McLendon's sprawling five-hundred acre ranch property north of Dallas on Lake Louisville, near the small town of Shady Shores. Don Keyes once wrote, *"Gordon never tried to impress people with his wealth, but Ceilo was different. Ceilo was to Gordon what the corporate jet and Rolex were to others; it was his pride and joy."*

The next morning, Bill and I took seats in the back of the taxi and waited for the program director from Buffalo, who was a bit slow getting started after the previous evening's extended happy hour. That's when Bill popped the question I had dreaded; *"what are your problems in Houston...is it Dickie?"* (new manager Rosenfeld). I had mentally prepared myself for the question, but surprised when it came so quickly. Rumors had become part of company legend about how staff members of newly acquired stations were called in and encouraged to share their criticism of the station, then were fired the next day. I was prepared for the question.

"Bill, my only problem is time, it just takes a lot of time to build

the kind of station I know KILT can be. I'm working to get the right air-team in place and revisiting all the internal systems, but we just need more time." I suspect that was not the type answer Bill Stewart wanted to hear, but I do know that he did not speak another word for the hour long drive to McLendon's ranch. It was a very uncomfortable cab ride.

~

Much of the early McLendon fortune came from a chain of outdoor theatres. Gordon's father, B.R. McLendon, was an attorney and in 1932, assumed ownership of a piece of land from a client as payment for his legal bill. McLendon determined that showing movies outdoors was a clever way to make raw land pay for itself while property values increased. In time, the McLendon's added even more drive-in theater properties and eventually expanded to multiple screens in many of their locations, setting a record of sorts at their I-45 drive-in in Houston with six screens and room for more than three thousand automobiles.

The theatre business had become a sizeable chain called Tri-State Theatres with as many as seventy properties in Texas, Oklahoma and Louisiana. In 1948, B.R. McLendon built the opulent Casa Linda Theatre near White Rock Lake in Dallas with its lighted cylindrical tower. It was later hailed by Entertainment Weekly as the *"best theatre in America."* Because the company booked so many motion pictures into their theatres, they had access to private screenings of virtually every new film. The viewing room at Cielo became the center of special screenings with an impressive list of friends, actors, celebrities and business associates. The room was huge with an opulent fireplace, fine rugs, a huge–fully stocked bar, lush fabric and leather couches and recliners plus a separate projection room with operators -- just like the finest theatres.

Gordon himself produced the commercials for the movies

they featured at the Casa Linda. He used his own voice and the power of his immense language skills to paint 'word pictures' in the listener's mind. His commercial for the classic western *High Noon*, for instance, was incredibly powerful. You could feel the tension as he described Gary Cooper, the small town marshal, standing face to face against a gang of killers hell-bent on sending him to the grave. One could feel the tension, the blistering New Mexico heat, and share the fear in the eyes of the small town's frightened residents. Just as McLendon had earlier described the excitement of a baseball game taking place hundreds of miles away, he used that same power of language to describe a showdown at High Noon.

Within no time, the success of McLendon's commercial work attracted the attention of Hollywood producers themselves and he was hired to create commercials for hundreds of first run movies, including the blockbuster James Bond thrillers *Dr No* and *From Russia with Love*. Between 1963 and 1966, McLendon was under exclusive contract to United Artists to produce radio ads for most all of the company's pictures. Gordon and Don Keyes would view the movie while making notes, Don would write some copy lines, engineer Glenn Callison would capture sounds and dialogue from the soundtrack, and Gordon would voice the copy.

To Gordon McLendon, no canvas was as large as the imagination, and the giant screen provided an ideal pallet for his immense word imagery. At one point, he became the largest shareholder of Columbia Pictures, and was Executive Producer of 'Escape to Victory,' starring Michael Caine, Sylvester Stallone and directed by John Huston.

There were actually three movies that McLendon himself produced that were shot at Cielo. 'Giant Gila Monster', 'The Killer Shrews', and 'My Dog Buddy' were McLendon produced movies that were released nationally. Some of them still show up occasionally on Comedy Central and other late night channels. The New York Times once labeled *Giant Gila Monster* as the 'worst movie ever made' prompting Gordon to respond with, "that's just not true - I made two other movies that were much worse!"

~

When we arrived at McLendon's ranch, the managers were already in the midst of some heavy duty discussions and we quietly took our place on the couches lining the back wall of the viewing room. Gordon sat in a reclining chair facing the managers while his father B.R McLendon – *'Mr. Mac'* - sat a few feet away in a large rocker. I took a seat between Bill Stewart and KILT's new manager Rosenfeld.

Most of the discussion was about advertising revenues and business projections but one of the issues failed to include any mention of possible impact from a recent FCC ruling on political advertising. I whispered to Bill Stewart that the issue was being overlooked and he urged me to *"go ahead and ask Gordon."*

Never having even met the man before, my voice was a bit tentative when I raised my hand and asked how the new rulings might impact our commercial limits. McLendon appeared to be very responsive, beginning the answer with *"good question, thank you for reminding me Bill."* He then went into a very lengthy discourse about listener limits, placement and rate structures and I was feeling very important that he was spending so much time responding but after he finished, I was not sure that he had actually answered the question. Apparently, Gordon's father felt the same way. Mr. Mac came straight to the point - *"gawl-dammit, answer his question!"*

~

We wound up spending the entire weekend at Cielo and on

Sunday morning, just after the meeting ended, Gordon McLendon came out on the covered walkway as I loaded the taxi. He shook my hand and said *"Bill, I'm glad you're with us."* It was a big moment for a kid from East Texas. Bill Stewart seemed equally proud and actually conversed during the cab drive back to the Adolphus. I went home to Houston and the joy of programming KILT for over fourteen more years.

Chapter NINETEEN
"MORNING HAS BROKEN"

As my first anniversary at KILT passed, I was pleased with the station's progress, but change and all of its uncertainties continued to lurk just around the corner. First, Bill Stewart stepped in to move our top-rated morning personality, Alex Bennett, to a late-night talk show from 10 p.m. to 2 a.m. Joe Pyne was achieving enormous ratings success with a confrontational talk show on KABC and later KLAC in Los Angeles. Joe's publicity touted him as *'the man you love to hate'* for insulting hippies, gays and feminists, his support for the Vietnamese War, and his commitment to ultimately anger every listener of his show. The audience loved to hate Joe Pyne!

The late night audience in Houston soon loved to hate Alex Bennett also -- it's just that the size and spending power of that audience was not the most sought-after listener for most advertisers. Meanwhile, I was faced with replacing a winning morning show.

We first hired Cousin Thom Sherwood to replace Alex in morning drive. Thom was a man of a thousand voices and had a lot of talent but as we neared summer, I knew we still had work to do to dominate this important day-part.

At Bill Stewart's recommendation, we transferred Jimmy Rabbit from the company's KLIF-Dallas to KILT. Jimmy had worked for me at KDOK but left to take over the early evening shift at KLIF. His Dallas success was instantaneous. Because of his popularity, Bill Stewart moved Jimmy to mornings in Dallas after Charlie & Harrigan left KLIF for Cleveland. Stewart then convinced me to move Jimmy to Houston and take over mornings. While I had reservations about how his unique style would fit with the Houston audience, there were no better options.

Jimmy's delivery was conversational with a distinct edge and just a hint of 'bad boy' sarcasm. While I had never considered him a morning type...he was so unique and stylized that it just might work. It didn't. Jimmy hated Houston, missed his girlfriend in Dallas and the experiment was short-lived.

A successful wake-up show can, and should, anchor the entire broadcast day. Ideally, the station has a personality with long tenure in the market and is heavily involved in the communities served. Finding someone who can replace them however is not simple. Most all of us have set personal routines in the morning and, for some, a favorite radio host often becomes part of that routine. Building dominance is more complicated than just playing the right music; it's about building a relationship with the listener and sharing the most personal time of their day. While my first year at KILT had been successful, I knew that we still had some real work to do. Mornings were still a problem.

In the spring of 1967, another significant change occurred. Russ Knight, our successful nighttime deejay, resigned to move back to New England. While losing anyone of Russ's capabilities hurt, his obvious replacement was already in the building. Steve Lundy's move to the 6-10 p.m. slot was about to become a giant step in the construction of the new KILT.

~

The automatic top of the hour tone sets the stage for Charlie

Van Dyke's deep, resonant voice of God...

(The exact naval observatory time is six p.m. The following sound is a reference tone. Use it to tune your radio to precisely six-ten kilohertz for maximum reception of the Steve Lundy Underground Experience.)

A wall of rapidly changing tones cycle through multiple frequencies before settling on a strangely harmonic—yet discordant—blend for exactly 1.3 seconds. Suddenly, it's overpowered by the floor-shacking pounding of bass and drums - cut to the vocal lead-in from George Thorogood's "IN THE NIGHTIME"

In the Nighttime -- that's the Right time...
I say the Nighttime -- that's the Right time...
I wanna beeee with you, In the Nightime..." ©

<u>Steve Lundy VO</u>: *"Six p.m., in the greatest city in the South and this is Steve Lundy, baby, on the* (deep echo chamber) <u>*BIG 6-10!*</u>*"*

With what many still call the greatest rock 'n roll disc jockey voice in contemporary radio, Steve Lundy immediately took total control of Houston nights.

Steve had the rare ability to merge a classic Shakespearean command of language and voice control with a soulful street-level funkiness that would eventually take him to the top tier of mega-stations - WNBC-New York, CKLW-Windsor/Detroit, WLS- Chicago, KROQ-Los Angeles and KFRC-San Francisco. He was chosen 'Disc Jockey of the Year' by Billboard Magazine while hosting the afternoon drive show in New York city.

~

Steve's move to nights on KILT created an opening in early

afternoon. I hired Mac Hudson to take over the midday slot. Other than time spent in Austin, most of Mac's career had taken place at various stations in Beaumont, a large petroleum-producing area ninety miles to the east of Houston.

The combined cities of Beaumont/Port Arthur/Orange had a huge reputation for producing a remarkable number of music and radio achievers.

It was there in 1959 that John Hicks Jr., a former theology professor at Southern Methodist University in Dallas, purchased his first radio station, KOLE in Port Arthur. Under the eventual management and financing expertise of three of his sons, Steve, Tom and William, their combined radio properties evolved into the massive Clear Channel Broadcasting dynasty.

Beaumont's KTRM was the launching pad for disc jockey and Program Director J.P Richardson, who set a world record in May, 1957 for staying on the air continuously, for six consecutive days. He became known nationally in 1958 as *The Big Bopper* with the million selling hit song *'Chantilly Lace'*. Richardson died in the plane crash that also took the lives of Buddy Holly and Richie Valens.

The Winter brothers, Johnny and Edgar, soaked in all the ethnic, gospel and blues influences present in the area to build enormously successful individual careers.

Janis Joplin was a native of Port Arthur and attended Lamar State College in Beaumont before transferring to University of Texas, then became part of the Haight/Ashbury 'flower power' movement in San Francisco.

Huey Meaux of nearby Winnie, Texas - the infamous record producer and 'Crazy Cajun' character - was a frequent guest deejay on area stations.

Al Caldwell spent decades as a top-rated deejay and program director of KLVI. He was eventually chosen the Natl. Association of Broadcaster's "Small Market Personality of the Year" and later inducted into the Texas Radio Hall of Fame.

Beaumont was also home for George Jones, 'Ivory' Joe Hunter, trumpeter Harry James, Archie Bell, Rod Bernard, Tracy Byrd, Mark Chesnutt, Jimmy Clanton, B.J. Thomas, Clay Walker, Tex Ritter, Lee Hazlewood – phew - and many others.

Oh, and Gordon Baxter, a storyteller, author, columnist, pilot, and outrageous morning deejay whose eclectic style built a huge following at a number of Beaumont area stations.

~

Mac Hudson was also a Beaumont native and had been heavily influenced by Baxter. Mac made it very clear when he came to KILT that he wanted to be a morning deejay, presumably in the unpredictable Baxter mold. I was reluctant to experiment in this important day part and go head-on against KNUZ' Paul Berlin with anything less than a proven winner. Plus, by early summer Mac's mid-day numbers were doing well enough that there was little enthusiasm for change.

Morning radio hosts are a special breed. I know - I hosted a morning show for years in Tyler and hated every single day. For openers, your day starts about the same time you used to get home back in college; most of your fellow employees arrive about the time your work day is finishing; the sales staff often has you booked for lunch with an existing or potential sponsor where you're expected to perform and keep everyone entertained until the sale is made; if you're lucky, you squeeze in a power nap in order to show up that night as the guest emcee for the annual Potted Meat Producer's dinner. Successful morning jocks have lots of people tugging at their off-air time. If there is a family involved, the schedule makes it even more difficult to maintain parenting and marriage responsibilities. Mac had a very large family.

Honestly, Mac Hudson simply did not fit the vision that I had in mind for a *"time to rise and shine, it's a brand new day"* kind of morning deejay. There was no question of his intelligence, his sense of drama and timing or his mastery of humor, but occasionally Mac's humor--and his moods--could be dark and sardonic. Quite frankly, I also worried about Mac's ability to do the public relations thing. The truth was however, I had no better options at the moment. I moved Mac to mornings in mid 1969 on a *'trial'* basis. He did admirable work, had a sharp mind and I soon began to think that, with time, he just might develop mornings into a winner.

~

A few weeks later, an out-of-the-blue phone call from Paul Menard changed everything. Paul entered the radio business after attending KDJU, a Dallas radio school taught by KLIF's morning team—Jack Woods and Ron Chapman—known on KLIF as Charlie and Harrigan. After work at a few small to medium-sized markets, then three years at Todd Storz' KOMA in Oklahoma City, Paul - who had obviously made an impression on the school's founders - was hired to replace the Harrigan half of the team after Chapman left radio to join WFAA-TV in Dallas. The team later moved to Cleveland, Ohio but after dissolving the partnership, Paul was looking for a job, hoping to finally prove himself as a successful stand -alone deejay. In reality, there were not many radio teams still left around so Paul's wish made logical sense. In spite of his pitch however, I was already considering another scenario - Paul Menard and Mac Hudson - together.

Paul did not have a tremendous radio voice; what some would call a great set of pipes. His voice was nasally and average at best. He was a great story teller however with a brilliant sense of timing but then, he always laughed at his own punch lines. The laugh itself was infectious; it came off as a staccato, nasal –

snort of sorts that reminded one of an old Woody Woodpecker cartoon. But there was also something extraordinary about his timing, his comedic way of approaching things and especially that payoff - that laugh. I could not get it out of my head. Everyone who heard his audition tape had the same response; whenever Paul laughed -- everybody laughed.

When I first mentioned the team show possibility, both Mac and Paul individually became defensive and voiced doubts about merging their careers with someone they had never met. I sent a plane ticket to Paul anyway and gave Mac a company credit card, telling them to hang out together for a few days and see what happened.

We met three days later for lunch at the downtown Houston House restaurant. Within minutes, I knew we had our morning show. It was sheer magic! I wish I could say it was some brilliant idea that I had planned and developed, but the reality is, all I had to do was get out of the way and let the Hudson & Harrigan franchise become the most successful morning radio show in Houston history.

They kept the city energized, both on and off the air with bizarre promotions: a 6 a.m. jog-in in the Astrodome with famed Heart Surgeon Denten Cooley and racing's A.J. Foyt as the pace runners; convincing KILT deejay Todd Wallace to live outside - for weeks - in Houston heat - on top of the Astrodome; Harrigan's *'gored in the groin'* encounter with a killer-whale at Galveston's Sea-Arama; the opening night premier in the Astrodome to commemorate Mac Hudson's brief walk-on one-liner in the movie, Brewster McCloud.

No idea was too bizarre' and no one was afraid to suggest something new; no one was angry or pissed off at the government; and no idea was a bad idea, well - except one...

Chapter TWENTY
"SURFIN USA"

It was once written; *'In radio, there is nothing new under the sun.'* So the act of *'perfecting'* an idea that had originated elsewhere was common practice in the industry. Still is.

Full disclosure here, the Big Kanuka promotion was a direct rip-off from KHJ in BOSS Angeles, the major radio powerhouse programmed by the talented Ron Jacobs and super-consultant Bill Drake. But KILT's copy of the summer promotion was not unique – many radio stations within reach of a beach created some version of the *Big K*.

Surfing was hot on the West Coast and although the waves were considerably less spectacular, also very popular on the Gulf Coast. The surf around San Luis Pass, equal distance between Galveston and Freeport could—if you were there early enough on the right morning—make you feel like you were 'shootin' the pier' or 'walkin' the nose.'

KHJ's original promotion was called *'The Big Kahuna.'* Cliff Robertson had played the part of the "Big K"– the best surfer on the beach – in the 1959 film *Gidget*. KHJ's promotion would ask listeners to call the station's hotline each time they heard the Big Kahuna blowing on a conch shell. That would be the signal to call a special phone number and the designated caller would win tickets to a spectacular KHJ luau. The climax of the event was to be the Big Kahuna's grand entrance, with prizes and photo ops.

~

The KILT version was called the 'Big Kanuka' - named for an exotic wilderness area on the North Island of New Zealand. KILT's summer promotion's launch was built around a giant arrival party on Galveston's West Beach. Listeners were invited to join us on the Beach to welcome our Big K as he rowed ashore in his prize-packed 'waka ama' outrigger canoe. So long as you could suspend reality for awhile, radio allowed those of us in the production studio to create huge mental pictures. But let's face it, the odds of anyone actually rowing themselves in an eleven-foot outrigger across the South Pacific Ocean; through the Panama Canal; across the massive Gulf of Mexico and then navigate to one single fifty yard-wide Galveston beach property (which just happened to have building lots on sale that weekend) was possible only if you accepted the existence of a tooth-fairy!

We ran the promotional announcements for ten days before the Kanuka's arrival at two o'clock on a sunny, summer, Sunday afternoon.

Our muscle-bound Big Kanuka was hired from a local health club and he seemed to have all the right skills – most of all, his availability all summer to be *on-call* for impromptu appearances, which translated meant that he had no other current employment! *"BK"* certainly looked the part; perfect tan; long blond hair; lots of muscle; and a big smile that I envisioned would appeal to every lonely-girl radio listener in town.

~

After a week of building up the promotion, arrival day came and some of the KILT staff members joined me at our sponsor's Galveston Beach development site. A makeup artist was hired to smooth out Big K's tan, his hair was trimmed perfectly and his native head-dress of colorful feathers and beads gave him the image of a true Surf God. The plan was to have a tri-hull motorboat pull his solo outriggers canoe a mile or so off-shore, out of sight of the destination point so that our hero could enter the small boat, take advantage of the prevailing south-easterly winds and with minimal skill, use the long traditional oars to row himself straight into the private beach.

The planning and the setting were perfect. Damn this was going to be great!

~

I do seem to recall a moment when our Big K appeared to be a bit apprehensive, but some level of stage-fright was to be expected. In fact, I was beginning to feel some butterflies myself, but we were all too busy to check on him. Finally, as we walked him out to the tri-hull boat, I noticed that he was beginning to look ill. When I asked if he was alright, he answered in a heretofore unheard, high-pitched voice..."*I can't swim.*"

By this time, the waves -- which seemed to be a lot higher fifty feet out in the surf -- were beginning to cause the rented Kanuka's colorful feathers to bleed a really yukky blend of fuchsia, lime green and saddle brown into a mosaic somewhat reminiscent of *baby poop*. The rapidly changing colors merged with the goldenrod tint of his makeup, originally meant only to augment his natural tan. But suddenly, each new wave revealed large patches of very pale skin and an expression of sheer panic.

As I watched through binoculars, the motorboat towed the brave native (now clinging to his life jacket) a mile or so offshore and I could swear that I saw his head leaning over the side of the boat. What was happening?

My first big promotion at KILT was suddenly in jeopardy of becoming a worst-case scenario come true. I should have listened when Mom taught me that commandment *"thou shalt not steal."* It was not just that I had been caught ripping another radio stations' promotion, I had not even ripped it off correctly. All my ambition, all the dreams of success in big market radio would now be marred by one huge career footnote: *"Young's career is distinguished for producing the only national screw-up of the Big Kahuna promotion, which incidentally—he stole from KHJ."*

~

During the arrival of the Big Kanuka, I retreated to the back of the makeshift stage to repair a sudden failure of the public address system. BK's once muscle-bound body was now washed with streaks of reds and yellows in stark contrast to his pale white–facial expression of stark terror. Without a word or a glance, our surf god from the islands stumbled to his automobile on shore, spent a few minutes leaning over next to his car fender, and then simply drove away.

All future phone calls to Mr. Big went unanswered. No further mentions of 'what's his name' appeared on KILT, and hopefully, readers of this admission will – as the famous old saying goes... "let dead dogs lie."

Chapter TWENTY ONE
"LET'S GET IT ON"

Rock critic Dave Marsh once wrote — *"Sex is bad, and somebody singing about it would be really bad."*

Prior to rock music's success--which arguably began with Bill Haley's *Rock Around the Clock*, song lyrics were easy to understand and remember. Dean Martin's *That's Amore* was a perfect example of smash hits with the singer's voice out front in the mix.

By the mid-fifties however, Rock n Roll had given ownership of popular music to a much younger audience. The new music was loud, compressed and the lyrics were increasingly bold and suggestive -- oh and it ratcheted even higher during unpredictable live performances.

Elvis Presley's first television appearance on the Ed Sullivan Show on September 9, 1956 was seen by an estimated sixty million people. Simply shaking his leg or tweaking his upper lip would cause screams and fainting from the mostly teen-aged girls in the audience. In Elvis' last appearance on the Sullivan show in early 1957, CBS censors required that he could only be shown from the waist up.

~

Dirty lyrics were frequently rumored to be a part of rock songs since many of the lyrics were "buried in the mix", a term meaning that the singer's vocal levels were compressed into the driving instrument track. If you listened really close, maybe even changed the speed or played the song backward, you might hear really shocking things. The Kinsmen's definitive hit in 1963 – 'Louie Louie' – survived for years with an incoherent lyric that was *supposedly* chocked full of sexual references. The FBI conducted a thirty month investigation of the song's lyrics with no final conclusion. The governor of Indiana labeled it *'pornographic'* but the Indianapolis Star wrote *"As a music critic, Governor Matthew E. Welsh is probably a good lawyer."*

Gordon McLendon led a campaign in early 1967 against *"smutty and drug-promoting song lyrics."* A headline in industry publication Billboard Magazine on May 27, 1967 read *"McLendon vs. Labels."* McClendon placed full-page ads in national trade journals against records *"rife with raunchy lyrics"* and urged other broadcasters to join the campaign. In a speech to the American Mothers Committee at the Waldorf-Astoria in New York, he said *"The McLendon radio stations will not air records that offend public morals, dignity or taste...we've had all we can stand of the record industry's glorifying marijuana, LSD and sexual activity."* I was quoted in numerous publications about the new policy; *"the program director of McLendon's KILT in Houston commented, 'the hippies know what they are saying on these records, but John Q Public doesn't.'* The McLendon's chain banned the broadcast of Mitch Ryder's 'Sock It To Me Baby', The Rolling Stone's 'Let's Spend the Night Together', and other hit songs. Bill Gavin's influential music tip sheet singled out the Byrd's' lyrics to 'Eight Miles High' as encouraging and approving *"the use of marijuana or LSD."* Although the campaign was endorsed by numerous parents' groups, a hundred and twenty-five other radio stations around the country and the ABC radio network, it actually had little long-term impact on lyrics.

~

Again in the mid-eighties, song lyrics were back in the news. Surgeon General C. Everett Koop was one of the first public officials to speak out about what he called "trashy lyrics." A municipal judge in Newark, New Jersey banned rock concerts at an outdoor civic park. Various church groups organized record burnings while Reverend Jimmy Swaggart's attacks on the industry led Wal-Mart to stop selling major rock magazines such as *Rolling Stone*.

It was Tipper Gore, James Baker's wife Susan, and their congressional wives' group - *PMRC* (Parents' Music Resource Center) that took ownership of the crusade against porn rock in 1984 by calling for warning labels on records marketed to children. As a result of the campaign, record companies agreed to place the warning "Parental Guidance: Explicit Lyrics" on albums and cassettes containing such lyrics. In her book "Raising PG Kids in an X-Rated Society," Mrs. Gore wrote, *"As parents and as consumers, we have the right and the power to pressure the entertainment industry to respond to our needs. Americans, after all, should insist that every corporate giant, whether it produces chemicals or records, accept responsibility for what it produces."*

Mesdames Gore and Baker testified before the US Senate Commerce Committee's PMRC hearings on September 19, 1985, a committee on which Tipper's then husband, Senator Al Gore, served. The pair earned an array of nicknames from many quarters. Hustler Magazine's publisher Larry Flynt called them *'cultural terrorists.'* The late Frank Zappa, founder and lead singer of the group *Mothers of Invention*, testified at the same hearing, *"Ladies, how dare you? Bad facts make bad law, and people who write bad laws are, in my opinion, more dangerous than songwriters who celebrate sexuality."*

~

Radio is free and readily available to listeners of all ages. In reality, it has no way of knowing, at a given moment, if it's broadcasting to a mature forty year old or a developing twelve year old. Music radio never claimed to be Sunday school, but for me, it was at least expected to be a good citizen.

Music lyrics are still a subject of debate. A frequently cited 2009 policy statement by the American Academy of Pediatrics stated..."*The effect that popular music has on children's and adolescent's behavior and emotions, is of paramount concern."*

Chapter TWENTY TWO
"WRECK ON THE HIGHWAY"

It was a sleepy Sunday morning in April, 1967 – 5:15 a.m. The telephone shook me out of a deep sleep and after dropping the receiver a few times, I mumbled something that sounded like *"hello."*

> *"Mr. Young, this is John Foshee. I'm Jack's...well, I'm Steve Lundy's cousin in Tyler. I'm sorry to wake you so early but Steve had an accident last night and he's in critical condition here at Mother Frances Hospital. They will make the decision later this morning, but it's very possible that he will lose his left leg."*

We discussed the accident for a few minutes before I took his number and asked if he would keep me informed through the day. Later that morning, I called manager Dickie Rosenfeld and some of Steve's closest friends at the station.

By afternoon, the details began to trickle in. Steve had left Houston Saturday night about midnight to visit his dad in Tyler. Driving through the thick, dark, lonely piney woods forest of East Texas, Steve swerved his sports car to miss a deer in the road and slammed into a huge pine tree. The impact was so severe that the rear engine separated from the car's chassis and landed in the top of a nearby tree, spilling fuel and debris all over the crash site.

There is no way to describe my feelings that morning. Steve was more than an employee. Our time together in Tyler and now in Houston had become close to a mentor/student, father/son relationship. He loved intense conversation and we debated anything and everything. We openly discussed his positives, and the negatives, sometimes with graphic language, but he thrived on constructive criticism. Together we dissected each detail of his work by listening to his recorded air checks. Likewise, we debated the strengths, weaknesses and talents of other successful deejays.

Steve was originally influenced by the style of Dan Ingram, but out of that study, Steve developed his own unique style. He had a mind like a sponge and inherent talents: intuition, timing, commitment, plus a tough and self-critical objectivity that drove him to become one of the best talents to ever open a microphone. (Ironically, Steve's show on WNBC, New York competed directly with his career idol - WABC's Dan Ingram - but in head to head competition, it was Steve who was selected Billboard Magazine's 1970 Disc Jockey of the Year.)

Later that day, the doctors in Tyler removed Steve's left leg just above the knee.

On Monday morning, I called McLendon headquarters in Dallas and told them that, although Steve's recuperation could possibly take a year, I wanted to keep him on staff at full salary. My respect for the McLendon's was forever cemented when I was told that they supported that decision. The KILT deejays talked openly about the accident and Steve's recovery on the air and the audience support was overwhelming. Within a matter of weeks, Steve started making daily on-the-air call-ins to the station. He occasionally joked about his situation, voicing in one interview that his biggest concern was that he might *"swim around in circles"* once he could get back in the pool.

But off the air, his recuperation was slow, painful, and the intense regimen of medications kept him on a frightening roller-coaster between panic and depression. Steve spent numerous days, even some nights in our home and he became part of our family at times. I frequently took him to his doctor's appointments, kept his family in Tyler advised of his progress and listened when the medications kept him awake and he just needed to talk.

~

On October, 18th of that year, Steve returned for a sold-out *'Steve Lundy Appreciation Night'* at the Sam Houston Coliseum, starring Eric Burdon and the Animals. He proudly walked out on stage with a shiny black peg-leg prosthesis and a colorful swash-buckling flared shirt. The crowd rushed to its feet and gave him a long, enthusiastic standing ovation. Only backstage did I notice Steve's hands shaking and the moisture in his eyes.

Steve openly confronted and became master of his disability. His talent matured through the process and his career would soon mushroom, taking him to some of the nation's most respected radio stations — WLS, Chicago - WNBC, New York - KFRC in San Francisco's and at KROQ in Los Angeles. Many agree however that Steve's best moments came when he was on the air at KILT. Late in his career he returned to Houston and became a successful voiceover for many national advertisers.

I watched the kid from Tyler's extraordinary talent blossom from the age of seventeen to success at some of the best radio stations in the county. We debated technique frequently and I was never able to convince him to show up on time for appointments, but we shared dreams and fears and the building of two successful radio stations together. Steve was my star pupil, but most of all, Steve Lundy was my friend.

Steve ended each day's show with three words that described his own life's commitment: *"Walk on world."* Steve Lundy died while asleep in his Houston residence in 1999.

Chapter TWENTY THREE
"WHAT'D I SAY"

There is nothing permanent except change.

Dogenes Laertius

Touring concert events of the late fifties and early sixties consisted of an eclectic lineup of popular artists touring together, performing three or four of their hit songs and usually backed by a traveling *'house band'* of musicians. Artists that appeared on American Bandstand were frequently booked for these tours.

It was one of these packaged tours, "The Winter Dance Party" in early February, 1959, that featured Buddy Holly, Ritchie Valens and J.P. Richardson aka *'The Big Bopper.'* After a performance in Green Bay, Wisconsin, the three boarded a chartered flight to the next stop in Clear Lake, Iowa and crashed shortly after takeoff in snow and gusty winds, killing all on board. The event was enshrined in 1971 by Don McLean's classic song *American Pie* as *"the day the music died."*

~

During the mid sixties, KILT actually booked and produced most of its concerts directly through managers and agents. Ticket prices were usually five dollars for general admission seats and the profits went to local non-profit organizations.

In the summer of 1967, the KILT Appreciation Day Spectacular was headlined by Jefferson Airplane, one of the new-age progressive rock bands from San Francisco. The group's 'Somebody to Love' was the number one song in the country when they came to Houston's Sam Houston Coliseum and appeared with a number of artists who also had hit songs on the KILT 40 Star survey at the time. Artists on a typical KILT show featured a broad diversity of hit artists, such as Neil Diamond, Pozo Seco Singers, The Four Tops, usually a local band such as the Coastliners and one major headliner, which for this particular event was Jefferson Airplane. The general admission tickets were priced at five dollars and the seating priority depended upon how early you showed up at the gate and then how fast you could run to the front rows.

Jefferson Airplane had actually appeared in Houston a year earlier when the group's record label, RCA Victor, presented a private, industry-only, new-artist presentation at the Houston Country Club in Southeast Houston. The band set up their equipment right there on the floor of the meeting room with no stage, no big speakers, no light-show effects, and no funny smelling smoke in the air. It must have been frustrating for the band who was accustomed to receiving enthusiastic feedback from an audience of passionate fans, but the local suits present - cocktails in hand - spent more time one-upping their competitors than listening to a band they had never heard of anyway. A year later however, we were all singing along to 'Somebody to Love', their first single release that went to number one in the country.

The Sam Houston Coliseum, which held some eight thousand people, was sold-out for both performances. The afternoon show drew a typically younger crowd with each supporting artist playing their handful of hits and it all came off without a hitch. The evening crowd, however, was a more eclectic audience that looked as if they might have followed the group to Houston directly from the Haight-Ashbury district in San Francisco. Jefferson Airplane's core fans were a very different type of Houston concert crowd that was clearly not in the Coliseum to see the Pozo Seco Singers.

~

The band took the stage at about nine thirty that evening with a set of unrecognized music and soon, most of the typical KILT audience started calling for them to perform their hit single release - *"Somebody to Love."* The crowd waited and waited while the band virtually ignored them, occasionally even turning their backs to the audience and playing long, esoteric riffs of whatever that thing they were doing was called. Most of the fans simply gave up and left the building. The few that remained were crowding the stage and becoming part of the performance itself. *No problem* I thought, it will be over by ten or ten-thirty and we'll all go home with everyone happy.

By eleven-thirty, the head of the off-duty police security force informed me that the show needed to be winding down since his crew of officers were *"off the payroll"* by midnight. Repeated suggestions, then appeals to the Airplane's road manager, failed to stop the cosmic connection the band was having with its handful of fans, some of whom were now on stage and virtually indistinguishable from the artists themselves.

They were all moving strangely in a slow, dream-like state of consciousness. I could see the contingent of Houston Police officers moving closer to the stage amidst a cloud of strange smelling smoke (apparently one of the group's visual production elements that had been omitted from the afternoon performance.)

"One pill makes you larger and one pill makes you small"

The road manager rolled his eyes and threw his hands in the air, admitting that he had no control over the band -- until the Sergeant in charge of the off-duty police officers suggested that, *"well, its ok, just let 'em play as long as they want, but in twenty minutes, all these forty police officers standing around here go on double-overtime...on your tab!"*

Within minutes, the Airplane left the stage and flew home.... and so did the rest of the crowd.

~

Fast forward a few years and the same audience that had walked out of Jefferson Airplane's private jam in 1966 packed the same venue for their return with Grateful Dead in 1969. The changes taking place in music found a willing audience. Jimi Hendrix, with local backup band Moving Sidewalks (featuring a young Billy Gibbons) sold out two straight shows at the downtown Houston Music Hall. I introduced both of them to the audience, then stood backstage, just ten feet away from Hendrix during the second show, as he set fire to lighter fluid poured on his guitar. Houston firemen immediately rushed to the side of the stage, roughly pushing me aside, but the flame only flared briefly. Grateful Dead, Quicksilver Messenger Service, Grand Funk Railroad, Jethro Tull, The Who and Cream's farewell tours were just some of the sold-out events that changed the Houston concert experience in the late sixties.

KILT no longer booked its own shows, instead forming advertising partnerships with concert promoters. They received package advertising rates in return for allowing us to exclusively promote the concert as a *"KILT Presentation."* With a string of groups coming to Houston, I was getting lots of experience creating radio ads for concerts. Concerts West, the major Seattle-based national promoter, asked me to produce the ads for their artists' appearances in other markets also.

~

The last half of the decade saw major shifts in the U.S. and its music. Hit music no longer came exclusively from traditional recording centers of New York or Nashville, but from smaller studios in San Francisco, Detroit, upstate New York, and from Houston. A new generation of producers - Brian Wilson, Phil Spector, Berry Gordy Jr. - and new artists from Abbey Road to Music Row began filling the charts with a wide variety of new sounds. Everything was being stretched to the limits.

By the late sixties, music and even the country itself seemed to be unraveling. Senator Robert Kennedy and Martin Luther King were assassinated - Timothy Leary was encouraging the use of LSD - Jimi Hendrix, Janis Joplin and Brian Jones died of drug overdoses - health warnings were placed on cigarette packs – and the most famous music event in history played to a crowd of half a million on a muddy hillside in upstate New York.

The times were indeed changing!

Chapter TWENTY FOUR
"BURNING DOWN THE HOUSE"

Nighttime radio was vitally important to top forty stations because of the large teen audience available. In most homes and cars, teenagers controlled the radio. The station that owned this demographic often won the total audience measurements also. That's why the competition for teens was so intense.

Rock music, which originally set off the music revolution of the mid fifties, began to splinter into a variety of genres by the mid to late sixties. While the Beatles scored the first and second place songs on Billboard's Top 100 hits of 1964, the rest of the top ten still contained traditional hits by Dean Martin, Barbara Streisand, Louis Armstrong and a young artist from my home town of Lufkin, Texas named J. Frank Wilson, who released the ultimate teenage-death song, "Last Kiss." Top forty music lists were all over the scale and contained bland Hootenanny music, Surfin' bands, and even worse -- Bossa Nova. Billboard magazine's number one song for 1966 was *'Ballad of the Green Berets'* by Sgt. Barry Sadler. But the British were still on the attack, and this time, there was no Paul Revere who could stop the invasion.

The first wave of British music was rather benign. The Beatles *'We Can Work It Out'* finished 1966 in the #16 slot, the Rolling

Stones had the #21 song with *'Paint it Black'* and the Troggs' *'Wild Thing'* finished at #24. Bob Dylan's *'Like a Rolling Stone'* challenged radio's commercial availabilities with a six-minute long single that shot up the charts. Columbia Records was hesitant to even release the record but it went to number two on the national charts. Some radio stations, including KILT, edited the song for use in hours with full commercial loads, but the number of complaints from those active music listeners was significant.

By 1968, the Beatles declared all-out war on traditional radio's time limitations with a seven minute long, highly repetitive single, *'Hey Jude.'* The must-play top band in the world forced a blatant challenge to music radio's high commercial commitments. There was no way we were going to edit a Beatles song! *Hey Jude* became the number one record of 1968 and forced those of us in radio to redesign our commercials structure and the hot-clock formulas.

~

For all the success of the Big 610, KILT's production facilities and engineering support was incredibly inadequate. The production room board was a monaural Collins 2-12 with round pots (potentiometers) to control volume. There was one Scully four-track tape recorder for assembling elements, two single track Ampex recorders for mix-downs and a cartridge recording machine for readying the finished ads for on-the-air use. Tape 'slap-back', a technique that took advantage of the short distance between the record and playback heads on the tape machines to create echo, was the only effects capability. In order to create a radio commercial with all the production value I wanted, each spot had to be bounced back and forth, multiple times between the various tape machines. It was surprising that there was any amount of dynamic range remaining in the mix-down by the time the spot hit the air. The final production was transferred to a 'Fidelipac' cartridge – an endless loop of tape encased in a small plastic box that re-cued itself after each use.

The original engineer when I arrived at KILT had very little concern for programming issues. No matter what I asked for technically, he just smiled, shook his head and walked away. After a year of hearing my constant complaints, the station manager offered hope; *"pahdnah, I'm gonna hire you da best engineer in the bidness."* He hired a friend that he had worked with many years before at Houston's KPRC. Things got worse.

KDOK, the little daytime station in Tyler, Texas, had far superior facilities and technical capability years earlier and WACO provided amazing engineering expertise compared to the big city. Both stations employed motivated, knowledgeable and creative engineers. But the new KILT *'Engineering Director'* was an 'Executive' and spent most of his time in his new office filling out forms but little time addressing the critically needed improvements. Our frequent confrontations ended one afternoon when he drove his fist through one of the hallway doors. He wore a cast for a few weeks which further limited his work load.

Just as loving music did not make a great deejay, simply holding a First-Class FCC license did not qualify one to be a competent audio engineer. Some radio station engineers had expertise and knowledge about transmitters and the legal responsibilities of insuring that signal emissions and radiation did not infringe on other frequencies. Others were good at troubleshooting and repairing equipment when needed. Some were responsible for the record keeping, diagnosis and repair of the equipment, compliance with the government's Emergency Broadcast System and zillions of other details that were critical to keep up with FCC mandates. KILT's new Chief Engineer took long coffee breaks!

A studio/audio engineer's responsibility is somewhat different. They are the ones responsible for the systems, the sound and the efficient operation and maintenance of the studio – as opposed to the transmitter equipment. A really good studio tech becomes part of the sound of the station itself. These are the people who translate the simplistic descriptions of the performer into engineer language; *"when I punch this button, I get this screeching sound in my headphones"* became *"the AC-3 bit stream indicates that the dialogue level is 25dB below the 100 percent level...zzz."* For over a year after I came to Houston, communication between programming and engineering simply did not exist at KILT.

~

The control room's mixing board was a Gates Diplomat, a well-respected console for its time, but one that had been pushed to its limits. Ten years of twenty-four hour a day usage gave little time for routine maintenance, usually relegated to an occasional Sunday night after midnight. Add to this the fact that cigarette smoke -- still considered cool in the sixties -- had deposited a sticky brown layer of gunk on all of the main studio's equipment and it was a wonder that anything functioned.

With no quality controls, no voice processing, no special effects, none of the kinds of things that made a big difference in the unique sound of a top-ten market radio station, I was starting to get a little crazy. Finally, one Saturday morning while on the air, the left turntable just stopped; dead; smack-dab in the middle of Aretha's R-E-S-P-E-C-T. That meant that only one turntable could be used with my right hand, manually removing/then replacing each forty-five ... all done by 'rote'. While leaning right, my right arm was stretched to the rear and my left stretched forward in an attempt to pull the microphone close enough to stay *'on mike.'* I must have looked like Moses trying to reconnect the Red Sea.

My ad-libs had to last long enough to remove the stylus arm from the previous record and locate--by brail--the opening grooves of the next disc. Unfortunately, all this pressure on the Electro-Voice RE-15 microphone and its four-foot, 12 pound, scissor-arm boom mechanism (with long springs that normally allowed unlimited positioning) caused the dammed mechanism to pull loose from its desk mount, launching the whole contraption into orbit around the room. The remainder of the day's show was a nightmare from hell! All the while, I had to sound 'up' and 'happy' and remind the listeners of all the great things happening at the Big 6-10.

~

On Monday morning, the audience in the management meeting heard graphic language from a very upset Program Director. I had always worked hard to maintain a calm demeanor when addressing difficult issues and usually brought organized presentation notes to these meetings, but I had run out of civility. Within a week, Dan Woodard--looking as if he had just arrived from Haight-Ashbury--became our new audio engineer. Simply put; Dan got it. Specifically, he knew how to tweak the transmitter, broaden the dynamic range and how to make an AM radio station sound louder and brighter while staying within the FCC's mandated limits. Dan loved music and treated that important program element with the kind of respect that made a difference to a listener. From each deejay and newsman's microphone processing with the Urei 1176 -- customized to showcase their unique voice qualities -- to the special tweaks of processing equipment that gave KILT a big, loud, dominating sound, Dan single handedly created the unique sound of KILT. By early 2011, Dan was the longest-tenured employee of KILT and its various CBS-owned Houston properties. He is also one of only a few engineers to be inducted into the Texas Radio

Hall of Fame.

The KILT control room was small with the back-side of the mixing board facing the entrance. There were two large standing/circular racks behind the disc jockey where the commercial cartridges and promos were filed by number. A tech rack, holding a variety of processing and test equipment was positioned just to the left of the entrance. While a record was being played, the deejay had two to three minutes to load all the commercials and station promos that were shown on the program log, plus select and cue the next record. If time was left, the deejay usually answered phone calls from listeners or prepped his ad-libs for the next break.

The main studio had two windows behind the cartridge racks. One of them could be opened to an empty lot, overgrown with native weeds. When the window was open, you could hear the traffic sounds from nearby Westheimer/Montrose intersection. The building was designed in a square with a central atrium and a fish pond at ground level. The only upstairs restroom was on the opposite side of the building from the main control room. Bad design! The average song lasted roughly two and a half to three minutes, meaning that if one felt the call of nature, it required a mad dash to and from the *john*. Normally, this could only be executed with any confidence by playing a very long record, such as *Hey Jude* or *MacArthur Park*. Station rumors suggested that the open, second-floor window itself had served as an option in a few cases of dire emergency.

In the mid seventies, Dan Woodard designed and built new studios for KILT FM (closer to the johns) plus two separate multi-track recording studios, one of them with a raft of bells and whistles for my production use.

~

Summer 1967 began with a string of changes. Chuck Dunaway

left KILT to return to Cleveland, Ohio, one of numerous markets where he had achieved past successes. Chuck was replaced by Johnny Michaels, a rapid-fire, pleasant-voiced, *'time and temp'* disc jockey who himself came from Cleveland by way of Beaumont, Texas.

KILT's ratings were consistently growing and the station's national reputation was garnering more and more industry press. Even though I had early concerns, Bill Stewart became a supportive national program director and KILT was becoming more autonomous than anyone had expected. For longer periods, I heard little from Bill but was frequently assured that he was pleased with the direction we were taking the station.

~

Radio's broadcast day is divided into specific day-parts. That's done for a variety of business reasons; a set amount of time within which an advertisement can play; the total audience available; the commercial spot load demand for that day part; consistency with the established ratings services; and as a tool for setting ad-rate pricing. The larger the audience during a specific day part, the higher the cost for a commercial to be aired during that period. That was known as CPM, 'cost per thousand' listeners.

Audience ratings were conducted by various services -- Aribtron, C.E. Hooper, Birch and Pulse -- each with different methods of collecting the information and in the way each provided its information. Hooper, a monthly service, utilized as a simple random telephone sampling; *"what radio station are you listening to now?"* Pulse and Birch depended upon listener recall while Arbitron gave participants a one-week diary with instructions to record all of their radio listening. The services usually deliver the reports in a number of ways, for instance Arbitron made estimates available for: Gross Rating points –

Gross Impressions - Average Quarter Hour' persons – Average Quarter Hour' ratings – Cumulative' persons - Cume' ratings - Exclusive Cume' - Share' of audience - Net reach - Frequency (of reach) - Time Spent Listening (TSL) - Cost Per Thousand (CPM) – Cost per rating point, and all of them available separately for specific day-parts -- mornings, mid-days, afternoon drive, and evenings. Oh, and all information could be presented for the Metro area, the Designated Market area or the Total Survey area.

The broadcast day was broken into the following day-parts:
Morning Drive: 6 a.m. - 9 (or 10) a.m.
Mid-days: 9 a.m. - 3 p.m.
Afternoon or p.m.. Drive: 3 - 7 p.m.
Evenings (Weekdays): 7 p.m. - Midnight
Overnights (& Weekdays): Midnight - 6 a.m.

~

KILT's successful morning Hudson & Harrigan show ran from six to ten a.m. In reality, a high percentage of a station's total cumulative morning audience is often concentrated within just one hour, the important seven to eight a.m. period. To increase revenue with this prime real-estate, stations could effectively raise the rates further with guaranteed placement for advertisers willing to pay a premium for 'fixed-position' ads, those placed at or as near as possible to a specific time during the hour. This way, those ads would reach the largest amount of client's preferred audience. Only when fixed-positions ads were not sold out did a 'run of schedule' buyer even have a chance of appearing in this golden hour.

With Hudson & Harrigan in a dominant ratings position in Houston's morning-drive, their four-hour period became a major cash-cow for the station. But morning dominance for a successful station is about much more than just revenue. A consistently winning morning show anchors the rest of the day and increases the important recall of the station in the listener's mind when a ratings' service conducts its survey sweep in a market.

In most major markets, the Arbitron ratings sweeps occurs each quarter. The Hooper ratings were released monthly, but for all practical purposes, Hooper was only used by programmers to get an early picture of audience trends. Salesmen sometimes used the Hooper to alert a client of audience movement - or a downward trend in the case of a competitor - prior to release of the ARB. The advertising agencies were most concerned with the spring and fall ratings sweeps, coinciding with the agency's budget planning stages. But I had to be able to see shifts in audience long before the sweeps, and that help came from the Hooper ratings. If I could see trends early enough, we could react accordingly. Likewise, if we saw a dramatic growth in our own audience before the ratings sweep, the sales department could alert sponsors to the positive trend, allowing them to get their schedules in place before rates were raised in response to the growth.

Contests, promotions and targeted features became an important part of a programmer's unique arsenal. These might include the use of cash or merchandise giveaways, free vacations, concert tickets, free concerts in the park, first-caller wins contests, or, in an area where McLendon himself spent a lot of effort; *'exotics.'* That was the word Gordon used to describe the disconnected and sometimes confusing announcements that motivated listeners to tell their friends about what they had heard on KLIF.

Bill Stewart may have created the first *'exotic'* at KLIF in 1954. According to the book *'The Hits Just Keep on Coming'* by Ben Fong-Torres, Stewart ran this announcement on KLIF and in full-page ads in Dallas Newspapers:

"KLIF WISHES TO OFFER THIS APOLOGY FOR THE UNFORTUNATE LANGUAGE USED ON AN INTERVIEW DURING AN ON-THE-SCENE BROADCAST OF AN ARMED ROBBERY FRIDAY NIGHT AT 8:44 PM. TO ALL OF THE MANY WHO CALLED THE STATION, KLIF WOULD LIKE TO SAY THAT WE'RE SORRY. BUT IN COVERING NEWS ON THE SCENE, AS WE DO, THE REMARKS OF A WITNESS, WHO MAY BE IN A HIGHLY EMOTIONAL STATE CANNOT BE GOVERNED. HOWEVER, IN ALL HUMILITY, KLIF TENDERS THIS APOLOGY."

In reality, few if any of the KLIF audience heard a broadcast of *'unfortunate language'*, but once the exotic aired and the rumors kicked in, the whole city of Dallas was talking – *"did you hear what that guy said on KLIF?"*

Gordon McLendon later used off-the-wall exotics to promote his beautiful music station in San Francisco. The strange, disconnected announcements might appear to be totally out of character for a beautiful music station, but McLendon had an interesting theory. He had a very romantic image of San Francisco, spent a lot of time there, and wanted to create a station for listeners who had the intelligence to appreciate it. KABL exotics were one of the ways he created that impression. A contest might offer *"ten cents in cash for the best letter theorizing an explanation of the Joliot-Curie craters on the backside of the moon."* The city's educated elite found these tongue-in-cheek promotions to be over the head of the masses and something only they could appreciate.

Officially, KABL's FCC license was granted to Oakland, across the bay from San Francisco. On KABL however, Oakland was relegated to only being mentioned during the legally required top of the hour station ID ... a very quick *"K-A-B-L Oakland"* (Harp glissando) *"You're listening to Kable Music, In the air, everywhere over San Fran-cisco."* To Gordon, the real magic was the romanticism of *"San Fran-Cisco"* and he delivered those precise syllables with theatrical finesse.

To be a winner in the radio wars, a program director had to know how to *'program to the book.'* That meant understanding the methodology of how the ratings were conducted. The A.R.B. supplied weekly diaries to a number of listeners, so stations designed contests that would encourage listeners to *"write it down."* To insure recall, a deejay might say, *"be the tenth caller and tell us the first three songs we played this hour."* Or, he might subtly suggest, *"if anyone asks, tell them you're listening to Z-101."* But regardless of the many twists to keep listeners tuned in -- none were as successful as *The Last Contest.*

~

Jack McCoy, the program director at KCBQ San Diego, created the ultimate ARB ratings-buster when he developed and syndicated -- THE LAST CONTEST. McCoy and a friend, a Milwaukee newscaster named Doug Harmon, developed what would become the most ripped-off radio contest in history. Over a few weeks (while the ratings were in progress), listeners were presented with a huge selection of prize packages from which to choose, with a new package every hour for the entire four week ratings sweep. Each prize was described by McCoy's mysterious voice with eloquently-written descriptions. All a listener had to do was to wait for the signal and be the first to call and choose their favorite prize package. While it may have sounded as if the station was giving away all those millions in prizes, only one prize was actually awarded and that was likely a no-cost station *trade-out* with a prize provider in return for free commercials. The contest required the audience to listen for long periods of time in order to hear that signal to call in and win, and that translated well to the ratings' methodology.

After the signal, the entire San Diego telephone network and a third of the city's phone system was blown out of order. The biggest winner of the *"Last Contest"* was KCBQ's ratings for the month - and the two creators, who quickly syndicated the "Last Contest" to stations in other parts of the country.

In reality, a small percentage of most listeners actually participate in radio contests. But since everyone loves a winner, hearing an exciting listener break down in tears because she just won a prize, made everyone happy. There was one other important benefit to contests - they increased the confidence of the deejays - which translated into a more exciting sounding station.

Chapter TWENTY FIVE
"UP UP AND AWAY"

On the day I write this, US Airways flight 1549 ditched into Hudson Bay after apparently encountering a flock of geese on takeoff from LeGuardia Airport. New York residents watched live TV as all one hundred fifty-five passengers aboard crawled out on the wings of the partially submerged Airbus A320 in frigid 20 degree temperatures and were picked up by rescue boats. While all aboard survived, those of us admitted acrophobia's still find news like this 'proof enough.'

My first flight to San Francisco revealed a latent, lifelong fear of flying. It was a well-known fact within my company that limited my professional options to say nothing of the missed joy of opportunities that came with my job and personal success.

A 1993 report in Fortune claimed that creative people often suffer from a fear of flying, adding *"most creative types are neurotic and proud of it."* Perfectionists are known to be among the most nervous flyers, probably because of the need to control what's going on. The article suggested that it is the creative type's active imagination that leads them to perfect the *"what if"* scenario. David Ogilvy, the advertising genius who founded Ogilvy & Mather, was terrified of turbulence and repeatedly invented excuses not to visit his company's two hundred and fifty offices in fifty seven countries. Film and TV producer Aaron Spelling refused to fly, even though he had served in the US Air Force. John Madden, the Super Bowl winning coach of the Oakland Raiders before becoming the announcer for ABC's Monday Night Football, traveled to games each week in his own coach-bus. Actress Penelope Cruz panicked before takeoff of a flight from Newark to Barcelona once and had to return to the terminal.

Hey folks, aerophobia is a very real issue for some of us. For openers, we have to board in a *terminal* before we can arrive at our *final destination.*

I suspect my fear of flying machines actually began at the age of four, by hearing those giant wall-shaking B24 bombers take off and land each night at Fort Worth's Convair factory. Plus, it all mixed with the sounds of war planes and sirens on nightly radio reports from the war front.

But real basis for fear was fried into my memory cells during the summer afternoon of May 16th, 1959. It was Armed Forces Day and the Waco, Texas celebration was being broadcast on WACO Radio, where I was program director at the time. One might legitimately question the appeal of radio reports of airplane flyovers, but for WACO, any event was an opportunity to sell more advertising. Bird/Kultgen Ford sponsored reports every quarter hour that day from James Connelly Air Force Base.

"This is Bill Young from Connelly Air Force Base, brought to you of course by your friendly Ford Dealer in Waco, Bird/Kultgen where you can test drive the new Ford Galaxie today. We are about to witness a very exciting demonstration. A Bell UH-1 Series Iroquois, known as the Huey Helicopter, is currently hovering about 1000 feet over the runway in front of our Bird/ Kultgen broadcast

booth and in just a moment, the pilot is going to turn off the power and demonstrate a rapid free-fall. Then at the last minute, he will restart the engine and - oh, here he comes now, gaining speed, we can hear him restarting the eng - oh my God, he just hit the runway!"

When the pilot attempted to re-engage the blades, the chopper tilted to the right, causing its propeller to hit the ground and send the craft skidding for hundreds of fiery yards down the runway. Miraculously, its path ran parallel to the people watching from the sideline. Sirens were heard rushing to the scene from everywhere. I could see the pilot, crawling out and then running away from the chopper, now being hosed with water.

I was speechless. My experience was insufficient to respond to this level of real-deal trauma. Fortunately, the station's crack news director, Bob Vandeventer, had seen it all from his vantage point a hundred yards away and ran to the cruiser, grabbed the shaking microphone from my hand and did what great news reporters get paid to do—described in detail what was going on.

~

My flight-phobia did not become apparent until my early thirties, simply because there was no need to travel by air. Driving to Dallas from Houston was simple, less expensive and without the Hobby and Love Field traffic.

When Bill Stewart told me to report to KABL Radio in San Francisco within three days, I purchased my first plane ticket ever, packed my bags and came face to face with fear.

I had it all; racing heartbeat; chest pains; hyperventilation; choking sensations; light-headedness; tingling and numbness. The thing that perhaps saved my life was that I drew a seat next to an even more fearful flier, a very attractive young lady who needed comforting on the long flight. Amazingly, my masculine protection genes kicked in and I was able to, at least temporarily, set my own fears aside in order to help calm this damsel in distress.

The reality was, I sometimes had to fly, occasionally to really important events; speaking at conventions; a meeting of Broadway show producers in Miami; meetings of national boards on which I served; joining an elite radio panel in Hollywood; accepting personal and station awards; meetings in New York on the new Genesis tour; the opening of a Broadway musical that I helped finance; directing a country superstar tribute in Nashville -- all required me to feel the fear and do it anyway. But flying never came easy.

~

In the mid-seventies, Walt Disney World planned a series of major market promotions surrounding their spectacular Space Mountain ride in Orlando. They invited a handful of radio managers and program directors from around the country to be their guests for individual VIP tours of the park with back-stage access to its many rides and features. While there, we would also plan the upcoming promotions and the accompanying advertising campaign for Space Mountain. KILT Manager Dickie Rosenfeld, his wife, and Sharon and I were to travel to Orlando and spend three days and two nights at Mickey's elegant Contemporary Resort Hotel. Disney even sent one of their private jets to fly us to and from the park. Sharon and the Rosenfeld's were excited but, as usual, I was hyperventilating -- particularly so when I walked out on the tarmac to board the jet at Hobby Airport and discovered the name of the aircraft. Here I was in near panic mode and they expected me to fly halfway across the country in a jet named *'Mickey Mouse'*!

~

Captain T.W. "Slim" Cummings, a pilot for Pan American Airlines established a series of *'Freedom from Fear of Flying'* programs in 1975. It consisted of weekly meetings that ended with an hour-long graduation flight over parts of the Gulf of Mexico. The class was instructive, fun and it taught me much about how safe flying really is, though it still did not convince me to become a nonchalant world traveler. My fear cost me much in career growth and opportunities. I'm not proud of admitting this, but fear of flying is a part of my story.

Flying home from Los Angeles late one Sunday evening on a 737, I sat next to an officer in the Air Force who may have finally validated my phobia; *"counting all the cables and fasteners and rotors and nozzles - there are probably six million parts and one hundred seventy one miles of wiring that make up this aircraft— all of it supplied by the lowest bidder!"*

Chapter TWENTY SIX
"THIS COULD BE THE START OF SOMETHING BIG"

By the time the founders of Top 40 radio, Todd Storz and Bill Stewart in Omaha, Nebraska, and Gordon McLendon in Dallas, Texas came up with their formula of excitable deejays, contests, jingles, abbreviated news, and a playlist of forty hit records, the deejay ranks had swelled and changed.

Ben Fong Torres

From the 1920s 'til the early '50s - *'The Golden Age of Radio'*, the box on the table was filled with a variety of entertainment and information programming. By the mid-fifties however, stations without networks began programming recorded music almost exclusively. At the same time, the music itself was changing and reaching a much younger audience. While markets in all parts of the country eventually duplicated the concept, the earliest and most publicized beginnings took place at two radio stations: one in Omaha, Nebraska--owned by Todd Storz, and the other in Dallas, Texas--owned by Gordon McLendon. One person held the distinction of being in charge of programming for both radio stations. His name was Bill Stewart.

Bill Stewart was born in 1927 in Du Bois, Pennsylvania. He taught Speech and Diction at Emerson College in Boston, a prestigious Communications and Arts school founded by Charles Wesley Emerson in 1880 as a 'School of Oratory.' Bill became a classical music host at WBMS radio in Boston. His work as a commercial voiceover talent would appear on a number of other eastern radio stations. Sometime in the-early to mid fifties however, Bill Stewart heeded the call to *"go west young man."*

~

Todd Storz was born in 1924, an heir to Omaha's Storz Beer brewery. As a student at the University of Nebraska, Todd first made a name for himself by tweaking the campus radio station's operating signal far beyond the federally mandated 1.5 mile limit. Eventually, FCC agents came around to investigate. It seems the University of Nebraska station's transmitter had been 'altered' and was overpowering a commercial station in Ohio. After serving in the Signal Corp during WW-II, Storz entered commercial radio as an engineer in Hutchinson, Kansas. He soon returned home to Omaha and worked for a number of area stations in various capacities — engineer, salesman and announcer.

According to Marc Fisher's 2007 book *"Something in the Air,"* Robert Storz put up $30,000, son Todd mortgaged a farm he owned in Iowa for $20,000, and they borrowed the rest to create the Mid-Continent Broadcasting Company. In 1949, they purchased KOWH, a low-rated, daytime-only station in Omaha with no network affiliation.

The call letters "KOWH" stood for the Omaha World Herald newspaper, who had owned and operated the station from it's inception in 1939. The station's FCC license required it to sign-off each day at local sunset to prevent interference with more powerful signals on the station's dial position (a result of the earlier discussed 'troposphere ducting' phenomenon at night). Todd Storz immediately set out to improve the station's daytime signal and to create his own local programming.

The major radio networks were already committed to other stations operating in the Omaha market. To create its own programming, KOWH began playing recorded music of various styles in different day-parts. The selection included everything from big bands and popular vocalists to the most popular hits of the day. The deejays were friendly and locally focused. KOWH's programming increasingly found an approving audience, particularly after featuring more currently popular songs. According to the December-1951/January-1952 ratings cycle--C.E. Hooper's Omaha Radio Audience Ratings showed that KOWH had become the number one rated station in Omaha. This was a significant development, because it bested all the national network stations in the city simply by playing popular music with local deejays. By April, 1953--a full page ad in Broadcasting/Telecasting magazine boasted that KOWH was "America's Most Listened-to Independent Station" with 35.8% of the Omaha audience."

~

Gordon McLendon was born in 1921 in Paris, Texas. He studied Far Eastern languages at Yale before accepting a commission in the Navy as an interpreter, translator and interrogator. After the service, he briefly attending Harvard Law School but soon returned home to East Texas and partnered with his father, Barton Robert McLendon, to purchase an interest in radio station KNET in Palestine, Texas. They sold KNET in 1947 after purchasing a new radio station in the Oak Cliff section of Dallas, changing the call letters to KLIF. The original KLIF presented a variety of music, old soap operas and radio drama recordings.

Eventually, its programming also added re-creations of baseball games from professional baseball teams, located in the eastern half of the country.

Using one word descriptions from a spotter at the stadium and sent to the radio station via Western Union wire, McLendon added baseball game ambiance and sound effects, plus his own, imagined, extemporaneous descriptions of the game. McLendon's game of the day became very popular in Dallas. They were so successful in fact that in 1948, Gordon and his father founded the Liberty Broadcast System and sold the broadcasts to other stations outside the eastern part of the US - lots of other stations. By 1950, the network had close to 500 radio stations on line, enough to awaken baseball owners to the huge revenue being lost to a private entity. After Major League Baseball drastically raised its licensing fees in 1952, the Liberty network declared bankruptcy and ceased broadcasting. It was a surprised and devastating blow to the company.

McLendon's KLIF immediately had to create new programming and it began presenting a wide variety of music and news. Just as in Omaha, the music varied during certain parts of the day and was selected by the deejay on the air from a library that included standards and currently popular music similar to that being played on then NBC's popular radio's show - Your Hit Parade. The station also presented interesting and entertaining 'disc jockeys' and regular, hourly newscasts.

~

C. E. Hooper was the king of local market radio ratings. Its so-called *Hooperatings* were based on telephone sampling of listeners in thirty-six key American cities, including both Dallas and Omaha. Although Hooper never claimed he was producing accurate national ratings, the winning stations in each market publicized that the Hooper gave an exact picture of listening.

Although there were other ratings services around - Neilson, Trendex, American Research Bureau and Pulse Inc. - the Hooper became the authority for the winning radio station. To track listening and convince advertisers of their station's success, both Storz' KOWH and McLendon's KLIF began developing non-network programming that would impact the Hooper, and that led them both to popular music.

~

This is where the story gets a bit hazy, because Bill Stewart, the former Boston professor, would be employed by both trendsetting stations (KLIF-Dallas and KOWH-Omaha) during the early years of top forty radio's development. Because of his influential position at both trendsetting stations, Bill has been touted by some as the person who deserves credit for developing and/or refining 'top forty' -- the most successful local programming concept since the invention of the medium. For purposes of my study, the label Top Forty, Top Fifty or Top any-number was of less significance than the fact that a radio station committed all of its programming to rotating a short list of the top hit songs of that period. That was the real programming breakthrough.

The oft repeated basis for the early development is the 'juke box version', first described in a January 6, 1973 interview in Billboard magazine between Bill Stewart and Billboard's chief radio writer, Claude Hall. Right out of the box, Hall dropped the big question, *"who really invented the top-forty format?"*

> Stewart: "the way it happened actually was that one night Todd Storz and I were sitting in a bar in Omaha and..."
> Hall: "Do you remember the bar?"
> Stewart: "..it was across from Gilpatricks on 15th Street,

where our studios used to be. And we were sitting there and the jukebox was playing, and it kept coming up to the same song. I can't even remember what the song was, but it was a rock n' roll type song. We must have sat there four or five hours talking about various things and they got ready to close, I guess it was midnight or whatever time they closed, and everyone was gone and they were kinda' giving us motions like we were supposed to leave and the waitress went over and put a quarter into the jukebox - lo and behold she put her own quarter in the machine and played that same record three times in a row, and it was the same record we'd heard all night long. So that sort of tripped a lot of - well, it was in both our minds. I don't know whether you could say that Todd literally discovered Top 40 or whether I did or whether someone in the company did, I don't know."

Hall: "What year was the bar incident?"

Stewart: "About 1955."

Many in the industry do not believe that the 'juke box in the bar' incident ever happened, at least not in the way the article described. The late Storz' programmer Richard W. Fatherly, in the 'on-line' 2006 book *'Radio's Revolution & the World's Happiest Broadcasters'--a study of the Storz Broadcasting Group'* ©-- spoke with many of those involved and claimed that the epiphany in the Omaha bar simply did not happen; *"the bar room is a mythology!"* I spoke with Richard frequently prior to his death in February 2010 and he re-stated that claim. In fact all of the early management level employees at Storz' stations that I contacted or researched, concur with Fatherly's conclusions.

There is little disagreement however that the first major ratings battle in Top 40 did take place in Omaha. Because Storz' KOWH broadcast license required it to sign-off the air at local sunset, his station's dominance came under brutal attack when twenty-five year old Don Burden from Pocatello, Idaho purchased KOIL, a full-time - 24 hour a day station at 1290 on the AM dial. Burden made a $5000 down payment, signed a ten year note to the existing owner, and took ownership of KOIL on January 1, 1953.

With very aggressive on-the-air contests and a deejay staff that included then seventeen year old morning deejay/ newsman Gary Owens, Don Burden's KOIL floundered in the beginning but eventually found its footing and came straight at KOWH's audience.

The competition between the two stations was fierce. A full page ad in 'Broadcasting-Telecasting' magazine dated April 13, 1953 – over three months after KOIL's debut – boldly claimed that KOWH was *"America's Most Listened-to Independent Station -- Number one in Omaha with 35.8% of the audience, the largest total audience of any Omaha station, 8 a.m. to 6 p.m. Monday thru Saturday"* (C.E.Hooper - Oct. 1951 -Feb. 1953). A close study of the published dates for these ratings reveals that much of this claim came from ratings that were collected before Burden's 1953 takeover of KOIL.

In an undated document titled *"Hooper Record Of The Storz Stations"* a company release of all Storz' station's ratings reports from C.E. Hooper. Inc.' -- winning ratings were shown at Storz stations WDGY in Minneapolis-St. Paul, WQAM in Miami, WHB-Kansas City and WTIX in New Orleans. But there was a real battle underway in Omaha at the company's flagship station. The document claimed winning daytime ratings in 1952 and again in 1956-1957, but most of these years were known to have been a tough period for the day-timer. Don Burden proved to be an aggressive, 24 hour a day competitor. When a KOWH contest went on the air offering a prize, KOIL would double the prize amount within minutes. If KOWH offered a new car, KOIL countered with two new cars!

~

In a Mid-Continent Broadcasting Company general memo on June 18th, 1956, Todd Storz announced a number of company changes, including the appointment of Bill Stewart as program director of KOWH, replacing Jim O'Neill. Bill's success in Dallas at KLIF and his tenacious competitiveness in New Orleans against an earlier acquired Storz station, had apparently made a strong impression on Todd Storz. Stewart made a number of changes at KOWH. New personalities Kent Burkhart and later, Bud Connell were brought in to join the staff that still included the market's popular Sandy Jackson.

The changes worked; for awhile. The October/November 1956 ratings showed in the company's 'Share of Audience' release mentioned earlier, boldly cited KOWH on top in Omaha with 39.0% of the afternoon audience to KOIL's 23.1%. By the February/March-1957 report however, KOIL was closing in again.

Competing against KOIL, an aggressive twenty-four hour operation, put Storz' flagship station at an enormous disadvantage. Kent Burkhart said that *"by March of 1957, KOIL started taking over the day-timer while Todd agonized over even adding Elvis records, afraid of losing his adult base."*

The writing was on the wall. The end of KOWH's reign was near. Storz sold the station to William F. Buckley in 1957 at a price over ten times what he and his dad had originally paid. The other radio stations that Todd Storz had acquired however were becoming enormously successful. Company-owned acquisitions in New Orleans, Kansas City, Miami, St. Louis, Minneapolis-St Paul and later in Oklahoma City would all become huge winners in their markets. Bill Stewart was promoted to National Program Director and brought in top local program directors that helped solidify Storz' place in the rapidly growing top forty battles.

~

A second version of top forty's beginnings also includes Bill Stewart, but earlier--in another setting. This we will call -- the 'Texas Version.'

The first time that industry consultant Kent Burkhart became aware of Bill Stewart was during the summer of 1953. Kent was briefly attending the University of Houston and working at KATL over the summer. Stewart came to Houston and applied for a job with then program director Webb Hunt who told Burkhart, *"that guy you just saw walking down the hall was after your job."* Still searching for work in Houston, Stewart applied to KLBS (the early call letters of 610 AM), then owned by Gordon McLendon. Stewart was hired by the manager, Glenn Douglas. While on the air at KLBS, Stewart shocked the city by playing a Stan Freberg record over and over, for days in a row.

As earlier mentioned, the year 1952 had not been so bright for McLendon's Liberty Broadcast Network. In spite of the network's existing contracts with baseball owners, the cost of the new season's broadcast rights from all but three organized baseball teams was raised from $1,000 to $225,000 for the new season. Falstaff Beer, a prime Liberty advertiser, pulled its sponsorship. Western Union refused to provide services any longer. Lindsey Nelson, one of Liberty's sportscasters at the time called it the *"beginning of the end."* A series of lawsuits between the various parties were filed but by the end of the day, the Liberty Broadcasting Network's only remaining option was bankruptcy.

Before Liberty's problems surfaced, Gordon and B.R. McLendon had purchased KLEE Radio in Houston just prior to the 1952 season. They changed the call letters to KLBS with, according to author Ronald Garay, the *"intent to transfer the flagship operations of Liberty Broadcasting System from KLIF to KLBS."* Left with no network however, McLendon immediately put the Houston station up for sale and started developing new programming for his radio station in Dallas. That's where Bill Stewart enters the picture.

Gordon McLendon did not know Todd Storz, but he had definitely heard about the success of Storz' non-network radio station in Omaha. One of the existing deejays at McLendon's KLBS in Houston -- Bill Stewart -- was reportedly utilizing program and promotional ideas similar to those being used in Omaha, resulting in heavy audience response. Before the sale of KLBS was finalized, McLendon transferred Stewart to Dallas and named him Program Director of KLIF. Already playing recorded music in all day parts, the station quickly tightened it's music list and focus on the most popular music became its primary programming. The exact timing of this decision depends upon who you are talking to. According to *'The History of KLIF Radio,'* a Dallas radio history website at 1650oldiesradio.com, *"Gordon set the earliest Top 40 arrival date as 1952."* Sponsor Magazine pegged 1953 as the year that KLIF *"burst into national prominence with its formula of music and news plus razzle-dazzle promotion."*

When Stewart arrived at KLIF in 1953, shortly after his brief summer at McLendon's station in Houston, KLIF was floundering with only a 2% share of the audience. Repeating the attention-getting promotion he had used in Houston, Bill played a single selection -- Ray Anthony's Dragnet theme -- for a full day. Within hours, word of the stunt became the talk of Dallas.

A direct quote from longtime McLendon national Program Director Don Keyes before his death stated, *"the real catalyst in the development of a true Top 40 format at KLIF was Bill*

Stewart and the ideas that he brought to the station from his earlier association with Todd Storz." (Note: Keyes' reference to an *'earlier (Stewart) association with Storz'* is inconsistent with most sources).

Keyes told the story, *"Stewart came in knowing what he was doing and that's when he really tightened the playlist. That's when we really went Top 40 – hard Top 40. Then we took off something fierce and played a shortened list of popular songs."* Keyes continued, *"KLIF went from tenth or eleventh place in the market to number one in sixty days!"*

Soon after arriving in Dallas -- Stewart, McLendon and station manager Bill Morgan flew to Omaha to monitor Todd Storz' KOWH. During the visit, McLendon met with Todd Storz to exchange ideas. According to media consultant and long-time McLendon associate Art Holt, Gordon and Todd began and maintained a long and cordial friendship after that visit. This is an interesting piece of the puzzle, and leads one to believe that KLIF was looking to KOWH for experience.

~

With success at both trendsetting stations, McLendon and Storz individually began to stalk for new markets to conquer. Although they avoided direct competition, New Orleans became the closest thing to a head-to-head confrontation between the two.

Todd Storz' purchased classical music station WTPS at 1450 in August, 1953 from the owners of the New Orleans Times Picayune-States newspapers. It was there in autumn, after changing the call letters to WTIX, that Storz switched the music format to one similar to his original daytime-only station in Omaha. A particular programming advantage of WTIX was it's willingness to merge the more credible black versions of the current hits, such as Little Richard's original version of Tutti

Frutti, rather than the pop version by Pat Boone.

According to recorded tapes of Bud Armstrong -- whose first role with Storz was station manager of WTIX in New Orleans -- the term *'top forty'* first came up in a 1953 conversation. Bob Walker, then WTIX program director, mentioned a popular top-twenty countdown show that was already on the air at WDSU. Bud Armstrong then suggested that *"if WDSU's top-twenty program is so popular, then why wouldn't a "top-forty" show be twice as popular?"*

Storz' entre' into the New Orleans market and its immediate success, in spite of WTIX's limited area coverage, set in motion a stampede of radio format changes in New Orleans. WNOE, with 50,000 daytime watts at 1060 on the dial, and a powerful 5000 directional watts at night joined a rapidly growing group of Crescent City stations joining the fray, which also included WJBW and WWEZ with popular local deejay Jack "the Cat" Elliot.

Sometime in 1955, after Bill Stewart had led KLIF to the top-rated position in Dallas, he moved to New Orleans' WNOE as Program Director to compete head-on with Storz' WTIX. WNOE was owned by the former Louisiana Governor James Noe, who also happened to be Gordon McLendon's father-in-law. While the stations were separately owned, they did share an advertising alliance called "NOEMAC" which allowed a national radio time-buyer to place advertising on all stations represented by the alliance at a package price. Gordon frequently loaned ideas and personnel to his father-in-law's station, so after KLIF settled into its firm leadership position in Dallas and Noe's station in New Orleans was in a battle with the new WTIX, Bill was dispatched to WNOE as Program Director.

New Orleans became the closest thing to a direct competitive confrontation between the two innovators. Locally, Storz' WTIX was the leading top forty station, but WNOE's massive night-time signal made it the popular choice for most of Louisiana, Mississippi, Arkansas plus the eastern half of Texas and many other areas throughout the south.

Again, Stewart repeated his successful, attention-getting promotion by, this time, playing the hit 'Shtiggy Boom' by Joe Houston over 1,300 times straight during the next few days! Within weeks, the radio *Battle of New Orleans* between 'TIX and 'NOE had become intense. The competition even turned personal when WTIX manager Bud Armstrong began preparing intent to file an action for $250,000 against WNOE and Bill Stewart. Stewart got word of the impending suit and jumped the gun on Armstrong by filing a $50,000 lawsuit against WTIX, making the same charges as WTIX's forthcoming suit. Reportedly, the lawsuits had something to do with copying a promotion and alleged bad-mouthing each other, a fairly benign occurrence between competitive radio stations.

~

Two trendsetting radio stations, competing against each other in the same market, brought a new dynamic to top forty's evolution. Competition made both of them better and the audience was the big winner. Our industry has been arguing for decades about who invented the darn thing, who was the first, who was the smartest, and who did it best. Whether or not the story of the Omaha tavern was Top 40's Holy Grail or whether the naming of a music countdown show in New Orleans was the big epiphany is not nearly as important as the willingness of both Storz and McLendon to experiment and go it alone. Bill Stewart and a whole class of first-generation radio rebels; Don Keyes, Bud Armstrong, Kent Burkhart, Chuck Blore, Bud Connell, Bob Whitney, George Wilson, Chuck Dunaway, Graham Richards, Ruth Meyer and others ... they all flourished with the freedom to try things, and turned a huge negative - no network to depend on - into a steamroller of radio, music and social change.

Who was the first? Does it really matter? Within a matter of weeks and months, the top forty radio format infected markets all over the country. Actually, they were all experimenting — they were all 'originals!'

There was no certainty of success for Storz or McLendon or any of the others, they simply shared the same dilemma; one radio station -- no network programming. There was an old saying that *'necessity is the mother of innovation.'* Todd Storz had literally bet the farm on a radio station with no network to supply programming, while Gordon McLendon's baseball network had just gone bankrupt. Neither KOWH nor KLIF had many options. David T. MacFarland, in his book *'Future Radio Programming Strategies,'* points out that *"just as a surgeon can take more risks on a cadaver than a live patient, so were Storz and McLendon able to feel free to gamble a little."*

From the perspective of years later, the various claims of top forty's beginnings may never be determined to everyone's satisfaction. The entire issue about the birth of the format may actually be hung up in the semantics; *"which station was using what terminology or what description first."* Perhaps the decision to devote a station's entire program day to rotating the most popular songs - regardless of what it was called - was the most significant development. Top Twenty, Top Forty, Top whatever: the number or name that was chosen, made little difference to the audience; they were there for the music and the excitement and being part of something new. That was -- plain and simple -- radio's big revolution.

~

While in New Orleans, Bill Stewart met and married his wife Marlene on November 20th, 1955. The newlyweds left New

Orleans in early 1956 after Bill accepted a job at a station in Cincinnati. While en route to the new job, Bill and Marlene stopped off in Dallas for breakfast with their friends Kent and Pat Burkhart. Before Bill reported for work in Cincinnati, Todd Storz tracked him down in Las Vegas and hired him to become his Program Director and Special Assistant in Omaha.

Within the year, Bill was appointed National Program Director for the growing list of Storz stations. One of Stewart's first acts was to appoint his friend Kent Burkhart, originally from Bay City, Texas, to become Program Director of the company's newest acquisition, WQAM in Miami.

~

By 1956, many other stations and groups were validating Top Forty's success with their own versions of the format. The Bartell, Balaban and Plough groups of stations showed up with similar programming. Instant success was taking place in Memphis, St. Louis, Denver, Atlanta and San Diego.

Because radio was such a local medium, stations freely borrowed, stole, copied, modified, enhanced and often improved programming ideas just enough to lay claim to parts of each new idea that then spread to even more markets. Just like epidemics, each new modification morphed with the last into a constantly evolving and improving radio format.

Radio, like many endeavors, has been both improved and damaged by its monkey-see, monkey-do attitude. Former Storz programmer Bud Connell explained the process of how one of his adult-contemporary concepts rapidly spread around the country, *"Indianapolis copied Anderson, Indiana - other major markets copied Indianapolis - New York, Chicago and LA soon copied the lower top ten and the funny part is, by this time no one even knew where it came from."*

~

In 1958 in Kansas City and again in 1959 in Miami Beach, the Storz stations sponsored national disc jockey conventions. In his opening welcome to the second event in Miami Beach, Todd Storz paid tribute to his national Program Director, Bill Stewart, for *'virtually single-handed'* planning of both conventions. Immediately after the Miami convention however, a June 1, 1959 Billboard article by writer Sam Chase wrote *"rumors circulated at the tail end of the meet of Stewart's departure (from Storz) to become the Vice-President in charge of programs for the radio-TV interests of the Metropolitan Broadcasting Company."* This was big news because, at the time, Metropolitan operated WNEW-New York and WHK-Cleveland, but Stewart never reached that pinnacle after news coverage of the Miami event quickly turned sour.

Variety described the convention as a *"drunken orgy."* Time magazine called the radio industry *"one of the most pampered trades in the U.S."* A June 5, 1959 headline story in the Miami Herald by writer Dan Brown called it *"an orgy of Booze, Broads and Bribes."* The article charged that the event was less about radio programming and more about, *"greasing the gratifications of deejays."* With all this negative publicity, coupled with the press's inherent hostility to radio and top-forty radio in particular, legislative threats of radio investigations came as no surprise.

Stewart left Storz Broadcasting shortly after the Miami Convention, and was quickly appointed national Program Director of Don Burden's cross-town Star Stations. Ben Fong Torres' history of Top 40 Radio *'The Hits Just Keep on Coming'* contains an interview with KOIL's popular morning man Bobby Dale(who I replaced at KOIL in January 1960), *".. and Bill Stewart, who had blown his job with Todd Storz, now worked for Don Burden."* Bill's presence with Burden was short-lived and there is limited information about his stay or accomplishments.

Bill Stewart moved back to Dallas and became a salesman for Pams, the successful radio jingle company founded by Bill Meeks, an early musical director for McLendon's Liberty Network. Over the next few years, Stewart showed up for brief periods with various radio groups and stations, but would frequently return to PAMS between radio jobs.

~

Todd Storz died of a stroke on April 13th, 1964 at the age of thirty-nine. Earlier that same day, Bud Armstrong, then president of Storz Broadcasting who had worked side-by-side with Storz since 1949, rehired Bill Stewart to return to the Storz station in Kansas City for *'promotional ideas.'*

Popular Los Angeles deejay Charlie Tuna remembers Stewart's May, 1966 visit to KOMA, the Storz-owned station in Oklahoma City where Charlie worked at that time. Bill scheduled a full program staff meeting at a local hotel. After the group arrived, Stewart informed them that he had invited them to hear the *"future of radio."* With that introduction, he played air checks of KHJ - Los Angeles, the new Boss Radio concept pioneered by Bill Drake and Gene Chenault. As Bill played tapes of the various KHJ personalities, he would stop frequently to make comments about one program element or another. He then played a tape of KHJ's popular morning man Robert W. Morgan and when finished, Bill looked directly at Tuna and predicted, *"Charlie, you are going to replace this man some day."* One year later, Charlie Tuna did indeed move to mornings at KHJ. He is still on the air in Los Angeles as of this writing, over forty years later.

~

By October 1966, I was nearing my tenth month with KILT. My working relationship with then National Program Director Don Keyes was one of the best learning experiences I could have imagined, but Don had bigger plans. For years, he had wanted to own and operate his own radio station. Don found that station in Canton, Ohio. He made the down payment, submitted the application and waited for months for FCC approval of the transfer of ownership.

In early conversations with Don, he voiced to me that he had never really felt adequate to fill Bill Stewart's shoes, so he made the decision to always work harder, whatever it took. Regardless of when Gordon called -- as he did in the middle of one year's Thanksgiving dinner -- Don dutifully left the family celebration and headed for Love Field to meet his boss for a quick flight to fix a problem at the Chicago station.

Finally, in early November 1966, Don's application for his Canton station was approved by the FCC. I had known the approval could occur anytime, but the news came quicker than I had hoped. In his last call to me, Don informed me that Bill Stewart had been hired to replace him as McLendon's new National Program Director.

No one in radio questioned Bill Stewart's huge accomplishments. His people skills however were less laudable. After voicing concerns based on all the Bill Stewart *rumors* I had heard, Don assured me that I would learn more working for Bill Stewart than from anyone else alive -- but he added one cautionary comment without explanation, *"just be careful."*

~

Yet again, Bill Stewart became the National Program Director of the McLendon stations. My initial experience with him was very cordial, albeit different from that with Keyes. My initial fears were unfounded. With few exceptions, Bill actually left me pretty much alone in the programming of KILT.

The relationship between Stewart and McLendon was complex, to say the least. Both of them were brilliant men with a deep respect for the other's talents but both also had quick tempers that resulted in frequent and intense conversations, resignations, firings, and re-hiring's -- oh, and they each shared an appreciation of alcohol. In fact, that was the primary contributing factor that permanently ended their working relationship.

~

Bill Stewart called me in late August, 1967 and instructed me to join him in San Francisco to help re-program KABL, McLendon's successful beautiful music station. When I asked how long it would take -- Bill said *"plan to stay awhile."*

Gordon, B.R., Bill Stewart and I, along with a number of other top McLendon personnel and a group of young trainees that Gordon called the *'Magnificent Seven'* -- all converged on San Francisco for a major overhaul of the music on KABL. The seven trainees were hand-picked by McLendon after submitting to rigorous testing if they made the final selections. After running ads in industry publications, the selected seven would undergo intense tutored by Gordon himself for future management roles. The initial seven included a young man who would later wind up as the Program Director of KABL - Don Barrett - now a highly respected Los Angeles radio news publisher.

I had been told to call Bill at the KABL studios when I arrived in San Francisco on Saturday morning. If not there, he said he would be in his hotel room. But Bill was not at the studio, nor at the hotel where most of the temporary staff was staying. In fact, by Wednesday of the next week, Stewart was still AWOL with little or no contact with anyone on the staff. Don Barrett recalls speaking to Bill briefly during this period at a barber shop near the studio. When informed that McLendon was looking for him, Bill told Don that he was on his way back to the office, but he never showed.

On Tuesday morning, Gordon called me out of a meeting with

KABL's local manager Heber Smith and quietly told me that *"Bill is having some problems right now so I am appointing you the acting national program director."* He also said he understood that I wanted to stay at KILT rather than move to Dallas and I confirmed that, realizing that I had probably just set a limit to my growth within the company. When I voiced my lack of knowledge of where Stewart had intended to take KABL, Gordon responded simply -- *"just do as you would do."*

Wednesday evening, I arrived back at the St. Frances hotel about 9 p.m. and received a call from Bill Stewart, asking if I would meet him downstairs. This was the first time in five days that anyone had heard from the man in charge, so I was nervous as I left the room. My immediate concern was that Bill would resent my increased role and interaction with Gordon himself. Bill, who appeared tired and somewhat disheveled, stood in the hallway as the elevator doors opened. He started walking toward the lobby bar and motioned for me to follow. On the way, he quietly handed me an envelope and motioned for me to read the contents. It was a company check, signed by Gordon McLendon for $5,000 with a simple handwritten note, *"Bill, you're fired, Gordon."*

I was stunned and told Bill that I really did not think Gordon had meant that but Bill said nothing except *"I'm through."* He flew back to Dallas the next morning and never returned to the McLendon Corporation again.

Bill Stewart did return to KLIF however, one final time-- in 1968--after McLendon had sold the station to Fairchild Broadcasting. There are reports that he also did later work for Fairchild in Minneapolis and with the Metromedia group of stations.

~

Ben Fong-Torres, in *'The Hits Just Keep on Coming'* wrote; *"Bill*

Stewart has been mentioned as an integral part of both Gordon McLendon's and Todd Storz's operations, but in the view of some industry veterans, he has not been mentioned enough."

Ken Dowe, the longtime KLIF morning personality and eventual McLendon national Program Director himself, worked at KLIF under both Stewart and McLendon. Ken says *"Bill had his demons, but the man sure knew his business."*

George Wilson, former Programming VP of Don Burden's Star Stations and the Bartell chain of stations once said *"Bill Stewart really started it all when he combined Storz and McLendon concepts."*

Don Keyes, the longtime National Program Director for the McLendon stations frequently spoke of his respect for Bill Stewart, who he said had been *"the catalyst that made top forty's initial success so dramatic."*

As the years have passed, many new names have been added to the list of radio's significant innovators - Buzz Bennett, Lee Abrams, Bud Connell, Bill Drake, Paul Drew, Scott Shannon, Ken Dowe, John Rook, Rick Sklar and others who delivered great radio for millions of listeners. The radio stations they created — all originals — gave us the gift of *connection* that was often absent in other parts of our lives.

~

Gordon McLendon ran unsuccessfully for the U.S. Senate in 1964 against the incumbent Texas Senator Ralph Yarborough, who McLendon dubbed *'Smilin' Ralph'*. It was a fierce race with McLendon using his own Texas' radio stations to repeatedly accuse Yarborough of connections with then federally-convicted financier Billy Sol Estes. Gordon's friends John Wayne, Chill Wills and Robert Cummings came to Texas to campaign for him. Yarboroughs' successful demand to the FCC for free 'equal-time' for advertising and news coverage on McLendon's own radio stations meant that an enormous number of free Ralph Yarborough commercials dominated Gordon's Texas stations during the last week of the race. It was a devastating blow to McLendon's campaign. McLendon ran again in the 1968 Democratic primary for Governor. The campaign was cut short however when he suddenly, without explanation, dropped out of the race.

By the mid-seventies, Gordon McLendon was out of radio and investing in land, gold, rare coins and precious metals. The now valuable land on which the McLendon theatres had entertained millions of people was being sold to become shopping malls and housing developments.

~

Back in Dallas, Bill Stewart entered the real estate business. On December third, 1985 at the age of fifty-eight, Bill ended his life with a self-inflicted gunshot wound in a wooded area of Collin County Texas, just north of Dallas.

~

Three days later, on December sixth, 1985, United Press International reported that *"Gordon McLendon, the Old Scotsman, who pioneered Top 40 radio is in critical but stable condition today from a self-inflicted gunshot wound to the head."* McLendon's son, Dallas businessman Bart McLendon, claimed that a .38 caliber revolver fired accidentally as his father was cleaning it at the family ranch at Lake Dallas. Denton County sheriff's investigators however said they had not *"ruled out the likelihood of attempted suicide."* He was said to have been in poor health. Gordon McLendon died of esophageal cancer on September 14th, 1986 at Cielo, his beloved ranch north of Dallas.

Chapter TWENTY SEVEN
"TEXAS RADIO"

Robbie Krieger's quick four-note riff kicks off an intoxicating bass line from Ray's fat bass patch as John Densmore's drums join the dark, mysterious riff...cue Morrison...

"I wanna tell you about Texas Radio ..."

In 1931, XER, the mongo, bad-assed, 150,000 watt border-blaster radio signal from Villa Acuna, Coahuila, Mexico -- identified on the air as Del Rio, Texas -- was the personal sales vehicle for Dr. John Romolus Brinkley's Medicine Show on the air. He blanketed the country with solutions for every ailment - physical and spiritual: virility elixirs, injections, and the ultimate limp-weenie cure, the 'Goat Gland Operation.'

"I'll tell you bout the heartache – about the hopeless night"

In 1960, Bob Smith--a fan of New York deejay Alan Freed-- convinced the owners of the re-named XERF to license a large block of time to he and an engineer friend, who tweaked the clear-channel, 250,000 watt transmitter to blanket the US, all the way north to Canada and over the pole into Russia. Smith used the air-name Wolfman Jack. He loaded his Cadillac each day with

45's and $100 bills to buy off authorities and crossed the Rio Grande to broadcast rock n' roll to every kid in North America.

"Some call it heavenly -- others, mean and ruthful"

"I bought the whole deal,
new towns—same sounds;
on top one day, then a cut in pay;
new jocks hired and good guys fired;
switchin' to country, switchin' to rock;
it's still all the same if you're a radio jock;
sweatin' the book - sent a tape to John Rook;
you just go with the flow, cause you love that damn radio.

When radio was good, it was very *good*, and when it was *bad*—
it was even better!

Chapter TWENTY EIGHT
"NEW KID IN TOWN"

By the late sixties, changes taking place in music were beginning to have a powerful impact on both Top Forty radio and the touring concert business. The audience that had walked out of the Coliseum when Jefferson Airplane first appeared in Houston, was now first in line for tickets to see Cream, Jimi Hendrix, Jethro Tull, Grateful Dead and Canned Heat. KILT had ceased booking its own concerts and was partnering with regional promoters, such as Concerts West. In return for sponsorship billing, KILT produced and aired commercials for the events at a full-package advertising price. While the year's top songs still included such diverse titles as *Hey Jude*, *Sittin' on the Dock of the Bay* and *Harper Valley PTA*, the concert audience was sending the message that the times were indeed changing.

When Terry Bassett took over the reins at Concerts West's Dallas office, he asked me to create the commercials for Houston and all of his markets which eventually included Dallas, San Diego, Denver and other markets. Because Concerts West's home office in Seattle would book those same acts into other markets, it meant that I could build a master stereo music track, add the script and simply change the localized date, venue and ticket information for different cities, a process that only took minutes once the first spot was completed and approved. Airing in multiple markets, the artists and managers themselves frequently heard the work and I soon started working with them directly to create ads for their artists' appearances in even more markets.

Creating commercials for rock concerts had been a fantasy since first hearing a Chuck Berry commercial a decade earlier. Suddenly, the dream was becoming reality. The company promoted the work since it was bringing in more advertising dollars and gave KILT an exclusive connection with the most active radio listener. It also meant that my income was no longer dependent upon annual raises from the radio station. With my voice showing up on major tours, sponsoring companies-such as Budweiser, Miller Lite, Chevy Trucks and Canada's Labatt Blue eventually wanted that same voice on their music event commercials.

Personally, the new decade brought a new baby boy into the Young household. Eric Edward Young was born March 26th, 1970, and he came out of the nest with a smile on his face. Eric was a truly delightful gift, and thankfully, a healthy, handsome baby boy who slept through the night from the first few weeks. His ten year old brother Scott was the most excited person of all and his age gave him the ability to actually help with the *'changes'* taking place at home. Pat and I pushed recurring negative issues into the background and shared one of life's most precious times, the growth and development of our sons.

Chapter TWENTY NINE
"GOOD MORNING SUNSHINE"

Beginning in 1967 and for more than four decades to follow, KILT's Hudson and Harrigan show owned mornings in Houston.

"7:45 IN THE MORNING ON THE HUDSON & HARRIGAN SHOW HERE ON KILT WHERE ..."

Crash; the loud, intrusive sound effect of a door opening interrupts Mr. Hudson...

"AW GOOD MORNING EVERYONE OUT THERE"
(cheering crowd)

It was the voice of an obviously inebriated Seymore Broomwad, one of the many characters that showed up each morning to disrupt the best intentions of Mac Hudson and Irving Harrigan. A full 'A cappella' choir performed Seymore's daily theme-song to the tune of Handel's *Hallelujah Chorus*...

"SEEMOREBROMWAD, SEEMOREBROOWAD

S'more Broomwad, S'more Broomwad,

SEEMOOOORRRE BROOMWAD" (giant applause)

Seymore: (slurring words) *"UGH GOOD MORNING MR. HUDSON, HOW'S YOUR MORNING?"*

Hudson: (very detached) *"UH, IT'S FINE SEYMORE, HOW ARE THINGS WITH YOU?"*

Seymore: *"WELL, I'M IN A GOOD MOOD THIS MORNING, I WENT OUT HANKY-PANKIAN' AROUND LAST NIGHT AND..."*

Hudson: (disconnected) *"NOT AGAIN SEYMORE."*

Seymore: *"BOY DID I FIND A GIRL FOR YOU MR. HUDSON."*

Hudson: (condescendingly) *"FOR MEEE, SEYMORE? I'LL HAVE YOU KNOW THAT I HAVE NO INTENTION OF RUNNING AROUND WITH ANY WOMAN WHO WOULD HANG OUT WITH YOU IN A BAR,"* (escalating intensity) *"PLUS, I DON'T EVEN WANT TO TALK ABOUT IT, I'M A HAPPILY MARRIED MAN SEYMORE -- A HAPPILY MARRIED MAN!"*

Seymore: *"SHE SAID SHE WOULD REALLY LIKE TO MEET YOU, BEING A STAR LIKE THAT AND ALL..."*

Hudson: (now angry) *"SEYMORE, I HAVE NO INTENTION OF MEETING SOMEONE YOU PICKED UP IN A BAR - THAT IS JUST NOT MY IDEA OF A FINE, WHOLESOME GIRL AND..."*

Seymore: *"WA WA WAIT A MINUTE ... WHAT KIND OF GIRL?"*

Hudson: (yelling now) *"A WHOLESOME GIRL SEYMORE, THAT'S WHAT ... WHOLESOME!"*

Seymour: *"WELL, SHE WAS A WHOLESOME GIRL ALRIGHT?"*

Hudson: (sudden interest) *"UH ... SHE WAS?"*

Seymour: *"OH YEAH, ABSOLUTELY...SHE COULD 'HOLD SOME' TWELVE MARTINIS, TEN HIGH BALLS, FIVE ENCHILADAS..."*

EXPLOSIVE LAUGHTER, DOOR SLAMS – BLACKOUT

~

Corny? You Bet! -- Sexist? Absolutely! -- Popular? Enormously! KILT now owned the top-rated and most valuable morning franchise in the city and the first chapter of Houston's leading morning radio franchise for the next forty years!

From its beginning in 1967, the morning Hudson and Harrigan show attracted a huge audience. According to Arbitron—KILT's twelve-plus morning-drive ratings were a dominant number one in the Houston ADI, a term that denotes a market's area of dominant influence, and even better, the show's popularity was growing with the release of each new ratings book. Having a winning morning show also set the stage for top ratings in all other day-parts.

The show was wild, outrageous and always unpredictable - full of various character voices created by each partner and situation humor that gave the show a very theatrical environment. Mac had experience as an actor and was later cast in a voiceover role in Robert Altman's hit, 'Brewster McCloud' (while being filmed in Houston.) Paul was a stand-up comedian himself, so the show was full of visual-evoking content and theatrical timing.

While the first few years of the show were hugely successful, the number of riffs between the two original hosts increasingly required lots of maintenance. On the air, Mac and Irving were engaged and communicated well, but when the microphones went silent, they increasingly refused to even acknowledge each other.

Texas is a right-to-work state, meaning that workers were not required to join a union, so virtually all radio stations in the state were non-union. That meant that the deejays usually operated their own control boards. Mac Hudson ran the main board, so part of his responsibility was to preset the commercials and other mandatory elements that aired between each music selection. Irving Harrigan sat across the glass in another studio with a smaller control mixer and cartridge machines for blackouts and sound effects. Paul was responsible for inserting the various crowd responses and comedic blackouts. Both studios were equipped with an off-the-air talkback system that allowed them to discuss and plan the upcoming 'stop set'-- but increasingly, they chose not to use it. In fact, they rarely communicated anymore. While they each had unique responsibilities while the music was playing, they still needed to maintain some level of direct communication. More and more however, they were not even acknowledging each other's presence except when the microphones were live. While the listener could probably not notice the growing tension going on in the studio, I could hear it clearly. Usually it was apparent in their timing or a very subtle voice intonation in their shared conversation. Human voice frequently reveals unspoken emotions. Problems rarely go away without intervention, so after a few days, I would confront the issue head-on and sit down with both of them to voice my concerns. After letting each of them blow off some steam, things would get back to sanity -- for awhile.

Off the air, Mac and Paul were very different personalities. Paul (Harrigan) was consistently jovial and friendly. Mac (Hudson) was frequently moody, distant, and appeared at times to be fighting a set of internal demons. During some of those confrontational meetings, Mac's first response would begin with *"I quit"* but then after talking the issue through, he and Harrigan were cracking jokes again. With a cast of character voices they each created--such as the frequently inebriated Seymour Broomwad (voiced by Harrigan), and the resident Katy, Texas bubba Jim Bob Jumpback (voiced by Hudson), the show rapidly became one of the country's most successful morning programs. Of no small significance, the show also featured the same popular newsman for most of those years - Robert B. McEntire.

Eventually however, the personal side of the partnership became irreparable. Paul left the show first in June of 1973, Mac followed a bit later. In a strange coincident, they both soon wound up in San Diego, but not at the same stations, and not with the same partners. Paul reunited with Jack Woods, his original Dallas and Cleveland partner as 'Charlie and Harrigan' on KCBQ in San Diego. Hudson soon left Houston with KTHT's Joe Bauer for San Diego's KFMB and the 'Hudson and Bauer' show. The ratings battle between the two former partners was intense but also provided the San Diego audience with some very exciting and entertaining radio shows.

Mac's long battle with addiction resulted in various stays in treatment centers, but in October, 1997, the morning after release from one of those visits – he left the show early, saying he did not feel well. Later that day, Mac was found dead in his residence.

~

Because the H&H franchise was so important to KILT, we experimented with a number of combinations in an effort to replicate the magic the show had initially created. Some of those that spent time on the show included Jack Mayberry - a stand-up comedian and frequent guest on the Johnny Carson Show, and the multi-talented Mike Scott who later became Billboard Magazines' Country Music Personality of the year. The show's ratings stayed strong, but I knew that none of the interim pairings would work for the long haul.

Jim Pruett was the Program Director of KLOL-FM, the first album rock station in Houston, whose studios sat literally next door to KILT's. When Jim applied for a job at KILT, I jumped at the chance to hire him for competitive reasons and put him on the air at KILT-FM. From day one however, Jim let it be known that he wanted to do *'that morning show.'* While Jim was pleasant enough on the air, there was no indication in his work history that demonstrated any ability to fit into the theatrical, humor-based environment the H & H show had developed. Nonetheless, Jim brought the subject up often enough that I began to listen more closely to his ideas.

~

Just prior to that time, I appointed a deejay hired from KULF in Houston to be Program Coordinator for KILT's new FM 100. His name was Glen Powers, originally heard on stations in Tennessee. Glen and his wife Sharon became friends of my Sharon and I and we spent many weekends searching for the best restaurants, movies and telling our favorite radio stories. Glen kept pushing me to go into partnership with him to consult other radio stations. Knowing my well-developed fear of flying, I was never going to chase that career but Glen said he would do all the travel on weekends and I could simply add my name, reputation and help devise the strategy. After checking with my bosses, I relented, Young/Powers programming's first client became WNOR-FM in Norfolk, Virginia. The station was owned by Arnold and Audrey Malkan from Corpus Christi, Texas. The Malkans were both attorneys and investors in radio stations. With a quick change in format to album rock, the Norfolk station's ratings shot to number one in the ARB ratings. At the time, it was reported to be the first FM album rock station in the country to achieve overall number one status in a rated market.

Impressed with the immediate turnaround in Norfolk, Malkan asked us to take a look at KFJZ in Ft. Worth, another station the couple co-owned with the longtime manager, Stan Wilson. Because Stan and I had met during my earlier days at WACO, he insisted that I be directly involved with KFJZ.

~

After Arbitron ratings service combined Dallas/Fort Worth into one media market called the DFW Metroplex, KFJZ's limited nighttime coverage and its 'Cow-Town' perception did not play so well in the newly-drawn market. Not surprisingly, the station's ratings began to steadily erode in the new environment. Glen and I set about doing as much as possible technically by tweaking the apparent loudness and pushing the signal to its legal limits, but the gains were marginal.

KFJZ's problems were varied and complex. For openers, it had a lot of sacred cows; practices and personalities that were considered immune to change. KFJZ was the base station for TSN - the Texas State Network - established in 1939. Its austere network voices included morning newsman Porter Randall, whose very-slow, very-precise delivery had defined the network since the early forties. The morning deejay was George Erwin, who had also joined the network in 1940. The network's member stations existed in small, mostly rural areas of the state, and those markets were not accustomed to change. There was little we could do to modernize that part of the operation.

Even the station's most contemporary personality was a concern. Mark Stevens had joined KFJZ in the early sixties and became known as 'Marky Baby.' During the Beatles invasion, Mark was the station's successful point-person for everything

Beatles; he walked, talked and dressed to fit the mold. Mark's program featured lots of loud, naughty, teenage humor with various bodily-function sound effects. In a 1988 Ft.Worth Press article, columnist Bud Kennedy described Mark's style; *"he laughs, screams, plays joke tapes, takes requests and generally barges into your living room like a belligerent drunk!"* After many years of no changes whatsoever, Mark's view of deejays as superstars was rapidly becoming extinct. Normally dressed in black and still wearing a Beatles mop-top with long chain-necklaces gave me the clue that Mark was not likely to make any major changes in fashion or the style of his radio show. While Stan's loyalty to Mark was admirable, it limited our ability to change the listener's perception of KFJZ.

In an effort to make change, we brought in some of the original team from McLendon's successful KNUS in nearby Dallas. Jon Rivers was hired to spend mornings on the air with George Irwin in an attempt to inject new energy into that important day part. Randy Brown, using the air name Christopher Hayes, was appointed the new Program Director and took over the afternoon drive slot. Beau Weaver answered my frantic call for help, yet again, by building the format structure and hosted the mid-day shift. We moved Mark Stevens back to nights.

~

Mark's show remained just as it had been for years -- good years at first -- but nearing the mid-seventies, that audience was busy building a life. Stan's loyalty to his employee was admirable and refreshingly rare in the industry, but it limited how far we could go in changing the listener's perception of KFJZ. In fact, Stan said we had to keep Mark Stevens -- unless we could find something better for him elsewhere.

Driving home to Houston one Sunday evening after a long weekend of meetings with Stan at his second home on Lake

Granbury, the obvious solution hit me. Mark's style may have been out of fashion and his perception in the market a bit dated, but with a slight audience re-focus, he might fit well in Houston as part of the morning Hudson and Harrigan world.

Not only did the move allow us to bring more consistency to KFJZ, but teaming Mark Stevens – a master of blackouts, double-entrende', and whiz-bang sound effects with Jim Pruett – an edgy, satirical humorist and master of clever ad-libs, breathed new life into KILT's morning franchise.

~

By the end of the year, Jim and Mark had re-energized and re-defined the Hudson and Harrigan show. From the very start, in June, 1974, the new team was a giant hit. First and foremost, they seemed to respect each other's talent, which was refreshing for a change. Unlike the original hosts, they worked well together as a team, both on and off the air. With Mark as the challenging setup guy and Jim's quick ownership of the show's popular characters—Seymour Broomwad and Jim Bob Jumpback—the H&H program was morning radio at its very best. Their frequent live promotional appearances added to the show's already large following. While they may have never reached the side-splitting comedic highs of the original team, the edgy new partners quickly took ownership of KILT's morning franchise.

Mark's style, out of step in the new world of KFJZ, was perfect for mornings at KILT. Having never heard him in a comedic role before, Mark was a big surprise for me. I had thought he would simply be the setup guy, but from day one, he was dead-on in his interpretation of the concept. The new team even exceeded previous numbers among the eighteen to twenty-four year old audience. KILT dominated morning ratings and only KIKK – the Pasadena station driving the pre-Urban Cowboy wave -- ever came anywhere close to the show's success.

By 1978 however, the show was exhibiting a bit more 'edge' than I had expected. Mr. Hudson no longer lectured Seymour for his outlandish escapades; in fact he wanted to hear all the prurient details. The original team's character had been less of an issue for most listeners. As always, Seymour spent nights out on the town, drinking too much and hanging out with loose characters. His unruly behavior always drew a lecture from Mr. Hudson, who became the moral conscience of the audience. By taking that position, it allowed the show's more virtuous listener, who might have felt uneasy with the subject matter, to find comfort that their favorite radio show still had a moral compass. With the new team however, the compass was demagnetized and spinning out of control in every direction!

The ratings were back strong, but internally, there were increasing discussions about the show's content. The battle line was clear -- I was uncomfortable with the direction of the show while Mark and Jim drew a line in the sand.

~

The shock-jock movement was growing in markets around the country with one consistent factor; the bad taste deejays all aired in morning drive. Howard Stern developed his free-form personality in the late seventies at WCCC in Hartford, Connecticut. After numerous moves, including Detroit and Washington DC, Stern wound up at WNBC in New York City, the flagship station of the prestigious radio network. A guest appearance on the David Letterman show put him into the national spotlight and he wound up with a huge new contract at WXRK in New York. The Stern show became even more shocking. Some of the show was syndicated on the E TV Network where Porn stars and strip dancers were regular guests. Eventually, Howard's program became syndicated in many parts of the country, but in 2006 - after a highly-publicized bidding war and a very expensive contract -

Stern moved his program to Sirius' satellite radio service.

With apparent looser standards by the FCC, the new generation of shock-jocks were making headlines and causing controversy all over the country with kinky sex jokes and naughty toilet humor. There seemed to be no limits anymore. WNEW New York's Opie and Anthony team produced enough outrage in 2002 to attract national news when listeners responded to a contest where the prize was to perform sex in the most outrageous public place. After a couple trying to win the prize was arrested in the vestibule of St. Patrick's Cathedral, the controversy finally convinced Infinity Broadcasting that things had gone too far. Opie and Anthony quickly wound up with huge contracts from Sirrus' competitor, XM Satellite Radio.

Within the unregulated world of satellite radio, these programs quickly found an audience with a win at any cost mandate. In an Associated Press article April 13, 2007, Larry McShane wrote *"economics often trumps emotion in an anything-goes business."*

~

The increasing amount of sexual content on the Hudson and Harrigan show was not the first difficult decision I had been required to face in my radio career. Because I was the one that usually had to take the calls from those who voiced complaints, the issue increasingly kept me awake at nights. Was 'winning' more important than my responsibility of citizenship? Could I, in good conscience, look at my wife, my sons, my neighbors, and justify the content being broadcast every morning on the program I had created. My parents taught me that integrity is not a quality one can simply turn on and off, like a switch. I remember asking myself; 'what would my Dad do?' The answer to that one was clear -- but no less difficult because it had implications for, not just my own career, but the investments of a large corporation and its millions of shareholders.

KILT's owner, the publically held Lin Broadcasting Corporation, had been acquired in 1967 by McCaw Cellular Communications which in turn would become part of AT&T. My once worthless stock options, initially awarded at $1.99 per share, had grown rapidly and split numerous times. The growth exceeded my wildest dreams. While I had the tacit support of KILT's management and Corporate officers about the show's direction, I also understood that I would ultimately be judged on the station's ratings success. It certainly was not the first or last time I would face difficult choices, but none with so many implications.

In a rare Saturday morning meeting, after numerous conversations with Mark and Jim -- together and individually -- the issue was clear and the showdown was here. Without a commitment to a more acceptable program standard, KILT would make a change in the morning show. Mark Stevens had drawn his line in the sand earlier, so I knew his stance, but I had hopes that Jim Pruett would stay on and rebuild the show. It was not to be. Mark and Jim moved briefly to KULF in Houston as Pruett and Stevens before accepting a job in Dallas at KEGL. Eventually they returned to Houston for a long, successful run at KLOL. An article by Helen Thompson about them in the November 1992 issue of Texas Monthly was titled *"Radio Foreplay."*

~

Immediately, I set about rebuilding the morning show. Time and again through my years at KILT, when I needed help, I called on Beau Weaver. A consummate radio artist, Beau had--at a very young age--worked weekends at KILT before moving to Tulsa's Bill Drake consulted KAKC. His resume was packed with the best of the best - KHJ/Los Angels, KFRC/San Francisco, KNUS/Dallas, KCBQ/San Diego and of course, KILT. In the late seventies, Beau was KILT's important afternoon-drive host. Later he replaced

Alex Bennett on KILT's late-night talk show, paving the way for people like Rush Limbaugh and Phil Hendrie. Now with our popular morning show on the line, I reached out to Beau again. He accepted the challenge. Beau teamed first with Tommy Kramer, a brilliant radio talent from Shreveport who had spent earlier years at KILT-FM.

Since neither of the two performed character voices, we added a de-facto third partner, Fred Kennedy, KILT's talented commercial director who had perfected many character voices. Later, in 1981, the show would pare down to just Fred and Randy Haymes, a hand-picked replacement by Beau Weaver. That team kept the franchise alive and successful for another twenty-eight years. In March 2010, in a very different radio environment, the Hudson & Harrigan franchise finally signed-off of the air for the last time.

~

Houston Chronicle writer Ken Hoffman called the Hudson and Harrigan show the *"longest-running, most successful morning team anywhere in America."* Even though the actors changed over the years (there were eleven different personalities in all), the show dominated ratings starting in 1968. Even the program's popular newsman, Robert B. McIntire, remained on the show throughout most of those changes.

~

Radio consulting today is very different from the constant owner/manager hand-holding necessary when Glen Powers and I were involved. With large blocks of stations owned by a handful of corporate owners, professional teams of consultants use new technologies to monitor a station's progress, maintaining contact and consistency in far flung markets. All of them are well-versed in the evolving audience measurement developments. Yet radio listenership is at an all time low.

Consulting works best when there is unique expertise in a programming movement sweeping the industry. Kent Burkhart and then twenty-year old partner Lee Abrams created a highly disciplined and sponsor-friendly album rock format in 1973 called SuperStars. While an increasing number of FM stations were achieving success with album rock formats, many of them were locally programmed with free-form music and subject to long drum solos. The rigidly controlled SuperStars format of select 'focus tracks' and longer versions of the more progressive pop hits was perfectly timed and very successful in all of its markets. Kent Burkhart continues to provide guidance for a large group of clients while Lee Abrams became the Senior Creative Officer of XM Satellite Radio before leaving in early 2009 to become Chief Development Officer at Tribune's publishing, broadcasting and interactive divisions. Abrams Left Tribune in late 2010.

The management/programming team of Bill Drake and Gene Chenault were the 'big kahunas' of consultants in the late sixties with their Boss Radio format. Unlike Superstars, the Boss format was highly dependent on the quality of its local talent, so some of its markets were more successful than others. Bill Drake passed away in 2008.

The Shulke stations were uniquely successful in many markets in the late seventies by developing a music format that took advantage of the ratings methodologies of the period. Shulke came to the conclusion that businesses and doctor's offices utilized radio as a free background music service for most of their day. The stations may have had a smaller number of total listeners in the 'cume' ratings, but they kicked butt with huge, all-day average-quarter-hour ratings.

Today, Mike McVay and his 'McVay Media' consult a large list of Adult Contemporary client stations around the country.

Rusty Walker has won Billboard Magazine's "Country Consultant of the Year" for seven consecutive years while 'Vallie-Richards-Donovan' consulting group of Hot AC and other formats keep stations up to date on industry trends and the constantly changing ratings methodology.

Sparknet Communications is a consultancy representing an interesting programming concept called Jack FM©. With a twelve hundred song library spanning four decades, the format is described as a computer with a playful and campy attitude that is always *'playing what Jack wants.'*

Chapter THIRTY
"PAYOLA BLUES"

"I don't know how to promote you." The remark came from Houston based independent record promoter Sammy Alfano who represented some of the hottest record labels. Getting his clients' new single added to radio stations such as KILT was important. A variety of influential national *'tip sheets'* looked to breakout stations like KILT, in markets similar to Houston, to set trends which could be duplicated on a national basis.

"What do you mean" I asked.

"Well, you don't do drugs or booze, you're not interested in meeting new ladies, can't get you to party, and you went public with the name of the only promoter who ever offered you cash -- there are no tools left!"

Radio airplay has perennially been the quickest way for an artist to get exposure, but with hundreds of single releases pouring into stations each week, labels needed a way to distinguish their songs from their competitors.

For decades, most major market radio stations reported the success of the songs it programmed to industry publications and tip sheets, such as Billboard, Cash Box, Radio and Records, The Bill Gavin Report and Kal Rudman's Friday Morning Quarterback. Since the number of times a song is played can influence its perceived popularity, a record's breakout in an important market could usually be duplicated in other areas, resulting in enormous sales and touring success for the artist and the lable.

~

Payola is defined as the *"illegal practice of payment or other inducement by record companies in return for broadcasting recordings on music radio in which the song is presented as being part of the normal day's broadcast."* Under US law, a station can actually play a specific song in exchange for money, but this must be disclosed on the air as being 'sponsored' airtime.

The term 'payola' (first used by Variety magazine in 1938) is a combination of *'payment'* and *'Victrola'* and refers to any secret payment made in return for radio play. Payola scandals in radio were not new to our generation; in fact payola in various forms was a common practice even during the big band era of the Thirties and Forties and in the vaudeville business back in the Twenties.

The payola scandal of the late fifties and early sixties occurred because of a number of factors; the emergence of rock music, the introduction of the forty-five rpm single, radio's shift from networks to locally programmed music, and the arrival of teenagers as an economic force. To the record industry, radio's influence on the record buyer became vitally important.

Record labels recognized that these new listeners had cash, loved rock n roll, and were influenced by popular deejays. Since less than ten percent of the hundreds of records released each week would ever become hits or even make a profit, radio airplay was the quickest way for an artist to get exposure and sell records. With singles pouring into radio stations at a rapid clip, labels needed a way to distinguish their songs from their competitors. A positive report from an influential radio station to one of the tip sheets could be the first step down the road to millions of dollars in record sales. With so much at stake, greed frequently trumped integrity.

In November 1959, Congress first announced that it would hold hearings on payola. Fearing the taint of scandal, radio stations across the country quickly responded and fired many disc jockeys. Legendary deejay, Alan Freed, the man believed to have first used the term 'rock 'n roll,' saw his career come to an end after he testified that he, too, had accepted payola. TV's American Bandstand host Dick Clark was called before a Senate Committee where he denied involvement in the practice.

By the mid seventies, a number of record labels owned by large, respected companies started hiring independent promotion personnel in order to remove the perception of involvement in payola. These *indie* promoters provided a layer of deniability for the label, since the people involved in the practice were not actually employees. Eventually however, payola even bypassed the deejays and music directors after the promoters started cutting deals with station management itself.

Press coverage of payola was back in the news in the seventies when former Capitol Records VP Roger Karshner published 'The Music Machine.' The book claimed to tell what *"really goes on in the record industry."* Most of the industry dismissed his claims until March 31st, 1972 when a headline from syndicated columnist Jack Anderson announced *"Payola Returns to the Record Industry."* He charged that deejays in the soul music formats were being supplied vacations, prostitutes, cash and cars as payoffs to play certain records. According to Anderson, payoffs were also being distributed as product under the guise of 'promotional copies' rather than cash, allowing the recipient of the free merchandise to then sell the albums at a lower cost to retailers who were happy to pay less than wholesale prices. Anderson also claimed that drugs were being supplied to certain deejays and music directors in return for play, giving rise to the new term, *"drugola."* After the Justice Department intensified its investigation, Clive Davis, the president of CBS Records, was fired.

~

In the years that preceded MTV, payola came in the form of direct payments of cash, product or favors to deejays. One incident however crossed the boundary and became an actual threat. A friend of mine, the highly-respected Program Director of a major market radio station (who will remain anonymous for obvious reasons), sat at my dining room table one evening and shared a hair-raising story.

My friend had been contacted by a local promotion executive numerous times one week and urged to add a relatively well-known artist's new record to his station's playlist. Although the artist was originally from that immediate area, his career was nearing the end of a string of hits and my friend did not believe that the new release would add value to his station. He gave the promoter his reasoning. Other calls followed.

After a few days of calls, the promotion man phoned again and said he urgently needed to talk to the Program Director immediately -- *"away from the station."* As they drove back to the studio from dinner, my friend was asked once again to add the record. After reiterating his position, the promotion man stopped the car, looked at my friend and said, *"I hate to tell you this, but if you value your family, you will add this record."*

A late night conference call between the justifiably panicked Program Director and officers of his public-held company determined that the threat was too risky to take chances. After advising the company's FCC Attorney, the record was added to the station's playlist with sufficient internal documentation each time the song was broadcast. In the finale analysis, the song never achieved a chart position on the local or national charts.

~

By 2000, payola, under a different name, became corporate. Clear Channel Communications paid an $8,000 fine for promoting a Bryan Adams single and billing his label, prompting Los Angels Times' writer Chuck Philips to call it a *"mere slap on the wrist."* The FCC was also forced to look into the practice after AM-FM/Chancellor Media, prior to being acquired by Clear Channel, charged A&M Records $237,000 to promote a Bryan Adams single.

By 2005, the practice had taken the form of direct bribes to the stations themselves, with airfare, electronics, iPods, tickets to sporting events and concerts as payments to radio stations for expenses and for use in contests. New York Attorney General Eliot Spitzer charged that record companies had hired independent promoters to act as conduits for payments to stations to increase airplay of some recordings that *"are supposed to be based on popularity among listeners."* Warner Music Group was fined five million dollars to settle its part of the investigation and Sony BMG Music Entertainment agreed to pay ten million dollars.

Other than a cash offer to add a local band to a company sponsored concert, which I declined and reported to my company -- I was never offered payola.

Chapter THIRTY ONE
"PLAY THAT FUNKY MUSIC"

Charlie Van Dyke's deep, powerful voice cuts through the night...

"KILT ROCK REVIVAL (massive timpani drum) THE YEAR -- 1961"

The opening from the Five Satin's classic love song *"In The Still Of the Night"* segues to the soft, swaying vocal riff from the background singers...

"SHOO SHOO BE SHOOBY DO – BA DOO - SHOO SHOO BE SHOOBY DO"

...and the soulful nighttime KILT disk jockey K.O. Bayley's deep, gravely, funk-filled voice mumbles a classic introduction..."This is K.O. on KILT nighttime, and you get down one of those times with a little tweak behind the juice man, hey and you 'member when you and momma were parked up 'err on 'da hill and you're telling her all those sweet thangs, with a little hit of the wine and the quiet, and..."

"IN THE STILL OF THE NIGHT, I HELD YOU, HELD YOU SO TIGHT"

I wonder where a listener could find anywhere near this kind of passion for music anymore. Radio artists like K.O. Bayley or Barry Kaye or Beau Weaver or Steve Lundy, all made the songs come alive on the radio ... and touched a place deep in our soul...

"WELL I MAKE IT ALL RIGHT,
FROM MONDAY MORNING TIL FRIDAY NIGHT,"

The best deejays understood the need for connection and the special relationship that existed between a listener and a voice on the radio. Connection is important...

"...BUT OOHH, THOSE LONELY WEEKENDS,"

There's an entire cottage industry out there still trading air checks of the masters from this era. Reelradio.com, Airchexx.com and other sites run by passionate radio curators compete to find the latest gem. I rarely saved my work, the best of which was created in the production studio. Some of it still shows up at times on YouTube and other radio websites, but the easy part of my work was that I had a tape machine, a splicing block and the luxury of lots of retakes. Talents like K.O. performed live, with no safety net. I miss the spontaneity of live, local radio -- it was magic.

"SHOO SHOO BE SHOOBY DO"

Chapter THIRTY TWO
"A SONG FOR YOU"

Of all the things unique to top-forty radio--albeit somewhat inconsistent--none had more power to inspire a staff of disk jockeys than a new set of *'jingles.'*

Hearing your station's call letters sung by a chorus with a large orchestra was just the ticket to sounding really big-time. Hearing your station's call letters sung by a chorus and a huge orchestra was also very inconsistent with your core programming.

Most early top-40 station's playlists included a broad range of hits from Little Richard to Conway Twitty and AC-DC to Alvin & the Chipmunks. The music rocked, and some of it rolled—but the station's jingles sounded as if they came from a Broadway musical.

That was always a *'disconnect'* for me. The youth-oriented listener tuned into our stations to hear the newest hit from the Dave Clark Five; yet we identified ourselves with big–band, group-sing jingles that sounded like the Mitch Miller Gang.

~

Bill Meeks in Dallas, Texas first began creating radio jingles in 1947 while working alongside Tom Merriman at Gordon McLendon's KLIF.

In 1951, Meeks left McLendon to created PAMS as an Ad Agency in Dallas but soon began offering syndicated packages of musical radio station jingles. Over the next two decades, PAMS Productions became very successful. Every six months or so, PAMS would create a new series of stock instrumental tracks and four or five staff singers would then re-sing each new client station's call letters. You can still occasionally hear those jingles on oldies programs from XM/Sirius satellite radio and on a number of jingle-groupie sites on the internet.

Program Directors from around the country would fly into Dallas and take their turn sitting in the Producer's Chair for the recording sessions. PAMS was a very creative environment, and since musicians had their own special language, it made a P.D. feel -- at least for an hour or so -- like Phil Spector. The entire PAMS' staff and sales manager Jim West treated you like a star producer by responding enthusiastically to every suggestion you made.

PAMS' created many clever concepts and styles for each new jingle set, with names such as Sonovox, Jet Set, Fun Vibrations', Go-Go and my personal favorite, the Pow-Pow-Power Series. The reason that PAMS' probably produced new sets of jingles each six months was twofold; first, it made good business sense to sell new packages of product, and second, because the deejays' and probably the listeners, would get really sick of hearing those same Pow-Pow-Power jingles, over and over, every few minutes, twenty-four hours a day, seven days a week!

Texas is a 'Right-to-Work' state, which means that a person cannot be denied employment because of membership or non-membership in a labor union. That meant that jingles could be created without union features such as residual payments to singers and musicians. The producer, in this case PAMS, could choose to hire 'non-union' talent for salary or free-lance fees.

PAMS' pricing was reasonable, usually about $2,500 per package, depending upon the size of your market. The company became enormously successful and sold their work to radio stations from New York to California, even in foreign countries!

The success of PAMS and the availability of competent talent, studios, and experience, spawned an entire jingle industry in Dallas and, to a lesser degree, in Memphis. Most of the other companies followed the PAMS' model; Toby Arnold Associates, JAM Creative, Century 21, Otis Conner and Thompson Creative in Dallas, and Pepper Tanner in Memphis.

~

For some of us, the real pro among Dallas music-makers was always Tom Merriman. Tom created the first jingle recorded in Dallas as an employee of Gordon McLendon's Liberty Broadcast Network in 1952. A former student at Julliard with established music credentials and an impressive list of main-stream ad agency clients, Merriman had less interest in becoming a jingle-mill. Most of his projects were custom made for each client. But in 1967, a former radio program director from Indianapolis named Jim Long formed a partnership with Merriman and created TM Productions.

Unlike the other jingle marketers, Long brought actual radio programming experience to the party. He knew how jingles could be used to increase awareness and he also understood radio's economics, the audience, and the rating's methodologies. Meanwhile, his partner had the respect of the top musicians and vocalists in the city. Many believed that TM was the best of its kind, winning awards and shaping the sound of commercials and radio for over forty years.

Because of his radio experience, Jim talked to programmers in an informed way that no other jingle salesman had ever talked to us before. He sought to provide jingles that actually addressed specific programming needs. It was in one of those conversations that Jim asked for ideas. For weeks, I had a single, simple jingle ID rolling around in my head. Not versed in the correct musical terminology, I described it to Jim in very simplistic terms — *"a super-quick track that opens with a rapid fire, explosive drum roll and a very fast and tightly-compressed vocal sing of the call letters only, oh and it has to end on an 'up' note - (never down)."* Within days, Jim called with a phone patch demo of the *'Shotgun'* jingle - and it was perfect. TM's Shotgun Series became one of the largest selling jingle packages ever produced. Realistically, its popularity soared after it was sold to one specific radio station.

Buzz Bennett - the brilliant programmer and consultant was garnering gobs of industry press. At KCBQ-San Diego, Buzz purchased TM's Shotgun package but used only one single jingle before every record played. It became part of the signature sound that made KCBQ one of the country's most emulated radio stations. Because of his success, Buzz won the Program Director of the year recognition at the 1971 Gavin Conference in New Orleans. Many programmers that attempted to emulate Buzz's success had to have that same jingle package.

~

After success in the mid sixties at KYNO in Fresno, California, owner Eugene Chanault and his program director Bill Drake formed a consulting partnership. Their success came from a simple, but highly disciplined top-forty concept of less talk - more music - less commercials - more contests. Their first major client was, ironically, the same KGB of Buzz Bennett's later success. The station was owned by General Tire and Rubber Company, eventually renamed *'RKO General'.* Radio was just one of the company's many holdings; it also dabbled in soft-drink bottling, hotel enterprises, hotels, appliances, aircraft parts, Frontier Airlines and RKO Pictures. KGB quickly went from fourteenth in the market to number one in San Diego. Since none of RKO's other radio properties were that successful, Willett Brown, the very happy manager of KGB, who also sat on the RKO board, recommended that the Drake-Chenault team be hired for the company's nearly obscure station in Los Angeles. Bill Drake's 'Boss Radio' concept, and brilliant program director Ron Jacobs' ideas and attention to detail, built the industry changing KHJ and their concept swept the country. RKO quickly repeated the success by hiring Drake/Chenault for its other markets which included KFRC-San Francisco, WOR-FM in New York, WRKO in Boston, WHBQ in Memphis and CKLW in Windsor/Detroit. The signature sound for all Bill Drake consulted stations was the use of that one simple jingle. Performed by the Johnny Mann Singers, the jingle, sang A-cappella - without instrumental backing - featured the frequency and call letters only — *'93 KHJ'*— and was played in front of each music selection. It became the identifying sound of the Drake stations and ratings exploded.

~

There remains a passionate group of collectors today who seek, swap and treasure radio jingles from the '60s and'70s. There is no doubt that humming along with a catchy music jingle subliminally reinforced a listener's recall during ratings sweeps and made the deejays who actually created good radio, feel better about what they were doing.

Chapter THIRTY THREE
"A DAY IN THE LIFE"

Richard Dobbin was an original. But Richard became the national poster boy of *'blood and guts'* radio news and it almost cost his radio station its license to operate.

Prior to the Telecommunications Act of 1996--the first major overhaul of telecommunications law in almost sixty-two years, a radio station's FCC *'license to operate'* required a significant percentage of public service programming, of which local and national news was a prime ingredient. Because newscasts were an obvious interruption to the core product of music stations, programmers were always looking for ways to make their newscasts less intrusive.

Most ratings services generated audience information through two prisms, Cumulative Audience--the total number of listeners to a given station, and Average Quarter Hour Listeners--the total number of continuous listeners for at least five minutes during any quarter-hour segment. In order to program elements that might be considered a negative to some listeners, such as commercials or talk segments, many Top 40 stations experimented with creative ways to program news.

Of course the ideal would be to make the newscast such a positive program element that it would attract an audience, of all ages. That's why Richard Dobbin's style of news delivery set the station apart from the competition. Richard was so popular with listeners that at least one of the big industries along the Houston ship channel had to shut down the assembly line each morning during Dobbin's 8 a.m. newscast, just so none of the shift workers would have to miss out. Richard drew a huge audience but kept company lawyers busy. While I had yet to hear him on the air, I had definitely heard *'about'* him.

Dobbin had a big voice with an intense, overly dramatic, over the top, rapid-fire, machine gun delivery; which also, incidentally, described his lifestyle. Richard's description of a drowning in a swimming pool might be delivered as *"...the claws of death reached from the depths of the Smith family's perfectly-landscaped swimming pool this afternoon..."*

Every newscast was like a Wes Craven horror movie and frequently caused one to feel the need for a shower, but listeners were talking and stayed tuned-in during the newscast.

When I arrived at KILT, Richard was the News Director. I only met him in passing my first day on the job, just as he was returning from a press trip to Las Vegas with the Houston Oiler's management. The Oilers office called manager Bill Weaver later with complaints that Richard had run-up an exorbitant bar tab on the trip. Complaints were frequent, mostly by those objecting to his bizarre news stories, but some of them for his real-life bizarre escapades. Life was a thrill a minute adventure with Dobbin; once driving the $35,000 KILT Headline News Cruiser, with flashing headlines on top, through the front door of a Houston residence.

Dan Lovett, the former ABC Sports Director at WABC-TV in New York, worked at KILT with Dobbin and tells of a morning when he was preparing to cover for one of Dobbin's apparent, infrequent no-shows. Just as the news introduction was beginning, Richard ran into the news room, out of breath and holding a towel over his left ear. Just before the microphone went 'live', Richard grabbed the news copy from Lovett's hands, pushed him aside and sat down at the microphone. Only then did Dan noticed blood dripping from his ear and asked if he was ok, only to be told that his female companion had *"shot me this morning."*

Did I mention that Richard enjoyed an alcoholic beverage or two on occasion?

~

On Sunday night of my first week at KILT, I called for a complete program staff meeting, which meant all on-the-air personnel. Everyone was present, with exception of newsman Dan Lovett, who was on assignment in Viet Nam--and Richard Dobbin who simply boycotted the meeting. I suspected a 'news vs. programming' turf war, which is not untypical between departments.

On Monday morning, I stopped by the manager's office and Bill Weaver asked, *"How'd the meeting go, everyone show?"*... *"Everyone except Richard"* I answered.

With no warning, Weaver immediately picked up the phone, dialed Richard's home number and simply said, *"Richard, I've had it, you're fired."* Whoa! I had never witnessed such an immediate response. I always considered the firing of an employee to be a serious act. There were those stories of a deejay in some northwestern city that, after being fired, walked straight out of the studio, into a building next door and jumped from a twelfth floor ledge. On TV's 'Apprentice', Donald Trump may have turned *"you're fired"* into a popular TV show in 2004, but to me, a job was an important part of most people's lives and should never be taken lightly.

In reality, Dobbin took the firing well; quickly found a new job in town and eventually helped make KIKK Country a major force in the Houston market.

~

Years later, as a member of the Gavin Program Conference planning board, I attended a prep-meeting for the 1969 conference to be held in Atlanta. Bill, a true gentleman who loved the radio industry, wanted to add a News Director's panel discussion to the annual meeting. He felt it would allow some large, respected stations to share with smaller outlets some valuable information about building a strong local news presence. The discussion then turned to who should be invited to serve on the panel and the most respected news operations in the country were immediately suggested--Atlanta's WSB was obvious, being the host city's respected powerhouse; WCCO in Minneapolis was mentioned; as was WGN in Chicago and a respected small market station there in Georgia. But then someone suggested that we should also include one of the more sensational types of news stations -- one of those using dramatic, hard-core news deliveries to build ratings.

I instantly raised my hand and suggested the perfect person. KIKK in Houston had hired Richard Dobbin after leaving KILT and he was a natural to complete the panel. Bill Gavin asked if I would contact Mr. Dobbin and invite him to the conference.

Richard was excited when I called. In fact, we had developed a cordial relationship since his exit from KILT and while I did not necessarily applaud his style, he was still a person who delivered a large audience to his station. Dobbin excitedly accepted the invitation.

~

As might be expected at a convention of program directors, disc jockeys and record promoters, a long, post-lunch news panel was not exactly a must-see event. The meeting was sparsely attended while the bar in the Crown Plaza lobby was packed.

There were probably twenty-five or so of us in the meeting room when the first three major station news directors began showing off their deep resonant voices and describing, in increasingly redundant detail, the major stories they had broken and the extensive capabilities their stations utilized.

"We have four reporters stationed at City Hall during midday, two at the State Capital, plus three people who work Police headquarters, a helicopter for morning traffic and stringers at all major intersections, etc, etc"... (zzzzz).

Then, it was Richard Dobbin's turn ...

"Well, I'm really impressed with all this stuff these guys have, but the KIKK news department has just me and an afternoon reader, and our most important local news source is a subscription to the Houston Chronicle newspaper."

Boom! After two long days of meetings and an excruciating parade of super deep-voices pumping up their importance, you could suddenly feel a new rush through the room. Dobbin had everyone's attention as he started delivering classic headlines from some of his past newscasts.

"She's under arrest in the county jail, while he's under a sheet in the county morgue."

I started trying to crawl under my chair.

"A Pasadena resident was pronounced dead last night after an accident while using a paring knife. We assume that he 'peeled' himself to death."

The Chicago News Director's mouth was wide open...

What we were watching was a classic *'sick joke'* standup routine. Nothing Richard said was actually amusing, but those trying to keep a straight face rapidly ratcheted the room into howls of hilarious delirium. The shocked panelists were clearing their throats and exchanging glances. Tears flowed as laughter roared; grown men and women - suddenly freed from the monotony of two long days of pompous speeches were suddenly swept away in a degradation of dignity.

> *"She was on top of the world with his ring on her finger...*
> *now she's flat on a slab with a tag on her toe."*

Dobbin's news stories had the audience in stitches...except for one person. At the end of the same aisle on which I was sitting was a man in a loose-fitting sports jacket, an open-collar and long hair in a pony-tail. He was rapidly scribbling copious notes. Someone whispered to me - *"that's Nicholas von Hoffman"* (a nationally syndicated columnist with the Washington Post, featured on CBS' *60 Minutes*, and a frequent columnist for Playboy).

The next week, subscribing newspapers around the country included von Hoffman's column about the state of radio news. Finally, print journalists had found the upstart media's Achilles' heel. KIKK was suddenly in the hot seat and its Washington attorneys said changes had to be made. Rumors were flying around Houston of a possible FCC investigation and something major needed to happen to call off the dogs. By the middle of the next week, Richard Dobbin was once again – as a result of my involvement – out of a job. I felt rotten.

~

Richard Dobbin was a man with enormous creative talent. A

slight career path adjustment could perhaps have made him one of the great satirist, a caustic columnist, a comedy writer for Saturday Night live or a screenwriter for horror movies. Instead, Richard loved the urgency of shock, and being quoted at his favorite bar - day after day.

Alcoholism and chemical addiction are a much too frequent problem in the lives of some in our business. I watched, helplessly, as many talented people drank, snorted or self-medicated their lives into personal and career failure, and all too often, into death itself.

Over the years, I would occasionally hear from Richard. It was apparent that his life choices had taken a toll, but he actually spoke proudly of his moment in the national spotlight. I tried to apologize for getting him involved, but Richard brushed it aside...

"doesn't matter what they say about you Billy .. long as they spell the name right."

~

Richard Dobbin ... lost in a world between genius and insanity, is buried in an un-marked pauper's grave in Southeast Houston.

Chapter THIRTY FOUR
"ON THE RADIO"

For the better part of fifteen years, KILT AM ruled Houston ratings. With a superstar lineup, the Big 6-10 was exactly where I wanted it to be.

The industry agreed. Billboard magazine listed KILT among its top contemporary stations in the country numerous times. In 1972, I received a rare industry Distinguished Service award at the Bill Gavin Program Conference. In 1973, KILT was awarded Radio Station of the Year recognition at the Century Plaza in Los Angeles. The following year, KILT swept the contemporary radio awards--Disc Jockey of the Year–Barry Kaye; Manager of the Year-Dickie Rosenfeld; Program Director of the Year-Bill Young.

Even now, forty years later, recordings of the Big 6-10 can still be found on various radio-history websites and are among the most sought-after downloads by a passionate group of collectors.

~

Hudson and Harrigan's morning success was actually the cumulative efforts of numerous people who later joined the team, each bringing their own personality to the franchise.

Mike Scott (*Michael Belile*) previously worked at KLIF-Dallas, KCBQ-San Diego and KFRC-San Francisco. He was recognized by Billboard as the Country Music Personality of the Year and inducted into the Texas Radio Hall of Fame. Mike was simply too nice a guy to butt heads with a partner each morning.

Jack Mayberry, a deejay and local stand-up comedian, also became a brief member of the H&H show. After moving to Los Angeles, Jack developed a unique comedy routine and appeared frequently on the Jay Leno show and A&E's *Evening at the Improv*.

~

Afternoon drive, 3-6 p.m., was second only to mornings in its revenue producing capability. Afternoon differed in that the listener's routine was usually less structured. For instance, on Tuesday's, the kids might have band practice or other school activities, some church's had mid-week services, factor in a late meeting with a new client, an occasional stop for a quick drink with friends, a stop by the grocery on the way home...the point is, afternoons were consistently inconsistent. The drive–home timeline itself is unique, starting for some as early as four p.m. and the freeways were still packed well after seven-o'clock.

Most afternoon listening came in shorter segments and the turnover of audience was larger. Lengthy comedy routines or content features just didn't work as well in the afternoon as they did in the morning. Most listeners could not invest as much time when life in the big city moved so fast. Building a loyal audience required a unique type of talent so a quick, get to the point, *'wham-bam, thank you ma'am'* presentation style had a better chance of holding on to an audience.

Chuck Dunaway probably defined the role of the perfect afternoon drive deejay. His career brought him recognition in Radio Halls of Fame in numerous states as both a deejay and program director. After successful stints in Cleveland, New York City, Oklahoma City, Houston and Dallas -- Chuck married a wonderful lady named Kendall, changed the pace of his colorful life and became a successful owner of a group of radio stations in Missouri. Chuck's book *"The Way I Saw It"* is a joy-ride through radio's most exciting years.

~

When radio groupies get together to discuss such things, the best of the high-energy deejays are quickly pared down to a handful. Obviously, the Real Don Steel at KHJ is chosen, Larry Lujack at WLS, Long John Silver (Bluebeard) in New Orleans and Charlotte ... Wolfman Jack's all-night show on WNBC in New York ... Scott Shannon at Nashville and New York ... Jackson Armstrong's wild stops at WPOP, 13Q or KFRC, and there are others. But many who know will agree that Barry Kay's work at KILT ranks among the best performances in the history of top-forty radio.

I hired Barry in early 1974 as host of the afternoon drive slot. Until I heard a tape of his work from KGB in San Diego, I was totally unaware of him. After a single listen to the tape, I was a believer. A native Texan, the *"ahhh-oooogah"* Boogie Man was an intense, butt-kickin', revved-up, dominant, in-your-face afternoon disc-jockey with the most impeccable timing of any radio artist I had ever heard. There was no way a listener could use Barry's show as background. His machine-gun delivery could cram an enormous amount to words into a five-second music intro. Barry's three hours each weekday was sheer adrenalin. His career took him to afternoon drive-time positions at KHJ-Los Angeles, KGB-San Diego and KLIF-Dallas. It was in San Diego where Barry first worked back-to-back shifts with K.O. Bayley.

~

KO's real name was Bob Elliot and the 'K.O.' pseudonym fit him perfectly. A former Golden Gloves champion as well as a boxing champion in the Marine Corps, K.O. had also been a P.O.W. during the Korean conflict. His radio career began at a classical music station in Carmel, California, but his 'get-down' rock and roll persona later took him to such major stations as New York's WOR-FM and Bill Drake's KFRC in San Francisco.

K.O. was a quiet, soft-spoken man, but incredibly imposing - 6'3" and 220 pounds - all sheer muscle. While K.O. was at KGB, Buzz Bennett was hired as the new Program Director. Knowing Buzz's reputation for bringing his own cadre' of deejays when he joined a station, K.O. immediately sought to know if his position was secure. After assurances from KGB's station manager that K.O. had "no worries about his job," Buzz did in fact fire K.O. during his first day on the job. According to radio's all-knowing rumor mill, the gentle-giant walked into the manager's office, said a few choice words, lifted the front of the desk and turned it over in the manager's lap.

~

During Barry and KO's shared time at KGB - from summer, 1971 to the spring of 1972 - they worked back-to-back shifts, identical to their show schedules at KILT. Whatever personality conflicts between the two surfaced in San Diego, followed them to Houston. The riff presented a new challenge that I felt inadequate to resolve. In one sense, I convinced myself that the competition between the two was only surface deep and might actually fuel their creative energies. Realistically however, I felt inadequate to play referee between two very large egos and two very large men - particularly knowing that one of them had been a boxing champion with a short emotional fuse. Eventually however, events left no options.

~

From the moment I arrived at KILT, I had a strict, published policy against drugs or alcohol use while on the air or in the building. My staff memo on the subject had said *"what you do on your own time is your business but what you do in this building is our business."* I made it clear to everyone that the *'no drugs or alcohol'* use was a zero-tolerance policy. Realistically, policing that for twenty-four hours a day, three-hundred and sixty five days a year was obviously impossible.

A call from one of the other deejays one night at 9:40 p.m. changed the playing field. The voice simply asked if I was listening to K.O. at that moment - which I was not. I turned on the radio. What I heard required no drug or alcohol testing validation, K.O. was smashed. With less than fifteen minutes left on his show I knew that there was nothing I could do that evening, so I decided to deal with it first thing the next morning.

Recalling the desk incident in San Diego when Buzz Bennett had fired KO, I chose to do the most prudent thing and notify him of the release with a phone call. Actually, I thanked him for his previous work for KILT, offered to give him a glowing recommendation and *"no, I did not actually think his suggestion of immediately driving to the studio to discuss the matter was necessary because, well, because I was running late for a meeting a very long distance from the studio."* All K.O. said was *"I'm comin' down man."*

In what I considered to be prudent management of the situation, I spent the next twenty minutes marshaling every large person on staff to be hanging out near my office during the meeting. In reality, K.O. was calmer by the time he arrived and while he appealed the decision, our discussion was physically uneventful. I hated to lose K.O., and I hated the circumstances that triggered the action, but there was really no other choice.

Actor Tom Hanks was reportedly one of K.O.'s biggest fans and used his name for a character in the film *'That Thing You Do.'* Ironically, K.O. was killed in a Michigan auto accident in 1978 - by a drunk driver.

~

In 1977, Barry Kaye resigned his position at KILT to move to our primary competitor at that time–KRBE-FM. The move forced a legal confrontation because of a non-compete clause in Barry's employment agreement. While never popular with disc jockeys, non-compete clauses in work contracts were nonetheless common in radio during this period. The use of such clauses is premised on the possibility that upon termination or resignation, an employee might begin working for a competitor and gain competitive advantage by abusing confidential information about their former employer's operations, client lists and business practices. Building a new deejay's popularity takes time, and often requires the radio station to spend significant up-front dollars in relocation and then in promotional support, such as billboards or TV advertising. Even then, it could be months or even years before the station could begin to recoup its investment.

In reality, courts are inherently uncomfortable with preventing an individual from working in a trade in which he or she has been trained. Some jurisdictions, such as California, do not even allow non-compete clauses at all. Because of the sensitivities, contracts must be very clear in the language and description of a breach, plus the burden of proof is on the plaintiffs' lawyers to prove intent.

Lin Broadcasting's home office saw the issue as an important precedent, so it was determined that KILT had to pursue enforcement of the agreement. The Station Manager Dickey Rosenfeld was never comfortable doing anything uncomfortable, so I was thrust into the horrific role of spending two days in court in an action against a friend whose talent I respected. After two grueling days of testimony and watching attorneys do whatever it is that they do, KILT lost the ruling on a technical issue. Barry was allowed to stay on the air cross-town at KRBE, a position he would leave voluntarily within a few months.

~

By the latter part of the seventies, the radio audience was increasingly moving to new music on FM radio stations. The handwriting was on the wall; to win and even to survive in the new radio world, KILT AM's programming had to be better - but my recurring nightmare was that simply being better might still not be enough. The landscape was changing. In order to compete against our former *ace*, I turned to the name I called on frequently during my career - Beau Weaver.

Beau is an immensely creative and enthusiastic radio talent. A transplanted native of Houston, he began working for KILT at the age of seventeen as host of a weekend deejay shift on Sundays. From the start, Beau's talent and enthusiasm were impressive. Soon, the offers started coming and Beau left KILT to join the Bill Drake programmed station in Tulsa, KAKC. His career eventually took him to KNUS-Dallas, KHJ-Los Angeles, KFRC-San Francisco, KRTH-Los Angeles, KCBQ-San Diego and he became one of the original pioneers of satellite broadcasting on the Transtar Network. While consulting KFJZ in Fort Worth, I brought Beau on board to help assemble the air-staff and then asked him to rejoin KILT in 1977 to replace Barry Kaye in afternoon-drive. In 1980, Beau took over the late-night talk-show that Alex Bennett first hosted on KILT. When I left the company in 1981, Beau replaced me as Program Director of KILT AM. Today, he is one of the country's most successful voice-actors and his work has appeared on many television programs, commercials and movie trailers.

Mid-days on KILT featured an illustrious group of talents.

Rick Shaw (Hugh Silvas) was a perfectionist. The tall gentle-giant came to KILT in early 1968 from KIMN in Denver. We agreed that his real name might be difficult for some listeners to recall in rating's surveys, but as the noon hour neared on the day he was slated to go on the air, we still had not settled on a stage-name. Hugh was very tall and a bit shy about his appearance, which included the near absence of a chin. Our station photographer, Lee Rodriquez, suggested his growing a beard - Hugh agreed. About ten minutes into the hour, a name used by a few deejays in other parts of the country surfaced - Rick Shaw. I rushed into the control to suggest it to Hugh? The new Rick Shaw broke into laughter and said he loved it. He modified the beard slightly to add a subtle Asian quality and we had a three-note jingle recorded for him that opened with a huge Chinese Gong. The name and beard stayed around for the rest of his career which took him to WOR-FM in New York, KNX-Los Angeles and KFRC in San Francisco. Rick lived a healthy life, free of smoke, drugs and alcohol, yet died in 1998 at the age of fifty-three of an aortic aneurysm. A 1998 post on *reelradio.com* from industry giant Terrell Metheny described Hugh best; *"he had a great deal of talent and a great big heart."*

~

John St. John (John Young) came to KILT in 1971 from Nashville's WMAK where he was a deejay and the station's music director. It was Bill Gavin of San Francisco's Gavin Report who first introduced me to John's talent, based on his belief that John and I would work well together. His smooth, deep voice and friendly style made him perfect for KILT's mid-day audience. We changed the last name to St. John, simply because of the confusion of two Young's on the same station. John returned home four years later to Nashville's WSM FM where he became Billboard's radio personality of the year before moving to the Program Directors position at Atlanta's Z93, the FM that finally toppled the long-reigning powerhouse, WQXI. John's rich voice appeared daily on Ted Turner's TBS Superstation, and later on CNN. He is still a highly successful national voice-over talent.

~

Jon Rivers moved to Houston in 1975 from McLendon's KNUS in Dallas. Jon was originally from Memphis but came to KILT in late 1975 to host the noon to three shift. John had a deep rich voice and the unique ability to sound calm and controlled even in the fast-paced world of top-forty radio.

In 1934, Congress passed the Communication's Act, which mandated that broadcasters were required to serve the public interest, convenience and necessity. The companion NAB Code was also written to guide industry practices under the ruling. The act explicitly included religious programming as a public service. From time to time over the years, I met with Claude Cox, a producer at the Southern Baptist Radio/Television Commission in Fort Worth to discuss providing programs to the industry that met their criteria, yet still addressed the station's core programming objectives. In late 1968, I suggested that the group consider creating a hit music version of 'Silhouettes.'

Silhouettes had been a late sixties radio project by John Rydgren, a Lutheran minister who played current album cuts interspersed with spiritual messages and near acid-head philosophy. His deep, calming voice and unique concept of using Rock as inspiration, became a part of many station's fulfillment of their FCC commitments. The show ceased to exist after ABC-FM hired and syndicated Rydgren nationally. They re-named him *Brother John* and he played progressive rock, intercut with mini-sermons on love, war, drugs and the new culture. Most of the hundreds of stations that had lost Silhouette as a result of the change were hungry to replace the popular, compliance friendly program.

Silhouette filled a major need in weekend programming and after it left the air, *'Powerline'* stepped in to fill the void in 1969. The show was clearly more Christian based, but also featured more popular music. I suggested Lee Randall, who had worked for me at WACO and at KILT, as a possible host. Lee was already working at KFJZ in Fort Worth and was hired as the first Powerline deejay. The show became syndicated to hundreds of stations around the country.

When Lee moved to KTSA in San Antonio as program director, Jon Rivers left KILT to take over Powerline for the next twenty years. Eventually, he created his own, successful, syndicated morning team show with his wife Sherry on K-LOVE, a newer Christian-based network that serviced a long list of radio stations throughout the country.

~

As late as 1977, few women made their living spinning records on major-market stations. KILT built its national reputation, in part, by doing things that were unique to the industry, so when Jon Rivers left, I started looking for new walls to break through. Even though much progress had been made in the seventies for women in broadcasting, most of those gains were in television news. Disc jockey jobs on hit music radio stations remained a man's domain. The problem was, very few women had broken the barrier, so no results existed for what a female top-40 disc jockey could accomplish. Finally, I heard a demonstration tape of a woman on the air at WHBQ in Memphis who crashed through the barriers. From the first time I heard Sheila Mayhew, it became clear that the time was right. I wanted her on the air in Houston. One listen to Sheila's air check immediately turned into one call to Sheila, who immediately accepted the job offer on the phone. She was dynamite on the air and the other deejays were proud of having her on the station. After two years at the big 6-10, Sheila moved to New York City where she became a successful commercial voice talent, actress and author of a published novel under the pen name Sheila York.

~

Ed Shane was a smart, superb programmer in his own right with success as a national radio consultant. He handled a variety of roles at KILT from newsman to deejay in the ten to noon slot after I fired myself off the air. Ed eventually crossed town to become the succesful program director of KRBE FM, our primary music competition and has since become a successful industry consultant.

Jay West had been recognized as the small market deejay of the year while in McAllen before taking over mid-mornings. A true gentleman, Jay spent many successful years at KILT.

Tommy Kramer was another KNUS grad that traveled south, first to KILT FM. A brilliant programmer with a variety of skills, Tommy joined Beau Weaver in the early eighties as a member of the Hudson and Harrigan show and he and Beau were responsible for convincing me to bring Randy Hames to KILT. Randy and Tommy took over the Hudson and Harrigan show in 1980. Fred Kennedy, a brilliant character voice talent was the KILT commercial director and joined the team to provide the character voices of Jim Bob Jumpback and Seymour Broomwad, eventually becoming one of the team members himself when Kramer left the station. Randy and Fred kept the show alive and successful until early 2010.

Night-time radio was becoming more complex. The broad, twelve to twenty-four year old target audience no longer shared the same music tastes. Donnie Osmond's *"Go Away Little Girl"* didn't play so well in a *'double-play'* with Deep Purple's *"Smoke on the Water."* While KILT's night-time listener preferred huge, larger-than-life deejays like Jim Wood, Russ Knight, Steve Lundy or K.O. Bayley – they increasingly connected with more laid-back deejays of the last half of the seventies-—Scotty Tripp,

Todd Wallace, Walt "Baby" Love, Catfish and Capt. Jack.

~

I still loved frequent flashbacks to high school listening habits of tuning the AM dial at nights to find new distant stations. It was on such an evening that I discovered XEROK--a 150,000 watt radio station in Juarez--just across the Mexican border from El Paso, Texas. The station, programmed by the talented John Long, was once home for three future KILT personalities...Christopher Haze, Randy Hames and Catfish.

Scotty Tripp came to KILT from San Francisco. His cool, laid-back nighttime style was connected to the growth of tie-dye shirts and alternative bands in the early seventies. He was also an avid cyclist and represented Houston in another of our joint promotions with the stations that had once been part of Gordon McLendon's Texas Triangle. The Great Texas Bike race, with stops planned in each sponsoring city, included Scotty, Woody Roberts from KTSA, San Antonio and a representative from KLIF in Dallas that worked on weekends (no one remembers his name). We loaded a motor home with spare equipment, refreshments and a Houston Policeman we called 'Officer Gambino' who would direct traffic and other local issues during the 319 mile race. The race got underway in San Antonio, cycled to Dallas and then turned south to Houston. San Antonio was leading at Conroe, some forty-five miles north of Houston.. Next morning, the race resumed and Scotty turned on the afterburners, overtaking Woody midway to Houston and arrived at the finish line at Houston's giant Memorial Park one minute ahead of second place San Antonio.

Walt *Baby* Love was the first black deejay to break the color barrier in Houston. I hired Walt from KYOK, the popular R&B station in town, and gave him the name which he later carried with him to KHJ and KMPC in Los Angeles, to CKLW in Windsor, and finally to WOR-FM and WNBC in New York City. Walt is a class act and his role in changing the industry remains a proud part of KILT's history.

In a two for one hiring, Rick Candea and Eric Chase found KILT by way of Pittsburg in 1979. Rick took the air name *'Captain Jack.'* More conversational than most night jocks, Rick was a smart, well-prepared talent that gave the station a very progressive tilt and competed well with the growing FM competition. Rick became program director of KILT-FM after I left and took the station to number one ratings in the city with a wall-to-wall country music format. Eric Chase was a deejay on KILT FM and produced many of the station's promotional announcements.

Chapter THIRTY FIVE
"UNFORGETTABLE"

The news was shocking and held parents frozen to radio and television screens around the country. At approximately 11:19 a.m. on Tuesday, April 20th, 1999 -- two male students entered the west entrance of Columbine High School in Columbine, Colorado. One of the boys started yelling 'go-go.' With cold, calculated precision, the two pulled out shotguns and a nine-millimeter handgun and embarked on a shooting rampage that left twelve students and one teacher dead. Another twenty-three were wounded before the two committed suicide themselves. It would not be until 4:30 that afternoon that the schoolhouse could be declared safe.

The country watched in horror as live television performed both the best and the worst of what our immediate access to media provides. On same-day coverage, a nation shared the gut-wrenching fear, graphically displayed on tears on the faces of parents as students ran screaming from the classrooms. We watched our kids live a violent hell that no child should ever have to experience. We watched the end of our long-held belief that our schools were a safe place.

April 20, 1999 was a chilling day in our country's history.

~

In Richardson, Texas, my father, W.R. *'Bill'* Young – a lifelong public school teacher and administrator – watched the horror unfolding in Columbine that day, and he wept.

~

Dad spent his entire adult life in education,
Work one has to love very deeply to experience,
Picking cotton and mowing lawns to earn his first degree,
Teaching six grades, all housed in a one-room schoolhouse,
Repairing tractors on weekends, trying to make the ends meet,
Driving morning and afternoon buses on roads yet to be paved,
Another hundred miles each summer day for work on his masters,
Tutoring kids with learning deficiencies, long before it had a name,
Nights at home with a ringing telephone -- an upset parent,
A teacher with the flu, a mom whose son was disrupting class...

Dad sat alone in his room that afternoon, losing the horrific battle with Acute Myeloid Leukemia that had so rapidly ravaged his strong body, and he watched television coverage of the darkest day in public education's history.

Back in Houston, I felt rage that actions so horrific could invade the innocence of a classroom — while in Richardson, Texas, a gentle, caring, dedicated, life-long educator watched the unfolding tragedy — and he wept.

~

I spoke with Dad that afternoon by phone. I could hear the sadness in his voice. Dear God, he sounded so frail. I assured him that Sharon and I were coming to be with him the next morning.

My father passed away at 9:50 a.m. on April 21, 1999, just ten minutes after we arrived. His labored breathing slowed while I lay next to him on his bed, holding his once strong hands and thanked him for what he had meant to my life. The Hospice nurse put her hand on my shoulder and quietly told me that they could no longer register a heartbeat — and I wept.

259

Chapter THIRTY SIX
"TOSSIN' AND TURNIN"

With success comes confidence--at least that's what they say. KILT was cookin' on all cylinders, consistently winning ratings, the station's commercial load was sold out and I wanted to change things. The poet and philosopher, Johann Wolfgang von Goethe once observed, *"only a creature as highly developed as man is capable of boredom."* Was I the one becoming bored? Or was I sensing that large blocks of my audience were becoming bored?

The boss in my first after-school job, a crusty butcher back at Lufkin's Q-P Grocery store, frequently pointed out that some people can *"just plain screw up a wet dream."* I had this recurring nightmare that something beyond my ability to control was taking place.

It was the latter half of the seventies and the more successful KILT became financially, the more worried I became. In spite of the ratings, I had the sense that the most active listeners were beginning to search for what's next and the lyrics from a hit song kept rolled around my head in the middle of the night.

"February made me shiver with every paper I'd deliver"

Don McLean's classic *'American Pie'* forecast the beginning of the end of what Bill Haley had started with *'Rock Around The Clock.'* Nothing was simple anymore. The world was spinning out of control. The good-time rock n' roll that spawned the Top 40 revolution had turned dark - angry. Meanwhile, my radio station still programmed music by John Denver and the Carpenters and most of our listeners wanted it to stay that way. But I could tell that we were losing the actives. I could feel it. They were on the move and searching for something new; Beatles were off playing sitars and released an album with a colorless cover, Pink Floyd created an album about the *Dark Side of the Moon*, Janet Joplin and Jim Morrison pushed the limits too far, and I had no idea how to stop the bleeding. Rock n' Roll's *'age of innocence'* and Top Forty's *'days of dominance'* were fading and our success had us locked in place. We could only watch it happen.

"...those good old boys were drinking whiskey and rye, singing this'll be the day that I die..."

Chapter THIRTY SEVEN
"FM (NO STATIC AT ALL)"

FM radio is a technology that uses *'frequency modulation'* to provide high-fidelity sound over broadcast radio. Actually invented in 1933 by Edwin Howard Armstrong, FM was initially used for educational programming and to broadcast classical music to an up-market audience. By the late fifties, a number of companies submitted systems to the FCC to add "stereo" to FM capability. General Electric and Zenith systems were considered theoretically identical and approved in April, 1966.

For decades, many owners of both AM and FM frequencies simulcast the same programming on both stations. By January first, 1967 however, the FCC mandated a rule prohibiting that practice and initiated a scramble for many dual-station owners to find how to provide profitable returns from the FM side without tarnishing their AM stations -- the existing gold-standard. Broadcasters fought the regulations but they could only delay the rules for another eighteen months.

In July of 1966, WOR-FM in New York got the jump on the FCC mandate and started programming a very progressive selection of rock music. After negotiating a new pay scale for union talent, the station added deejays Murray the K and Scott Muni, who already had strong identity in the market, and adopted a low-keyed, looser delivery style. The station featured a broad playlist of longer LP cuts, most of them in stereo, and the deejays spent a lot of time bashing the government for its involvement in Vietnam. The lack of extreme technical processing and compression, which AM radio stations used to insure a loud and consistent sound level, was actually refreshing and allowed the songs to be aired just as they had been recorded. Similar stations in Boston and San Francisco followed.

The San Francisco station, KMPX, took on a significant role in FM's explosive growth after release of a 1967 Rolling Stone magazine article written by Tom Donahue, one of the city's most popular top-forty deejays. While listening one night to the Door's first album, Donahue questioned why no stations were playing this kind of music on the radio. In April, 1967, he convinced a small Bay area FM station – KMPX - to play album rock 24/7, and a rock revolution began. His article in Rolling Stone, *"AM Radio Is Dead and Its Rotting Corpse Is Stinking Up the Airwaves"* became a significant milestone in Progressive Rock radio's beginnings.

Programmers on the FM band began using longer sets of music, by artists that only received minimal play on AM - Grateful Dead, Jefferson Airplane, and The Doors. On AM radio, Jami Hendrix sounded tinny and compressed, but on FM - in stereo - it was a revolution. The success of Woodstock in the summer of 1969 served notice to radio programmers everywhere that, to paraphrase Bob Dylan, the "times, they are a-changing." KILT built its dominance with the good-time surfer generation of the sixties, not the dark, drug-laced revolution of the seventies. It became clear that we were about to face the facts of what was happening in the neighborhood.

Progressive rock on Houston's KLOL-FM – known as K-101 – debuted in 1970 with the song *'I'm Free'* by The Who. The station's initial promotional efforts included a billboard campaign that featured a prominent cannabis leaf on its logo that lasted about ten minutes once the austere family who founded parent KTRH was informed. The billboards lasted long enough however to make a bold positioning statement to its target audience. One of the station's slogans said *"Houston radio sucks; we just suck less!"*

K-101's top personality was a deep-voiced, laid-back deejay by the name of Crash and its first Manager and Program Director was Pat Font. Jim Pruett became Program Director within time and used the air name Tony Raven.

Overnight it seemed, FM music stations all over town began chipping away at KILT AM's dominance, just as it was happening to successful AM stations all over the country. KLOL quickly established itself with the growing progressive rock audience. KRBE-FM–Super Rock 104, first programmed by Danny O'Brian and then the talented Ed Shane, took the hit-music route and aggressively came after KILT's core audience. Hudson & Harridan's dominance came under attack from a morning jock on KAUM FM, who called him-self Moby. Suddenly the slow but steady erosion of Hudson and Harrigan, KILT's morning cash-cow, became a concern.

~

KILT's FM station was KOST. From the beginnings in 1957, KOST had consisted of one playback tape machine with a handful of hour-long tapes of elevator music and an hourly voice recording of the call letter information. There were no commercials and the station was only on the air each day just long enough to keep the license; that is, on days when someone remembered to load the tapes on the machine. On days it was silent, not a single listener called to complain, not even management.

It was finally time to shut down the single-tape, human-dependent, best kept secret radio station in town, and build our own competitive FM station. Construction of the new KILT FM studios began within weeks.

In spite of its rapid national success, the initial underground-progressive music format still needed to reach a wider audience in order to appeal to major advertisers. The successful consultant Kent Burkhart, originally from Bay City, Texas just south of Houston, joined forces in 1972 with a brilliant young programmer named Lee Abrams, not yet twenty-one and still living with his parents, and the underground became mainstream.

Burkhart/Abrams created the Superstars format featuring 'album-oriented rock,' eventually at over two hundred radio stations. The programming featured a structure similar enough to top-forty stations to cut into our audience shares. The Superstar stations programmed a larger playlist of music and featured longer LP cuts that were impossible to be aired by most successful top-40 stations. Because of AM's large commercial commitments and the denial of many top forty programmers -- the market was ripe for Burkhart/Abrams' new radio format. By 1981, six of the top ten rated album rock stations in the country were Superstar stations.

~

While KILT AM was still winning most day parts, it was not as impressively as before and I could feel the pressure of change closing in.

Chapter THIRTY EIGHT
"BAND ON THE RUN"

From time to time over the years, I received job offers from other radio stations, some of them local competitors. As enticement to stay at KILT, the company built two new recording studios, one for my use in developing both company promotions and for my own concert production projects. My freelance work was encouraged by management because it meant more advertising dollars for KILT, and it also meant my income growth was no longer dependent only on the radio station. I may have been the lowest paid Program Director of a number one station in any major market, but when my free-lance voice-over fees were factored in, I was doing quite well, thank you.

The early Rolling Stones and later concert ads I created for KILT sponsored events began attracting the attention of concert promoters from other markets. Terry Bassett with Concerts West-Dallas was already hiring me to do commercials for his Houston events, but then, asked me to create ads for their shows in other markets. Terry was a partner with Pat O'Day, a Seattle deejay, Program Director, Station Manager of KJR and National Program Director for the other Danny Kaye/Lester Smith owned properties. In addition to his work at KJR, Pat started promoting concerts in the Northeast under the name *'Pat O'Day and Associates.'* With new backing, Pat and his partners eventually opened a Dallas office and later, appointed Terry Bassett to run the division. The company renamed itself "Concerts West" and quickly became one of the hottest concert promoters in the country, overseeing tours across the US and Canada for Jami Hendrix, Three Dog Night, Led Zeppelin, Credence Clearwater Revival, Bee Gees, Moody Blues and Bad Company.

Pat and Terry made a tremendous team. Their laid-back, casual demeanor masked an intense drive for perfection. The company's close relationships with such industry icons as Jerry Weintraub brought them top national tours, such as Frank Sinatra, Neil Diamond, Bee Gees and also created new audiences for then opening acts, such as Bob Seeger and his Silver Bullet Band.

~

Pat tells the story of a critical point in his company's growth when Jimi Hendrix came to him and said, *"Pat, I'm getting two and three calls a day from Eldrige Cleaver, Bobby Seale, and all the Panther guys, calling me an Uncle Tom. They want me to work for them and they say I'm an Uncle Tom 'cause I'm working with you guys. Pat, I love ya and don't want to change a thing, but what in the hell am I supposed to do?"*

Pat continued, *"its at times like this Bill when our years behind the microphone - with commercials to cue, phones to answer, logs to fill out, music to select, and entertaining adlibs to write - causes all those creative juices we've trained ourselves to release come into play."* I said, *"Let me ask you something Jimi. Wasn't Uncle Tom a slave? Here we are in Houston, where 10,000 people have paid to see you play. We bought the advertising, loaded the trucks, fed the roadies, arranged the airplane, booked the hotel, sold the tickets, hired the security and guard the box office, all because we work for you. Every cop, every usher, every one in this building tonight works for you, including me. You can fire me at this moment if you choose as you can fire all of us, because this is all yours. Uncle Tom was a slave Jimi, but here, we are the slaves and you are the man. We are the ones working for the man, and that man is YOU! So tell Clever, Seales, and the rest of them to go screw themselves!"*

Jimi started laughing, *"Pat, you're right. This is all mine."* He was still laughing when he went on stage. The next night in Dallas he just said *"Thanks Pat - that stopped 'em."*

~

I began supplying commercials for Concerts West events in Los Angeles, Denver, and markets throughout the western states. Some of those events were extensive tours by Led Zepplin, John Denver, Three Dog Night, Frank Sinatra, and a new group calling themselves Eagles.

After years of recognized supremacy in the concert field, Pat O'Day left Concerts West to buy radio stations. Terry Basset elected to go his own way. After moving to San Diego, Terry acquired ownership of radio stations and continued promotion work with The Eagles and manager Irving Azoff. Concerts West's departure left a vacuum in Texas which was quickly filled by other promoters."

~

In late 1969, Houston record promoter Bill Ham became the manager of a newly formed group that featured Houston's Billy Gibbons and two Dallas natives, bass player Dusty Hill and drummer Frank Beard. They chose the name *ZZ TOP*. Bill took leave from Daily Brother's Distributing and with a production loan from the brothers, produced an album and signed the group to London Records. The group's first two LPs had respectable regional success but their third album hit Gold, big time.

In January 1973, Houston television station KTRK-TV hired

a flamboyant former Consumer Fraud officer from the Harris County District Attorney's office. Marvin Zindler was the son of a prominent Houston clothing store family. His job at Channel 13 was as an 'investigative' reporter, exposing frauds and nursing home abuse, plus weekly drop-ins to local restaurants in search of *"rats and roaches"* or *"slime in the ice machine."* Zindler's exposes - usually in front of TV cameras - always featured the officer, sharply-dressed with flamboyant suits and his brilliantly coifed hairpiece. One of Zindler's early exposes' targeted the Chicken Ranch brothel in nearby La Grange, Texas. The ranch had existed for decades and was not much of a secret to folks in the immediate area or to generations of nearby college fraternity brothers, but in Maaarrrvin Zindler's hands, the story became huge. So huge, and apparently entertaining to the rest of the country that the expose went national and eventually became the basis for a major Broadway and motion picture musical – *'The Best Little Whorehouse in Texas.'*

For ZZ Top, it was their song about La Grange that launched that little old band from Texas into the stratosphere. The song was the first of a string of hits for the group and enormous success as a touring band. From the start, Bill Ham asked me to create the radio and TV commercials for all of ZZ Top's concerts. But it was a call about one particular ZZ Top concert that introduced me to Barry Leff.

Bill somehow convinced the University of Texas to change their previous policy against concert events at the massive Memorial Stadium, home of the Texas Longhorns' football team. On September 1st, 1974, *'ZZ Top's Rompin-Stompin Barn Dance and Barbecue'* with special guests Santana, Joe Cocker and Bad Company was a total, eighty-thousand seat sellout.

In preparing the advertising for the event, the University required that its Student Director of Event Planning for campus venues to be involved in all aspects of the promotion, which of course included creative oversight of the advertising. Barry Leff was the son of the 1921-founded family-owned chain of 'Leff Bros. Wholesale Dry Goods' stores located throughout the southern half of Texas. After creating the commercials and gaining approval from Bill Hamm, Barry would then tweak the ads with UT information and we would ship the spots to the radio stations. I was immediately impressed with the student's organizational skills. His media and publicity planning was far more sophisticated than I would have expected from someone with no previous advertising experience.

Apparently, the promotion company that Bill Ham had partnered with to produce the show was equally impressed. Beaver Productions, a national concert promoter out of New Orleans had become the primary promoter of most of ZZ Tops concerts. One of the partners of Beaver told Barry to contact him if he ever decided to get into concert promotion fulltime.

Barry made that decision right then and there. A few weeks later, after dropping out of UT, Barry showed up in the New Orleans office of Beaver, ready to go to work. However, the partner that Barry had worked with on the Austin show had left Beaver shortly after the event and the remaining owner, Don Fox, had no knowledge of any such offer, so this kid could *"just get on back home to Austin."*

Having gone through the tough job of convincing his family that he wanted to give up a college degree; a career in the family business; and become a rock and roll concert promoter - Barry now faced the worst personal scenario imaginable. He did the most obvious thing he could think of - he begged.

Don Fox, whose reputation was not usually associated with being a benevolent soul, relented. Today Barry Leff remains with Beaver as one of the touring industry's most brilliant promotion planners.

~

Back home in Houston, entrepreneur Alan Becker and his business partner Sidney Schlenker launched Pace Entertainment in 1966 to promote the Houston Boat Show in the Astrodome. The company then began booking unique events into the Dome such as Supercross and Monster Truck Pulls. From very early in their growth, I was asked to create the radio and TV ads for those events and they became high-profile commercials with intrusive sound effects and clever copy lines. One of my most quoted script lines came from a monster truck event in the Astrodome that started showing up on the city's top TV station. KTRK's News Anchor Dave Ward would cup his hand around his ear, furrow his brow and read the closing line from the ad, *"the roof of the Astrodome is coming OFF!"*

When the Louisiana Superdome was completed in 1975, Pace Management was hired to help produce the musical part of the opening event. Becker hired a local New Orleans concert promoter to be the Pace person on the ground in the Crescent City. After the event, Becker convinced the young promoter - Louis Messina - to move to Houston and develop an all-new concert division for Pace.

Pace Concert's first production in Houston was Barry Manilow at the Houston Music Hall. Because of KILT's close identification with Concerts West, Messina contracted with competing Houston station KRBE for commercial support. Chester Maxwell, one of the KILT salesmen, quickly called on the new promoter and asked me if I would join he and Messina for lunch the next day. We met at a popular restaurant on Loop 610 near the Galleria and Louie quickly voiced his concern about getting lost in the large volume of events already being advertised on KILT. I suggested that the station most known for being the source of concert information was, most probably, exactly where his advertising needed to be. Louie smiled and reached across the table to shake my hand. He gave us that shot with his next concert and it became the first of what is now over three decades of events with him at Pace, SFX and later with his own successful national touring company, The Messina Group -- a partner of AVG LIVE.

My own relationship with Messina and Pace took on a much larger role in 1975. Pace Concerts entered into an agreement to develop the first concert production for Houston's new Summit venue, later renamed Compaq Center. The sold-out opening event on November 20th, 1975 starred The Who. Our commercials blanketed the market and once tickets went on sale, the event was a first-day, sold-out event.

The opening was spectacular and so was the invitation-only celebration after the show at the elegant Houston Oaks Hotel, next door to Neiman Marcus. The Imperial Ballroom featured themed food and beverage courts located in every direction and mini-platforms with an eclectic group of dancers, magicians and entertainers performing at each one. An hour after the party began, members of The Who arrived and caused quite a commotion as the elite invited guests surrounded them for autographs and pictures.

One of the mini-platforms had three or four female dancers who were beginning to draw a rather vocal crowd so my friend, Dr. Ronald Hauser and I headed over to see what was going on, for research purposes of course. Houston was building somewhat of a reputation for its upscale men's clubs and apparently a few of the resident dancers had shown up for the event. While mildly provocative at first, the minute Who drummer Keith Moon decided to jump on stage and join the dancers, the performance became more graphic -- much more graphic. As the crowd grew larger and louder, my friend and I decided that we might want to consider leaving the building, immediately! Just as we reached the escalator, we heard police whistles and a rather loud crowd response from the area we had just vacated. The next morning's Houston Post and Chronicle both reported that the Who's John Entwistle and tour manager John "Wiggy" Wolff, had been arrested at the celebration.

Chapter THIRTY NINE
"HEADED FOR A SHOW DOWN"

There was never a void of information available to Top 40 stations about new music. The music tip sheets; Gavin, Hamilton, Rudman - and the glossies; Billboard, Cash Box, Radio and Records, Rolling Stone, Record World, Crawdaddy, Variety, Creem, etc, etc, provided breaking news about popular music and the people who controlled its presentation. Each of them, some more than others, became part of a music director's weekly research to check validation of current and future hits in other markets. Each song played had the potential to attract or drive away significant blocks of listeners. The more validation available, the more confidence I had in adding a new record.

The tip sheets also created radio stars. Unlike the major magazines covering the music business, the tip sheets reported which stations had added a particular record, the level of response they were getting from the audience and music director's evaluation of its potential. One could quickly identify hit potential for a new release in markets comparable to their own. Inherently, this created a lot of name mentions for the individuals that became proficient at picking hit songs early. The publicity initiated a race by many music and program directors to be the first to discover the next smash hit.

It was a self-perpetuating scenario. Being the first to break a new hit brought substantial press from the tip sheets for that program or music director. A promoter's calls to influential stations always mentioned, for instance, *"Jay Cook at WFIL says his listeners are all over this one!"* All of a sudden, a music director from a small radio station in Kansas might be getting industry press equal to a top programmer in Los Angeles.

The Gavin Report was considered by many to be the most credible of the tip sheets. Bill Gavin's impeccable ethics and objectivity set a high standard of integrity. His annual *"Radio Program Conference"* was the most important industry source for many years. But Gavin's inherent nature was cautious compared to most tip sheets flooding program director's offices each Monday.

Kal Rudman brought tremendous excitement to the process, although most understood that Kal was very active in the record promotion business itself. Rudman's reporting about a hot new hit was exciting and, at times, over the top. Kal's pre-release articles leading up to the first U.S. release by Elton John were, in my opinion, a major reason he achieved such immediate success.

The Bob Hamilton Radio Report was a hugely popular sheet from 1970 until 1974. While similar to the other tipsters, Bob's report placed more emphasis on radio happenings and trends, rather than just news of the week's new music. His own radio career in Elk City, Oklahoma with brief appearances in Tulsa, Oklahoma City and Long Island, New York gave Bob a first-hand understanding of radio issues that instantly helped establish the sheet's level of credibility.

~

Bob and his friend—super programmer Buzz Bennett— initiated a traveling series of regional programming seminars in various parts of the country. I was invited for be part of the panel at the meeting in Shreveport, Louisiana. I would serve on a panel alongside Buzz, Chuck Dunaway--who was programming an album rock station in Austin at the time, and Sebastian Stone--the program director of WOR-FM, the Bill Drake consulted station in New York City.

Buzz Bennett had an enormous reputation after a string of successes in Pine Bluff, Arkansas, Miami, and WTIX New Orleans and repeated in San Diego, first at KGB in 1969 and later across town at KCBQ. Buzz described his stations as *'money, music and magic.'* Listeners described his stations as *'rock and roll radio on speed!'*

Industry icon Lee Abrams worked with Buzz at WMYQ in Miami in 1970 and posted thoughts about him on his blog site on July 02, 2006 — *"...an absolutely brilliant programmer."* At a time when the underground rock press was already filled with the new language of drugs, sex and rock n' roll — a Buzz Bennett station took the culture mainstream. His management style attracted deejays who became more than just an employee; they became members of a family. A staff photo from one of Buzz's projects resembled a Woodstock era love-in.

~

Very quickly, the Shreveport meeting became something very different from any program conference I had attended before. In a brief meeting beforehand, Bob told us he wanted to explore more relevant issues than just formats and music rotations and to dig deeper into establishing a real connection between a radio station staff and its listeners. So, here we were in Shreveport, Louisiana with a group of thirty or so small-market program directors from places like Nacogdoches, Texas and DeRitter, Louisiana discussing how to relate on some metaphysical planet with an audience whose main focus was simply holding on to their job at the farm supply store.

Having spent both of our early careers in small market Texas radio, Chuck and I separately came to the same conclusion that these visiting program directors might have a tough time selling this type of radio to their local managers when they returned home to Crowly, Louisiana or Jasper, Texas - and even less success selling it to listeners like Bubba Pippin at the Friday night fish fry. Few radio programmers ever lost their jobs for underestimating the intelligence of the audience.

Pointing out such inconsistencies to Bob and Buzz made for a rapidly disintegrating level of decorum among the panel, and a reality check for a number of first year small-market program directors. Neither Chuck nor I found it possible to let pass what we considered to be unrealistic suggestions for beginning programmer's, without cautioning them of the danger in being out of sync with their employer and/or the audience. Most of all, we knew these guys had to go home with enough real usable information to justify the time and expense their managers had spent in sending them to a professional programming conference.

~

A high-point of the well-planned meeting actually came at the luncheon on Saturday, just before a live, mid-day appearance by the Nitty Gritty Dirt Band. Sure, the band was great - as expected - but the opening act was the big surprise! An unheard-of comedian by the name of Steve Martin strolled into the room unannounced. He first appeared to be some kooky, intrusive character crashing our lunch and making lots of bizarre comments. Martin's voice became louder and more dominant, interrupting radio-related conversations going on at the various tables, and he quickly wound up behind the Dirt Band's microphone. All of a sudden, the outrageous characters that would later surface on huge tours and network television had the attention of the entire room. After a riotous half-hour stand-up routine, Steve Martin left the room the same way he entered, by simply walking away, out the door of the banquet hall, through the hotel lobby, out the front door, and his voice could still be heard from the parking lot; *"I'm going away now, back to my room. It's lonely back there, where I sometimes do strange things to my dog with a spoon."* My first discovery of a true genius named Steve Martin was pleasantly outrageous!

~

At the end of the conference, Bob graciously thanked me for coming but added that my contrarian positions had been his biggest disappointment of the weekend. I thanked him for the invitation.

In hindsight, the discussion may have presented the group with clear choices for the type radio they should deliver to their listeners. The fact is, Buzz Bennett was - in spite of the sometime outrageous lifestyle rumors that surrounded him - an enormous talent and his accomplishments speak for themselves. His stations were full of excitement and his ideas were unique and legitimately won ratings battles against programming giants. English comedy writer Alan Moore observed, *"if you're going to be doing something new, then to a degree you're destroying whatever preceded it."*

Buzz Bennett became a programming consultant in 1972 and his last known industry project was in Dallas in 1986. He has since virtually disappeared from the industry. A great talent, sadly absent during the dire need of new ideas today.

Chapter FOURTY
"STARTING OVER"

By the early eighties, radio increasingly de-emphasized the role of deejay talent with dependence on research gurus and quarter-hour sweeps of music. The exceptions occurred in morning drive which went the opposite direction. Morning radio shows, with casts of characters even more outrageous than KLIF's Charley and Harrigan and KILT's Hudson and Harrigan started popping up everywhere. The new versions were even wackier than before, and some became known as "morning zoos." It started in 1978 in Dallas' at KZEW with John Rody and John LaBella. In Tampa, it was Scott Shannon and Cleveland Wheeler, then in New York with Scott Shannon and Ross Brillain, John Lander at KKBQ in Houston and Glenn Beck in Corpus Christi - yes, that Glenn Beck.

The 'zoo' concepts' rapid growth once again validated radio's recurring tendency toward *monkey see - monkey do* programming. In a more rapidly changing world, the thin lines between shock-jocks, zoo-hosts and Rush-clones are blurred by one very sad human hickey; shock sells. To attract attention, each new shock has to be more shocking than the one before and therein is what should concern us all. Is there a limit to how much a person or a society can absorb? Has the audience's excitement about new technology already told us that they would prefer to control their own programming, which may no longer include radio?

~

The radio industry was changing and I knew that I had to consider a life outside radio. I was excited about the growth of my concert commercial work, but I had always depended upon a regular salary. The fear of no safety net, no confidence in my business skills, and two households to support kept telling me to stay put. I was addicted to a regular payday and frightened of the uncertainty of letting go. 1980 was a tough year for AM music stations and KILT was not, as I had hoped, immune from reality.

Very soon, choice would be taken out of my hands.

In late December 1980, between the Christmas and New Year's holidays, the Arbitron ratings arrived and they were horrid. FM radio was growing rapidly - in audience and in the number of stations. Musical schizophrenia had set in and the hit music charts were all over the scale. According to Billboard Magazine, 1980's top songs included Pink Floyd's *Another Brick In the Wall'*, Kenny Roger's *'Lady'* and Captain and Tennille's *'Do That To Me One More Time.'* The once loyal pop music crowd was now riding barrel-bulls at Gilley's and AM radio could no longer succeed by trying to please everyone.

~

Sharon and I were spending the holidays with our Brittany's at our quail hunting lease near San Antonio when I called in to check on the news about the ratings. I asked Dickie for his thoughts and the sound of his voice said more than his words, *"we'll talk about it when you get back next week."*

Six weeks later, on February 15, 1981, I walked out of the KILT studios for the last time, fifteen years to the day after I had first entered the building in 1966. I drove home and the moment I opened the back door, Sharon could read the look on my face. I embraced my wife. Her strength and confidence in our ability to get through the crisis set the stage for the most successful years of my career.

My emotions were full of contradictions. On the one hand, our wins at KILT had provided more fun and recognition than I could ever have imagined. I had worked with some of the industry's best talents. KILT's success had validated my earlier small market success and offered a unique opportunity to prove my theories about how to reach a mass audience.

Getting fired happens frequently in our business. In fact, there is a level of inherent expectancy and casual acceptance that stalks the weekly trade sheets and the industry's all-knowing rumor mill. The bigger the fall – the more newsworthy it is. I never considered the loss of a person's job as something that could be taken lightly. I occasionally had to fire people but now, I was the one being fired. Its tough both ways. On February 15, 1981 – fifteen years to the day after I first entered the building... I walked out of the KILT studios for the last time.

We were only playing rock and roll records for God's sake, it wasn't brain surgery. But some of us still miss the days when radio was King. Our success and failure was often celebrated by an industry that first created and then replaced its superstars. We were judged by a ratings system we didn't trust; an audience constantly searching for what's new; and by the musical chairs turnover of corporate owners more focused on stock price than in serving a community. Radio made stars of the few who discovered some clever new way to coax an audience to stay tuned for one more quarter hour, but all too often, we overlooked the few who didn't have to give away concert tickets to attract an audience. But most of us would do it again if we had the chance.

~

Station Manager Dickie Rosenfeld always left the building when someone on staff had to be fired, leaving that task to Harry Rogers for sales or to me on the programming side. He was very nervous when he gave me the news. I may hold the distinction of being one of the first he actually fired. After all the success we had shared together, it was apparent that it was not easy for him. Rosenfeld knew, as I knew, that it would have been difficult for me to dismantle the KILT that I had helped create. The FM station would move to country and the AM would continue to air Hudson and Harrigan, the popular morning show we had developed, eventually moving it to FM also. I was also proud that Rick Candea and Beau Weaver, two wonderful talents I had brought to the company would get their shot at programming. I filled a box with a few personal photos, a largemouth bass mount that hung on my office wall and a handful of awards, along with my ever-present *slinky* and stopped by a couple of offices to thank some special friends. The afternoon sun was setting as the car turned east on Lovett for the last time and the day's events started sinking in. I was unemployed for the first time since the age of seventeen.

My contract with KILT required them to continue to pay full salary for six months so long as I did not accept another programming job in the Houston market. That was not in my plans anyway and although I didn't tell them, I was burned out. I also knew that realistically, a forty-year-old rock radio programmer probably needed to find a new line of work. That day would have been really tough had it not been for the positive support of my wife Sharon. She refused to allow either of us to focus on anything except a positive view of the future. My first two calls that afternoon went to my two concert production clients, Louis Messina at Pace Concerts in Houston and Barry Leff with Beaver Productions in New Orleans. They both assured me that they would continue to hire me to produced ads for their tours, but without a studio, without a base, I was still worried. A good friend and former KILT disc jockey, Jay West, had built his own commercial production studio just a few blocks from our home and he offered to rent one of his rooms to me in order to continue producing my commercials.

I believe in a higher power, and I am living proof that this power has perfect timing. One week before my six month severance agreement ended, Bob Chandler, the manager of KENR radio called, out of the blue, and offered me the Program Director's position. I declined the offer but after discussion, agreed to take a consulting position with the station for six months only, at the exact same salary I had received at KILT.

Meanwhile, I rented space from a new office strip center in southwest Houston and hired a studio design firm from Dallas to build two audio suites. With an SBA loan from Texas Commerce Bank for $88,000 - all the money in the world to me at that moment. I ordered equipment and spent evenings and weekends developing the type of company I wanted to be.

~

The certainty of a weekly pay check had actually prevented me from even imagining the possibility of where my talents might lead. It was time to let go, without a safety net, and see just how high the plane could fly. Starting a new business is frightening at any time, but in early 1982, the economy was dismal. Real per capita GDP had dropped by three percent and the unemployment rate peaked at nearly eleven percent. The interest rate on my new SBA loan was a staggering twenty-one percent. According to my banker, the recession was seeing two out of every three new business startups in Houston to fail or default on their loans. I began spending a non-stop string of long days recording commercials for my existing clients, and nights working to build new studios and new clients. Every day brought a new set of setbacks. No one prepared me for delayed deliveries and the boredom of stringing cable or how much fun it was to chase down pops and hums and feedback.

The most successful competitor in the concert advertising business was Superspots in Chicago. The founder, Joe Kelly, had a wonderful voice for such ads and he claimed most of the top promoters in the country as clients. Joe's company was operated much like a traditional recording studio. A producer would create the music track, a writer would write the script and Joe would walk into an announce booth and lay down the voice tracks on a multi-track recorder. The engineer would then mix those elements down to a stereo master which would be duplicated into enough copies to meet the number of radio buys and then shipped to the client. The process took time – far too much time. In my opinion, Superspots had two vulnerable weaknesses. Their ads were too expensive and the company's delivery time to promoters was out of step with two major new developments that were taking place.

Ticketmaster was a revolutionary new ticketing service that -- market by market, was changing the event business. The concert promoter and ticket retailer had previously been required to manually 'scale the house' around a performer's stage and equipment requirements. This then had to be re-configured for each different venue to create adequate sight lines and equipment placement. Only after this laborious process was completed could the hard-copy tickets be printed and then distributed to the various ticket outlets. Because the tickets then had to be divided between the various locations, the best seats might not even be available at your nearest ticket outlet.

With Ticketmaster's revolutionary new model, developed by three Arizona State University students in 1976, the entire process could be accomplished on computer and it took just mere minutes. That meant that seating priorities and availabilities could be quickly determined, allowing the best seats to be equally available at all ticket outlets. It also meant that tickets could go on sale almost immediately.

The other paradigm shift came in the area of delivery. Federal Express, operating out of a drafty airport freight terminal in Memphis, went into a head-to-head battle with the US Postal Service. Fed Ex began building its own jet cargo fleet and offered its own Express Mail service in selected cities. By the early eighties, small and large packages could be delivered -- first to major markets and soon to virtually anywhere in the United States, by the time offices opened the next morning.

Within a year, our little company was creating advertising for seventy-five percent of the major concert tours. Rolling Stones, Led Zepplin, Aerosmith, Paul McCartney, Michael Jackson, Bruce Springsteen, Genesis, Stevie Wonder and Barbara Streisand were just some of the artists whose managers hired us to supply their advertising. The bank loan was paid off in six months! Bill Young Productions had survived.

Best of all, my work was now focused only on the part of radio that had always meant the most to me...the music...the reason I came to this party in the first place.

Epilogue
"IT WAS A VERY GOOD YEAR"

Failure is not terminal; in fact it was a failure that set the stage for my biggest success. I've spent a lot of pages discussing ups and downs and the amazing creative diversity of my radio career, but I still have work to do in other areas of life.

I was not the parent or the husband I had hoped to be. That's a tough admission. It happens often in our business. Somewhere along the way, I came to believe that being a good provider was my primary responsibility. I was wrong. My parents gave me a much more important gift, the gift of their time. It was a lesson I somehow forgot when my work offered such recognition and success.

After all the tremendous highs and the frightening lows, I have come to the realization that the things that really matter are dangerously fragile and can be lost with an unkind word or the failure to simply be present. On our tenth anniversary, I had planned a special dinner with my wife and our best friends at a popular restaurant. At four that afternoon, our largest agency client called and needed to get into the studio to build a demonstration ad for a major client presentation the next morning. When I explained that I could not possibly handle the session, my client emphasized the importance of the project and assured me that it would only take one hour. I gave in. The session ended just after midnight. My wife and our friends all said the right words - *"we understand"* - but a significant moment was lost forever, just like my youngest son's first baseball game, my granddaughter's dance team appearance at the Orange Bowl, and my best friend's last hours. Its part of the story I would change.

My career rewarded me with lots of stuff; lots of friends, national recognition, awards on the wall, nice home, fine cars, and the means to mostly do what I want to do. But there's a hidden cost to all those things. Its called *time* - it vanishes quickly and at some point in our lives, we have to decide how we want to spend that precious gift.

~

It's a gorgeous Sunday afternoon sunset. Amidst the long shadows, a final ray of sunlight has saved its last burst of brilliance for the thousands of tiny, yellow flowers on the Mexican Palo Verde tree that exploded into full color in the front yard this week -- protected now from my pruning sheers by thousands of needle-sharp spines and hundreds of worker bees collecting nectar from the blooms while performing their *'waggle dance'* to communicate with each other.

The contrast is simple. Beauty — Danger! I need that extreme equation to remind me that my fears share the same space as my dreams.

Our life is frittered away by detail.
Simplicity, Simplicity, Simplicity!
Henry David Thoreau (1817-1864)

About the author:

From 1966 to 1981, Bill Young served as Director of Programming for KILT AM/FM-Houston. The station was originally founded by Top 40 radio pioneer Gordon McLendon. Under Young's 15 year leadership, KILT dominated Houston ratings and achieved national acclaim within the radio industry, including recognition as "Radio Station of the Year" and "Program Director of the Year." After radio, his company—BILL YOUNG PRODUCTIONS—became the standard for the touring industry's radio, TV and print advertising. Bill's voice has been featured on world-wide tours for Paul McCartney, Bruce Springsteen, Madonna, U2, Michael Jackson, Barbra Streisand, Sir Michael Crawford, ZZ Top, George Strait and many others. The company he founded—Bill Young Productions—still provides materials for hundreds of tours each year. Bill also directed national television ads and over 100 music videos, once having created ten straight number one music videos on CMT. Bill lives with his wife and Brittany's in Texas.

Comments by others:

"Dead Air" is a true story of how radio was, and how it became what it is today. In a business filled with massive egos, Bill Young was able to keep it all in perspective and remain "real". He never lost touch with the audience and programmed one of the nation's best top 40 radio stations masterfully. Over the years he became one of the most successful program directors in the industry, but he was a genius in the production room, which was his true passion. Bill's perspective of events in the history of radio should be required reading for college communication courses."
    CHUCK DUNAWAY – WABC/ KLIF/WIXY

"Bill Young -- He's not only a tremendously successful business man and elite broadcaster, but one of the finest 'gentle' men I've ever known, for 40+ years now."
    KEN DOWE – Natl. P.D. McLendon Stations

"I never really worked with a mentor, I just studied people that I admired from afar, and there were only two - Bill Drake and Bill Young!"
    SCOTT SHANNON – NAB HOF, Founder of Morning Zoo concept -
    WHTZ-FM New York, KOLZ Los Angels, WPLJ - NYC

"Bill Young showed me that empowerment can raise people to new heights. In an era when programmers are notorious for micromanagement and the totally misnamed 'constructive criticism', we can only hope that Bill Young will soon be cloned. Today's corporate radio could use several dozen Bill Youngs!"
    TOMMY KRAMER – Talent Coach

"Bill may not realize what a profound influence he was to us, not so much by what he said, but how we observed his character in action. The best teachers are like that, doing most of their teaching when unaware that the students are watching—but we were watching."
    BEAU WEAVER – KHJ-KCBQ-KFRC –Voice Actor

"Bill Young reignites memories and adds to the knowledge of those early years when--like a magnet--radio was largely responsible for bringing change to our society."
JOHN ROOK – WLS, KABC, KFI

"Bill Young completed exhaustive research regarding many of radio's grand moments!! I know, because he called or e-mailed me and others many times asking for recollection of certain events. You will enjoy this book written by a true radio broadcaster/legend."
KENT BURKHART – Owner, Consultant, NAB 'Legend'

"The Rise and Demise of Music Radio is a fascinating subject for a huge audience. I have never read anything described in such articulate and affectionate detail."
CHUCK BLORE – over 500 industry awards.

"This is a wonderful book! Dead Air will educate those who think satellite is the only history of radio."
RON ALEXENBERG – Prof of Music Marketing @ NYU

"Best production person in the universe! Bill Young is one of the few radio heroes that I grew up trying to copy. If Bill reads this, thanks for the inspiration."
TOM BIGBY – CBS VP (WIP, WNEW, KLUV)

"Bill quietly led, inspired, and attracted people who wanted to be their best."
JOHN YOUNG – WMAK, KILT, CNN, Georgia Radio Hall of Fame

"Bill Young has been to the mountain and not only knows how great radio can be, but is a reason for it's greatness."
SONNY MELENDREZ – Billboard "Personality of the Year" KTSA, KMPC, sonnyradio.com

Works Cited and Background Research Resources

Freeberg, Stan. Does Anybody Here Remember Radio "Freberg Undeground" Capitol Records T/ST-2551, 1966 reissued on SM-2551

Penniman, Richard & Dorthy LaBostrie -- Tootie Frutti "ah wop-bob-a-lu-mop..." - © 1955 Sony/ATV Songs LLC

American Public Radio. Hearing America-A Century of Music on the Radio http://americanradioworks.publicradio.org/features/radio/c1.html." Bob Dylan has said he owes much of his musical inspiration to listening to WLAC as a young teenager"

Johnson, Bradley. Advertising Age, January 10, 1994 "Ten Year's After The commercial that changed advertising" "Chiat/Day Inc.

Colliano, Jerry Del. Inside Music Media May 1, 2009 "Apple may be the only communications company that gets it..."

Irwin, Richard W. www.reelradio.com "so *what if you lose a point to your competitor...*"

Lefzetz, Bob. Lefzetz Letter "the *primary ticket buyer is no longer a fan*"

Mindlin, Alex. New York Times Business Section "Radio's Popularity Declining Unevenly" (June 9, 2008) "*Over the last 10 years, the average share of Americans listening to radio-has shrunk*" –

Azoff, Irving. PC Magazine 5.27.09 "*recorded music has become more of a marketing tool than a revenue source*"

Enders Analysis. "Music Downloads Don't Offset CD Sales Slump" http://www.marketingcharts.com/topics/entertainment/music-downloads-dont-offset-cd-sales-slump-281/

Christman, Ed Billboard.Biz.com 6/24/10 "Album Sales Plummet to Lowest Total in Decades"

Kafka, Peter. Business Insider SAI 8-18-2008"*Walmart Phasing out Music Sales..*" 8/18/08

McLuhan, Marshall. Understanding Media: The Extensions of Man Originally published, 1964 by Mentor, New York; reissued 1994,MIT Press, Cambridge, Mass.

Nilssen, Tore & Lars Sorgard. SBF Report No.3/00 "Flushometer"

Hoffman, Abby '..No greater high than challenging the power structure;;. -- *Soon to Be a Major Motion Picture* (1980, Perigee)

Nightingale, Earl. The Winner's Notebook -Keyes Publishing "You'll find bordedom where there is a lack of a good idea".

Oshinsky, David M. "Polio, an American Story" The progression of Poliomyelitis and "The March of Dimes" organization - 2006 Pulitzer Prize in History

Edward R. Murroww – CBS Radio "This is London" - my knees should have been strong enough..." Broadcast World War II –p

Internment of "Foreign Enemy Ancestry" http:// enwikipedia.org / wiki/Executive_Order_9066 or *Documents from the National Archives: Internment of Japanese Americans [Dubuque, Iowa: Kendall/Hunt Publishing Company, 1989]* –

U.S. Census Bureau "Oldest Baby Boomers turn sixty" --from 1946 to 1964, seventy-six million American children were born! Jan 3, 2006 -

Petigny, Alan. Illegitimacy, Postwar Psychology, and the Reperiodization of the Sexual Revolution -Journal of Social History - Volume 38, Number 1, Fall 2004, -

Bennard, George "The Old Rugged Cross" published 1915 "

Newton, John "Amazing Grace" First appeared in Newton's Olney Hymns (1779)

Roy Rogers Rider's Club Rules "Be Neat and clean..."

http://www.royrogers.com/happy_trails-index.html

McLuhan, Marshall Live appearance at Radio & Records Conference in Dallas, 1977 "...this speed-up of information is insanity" from authors recollection.

Steyer, James P. "The Other Parent" 2003 Simon & Shuster

Phyllis Schlafly – 'America's children: Addicted to blood" World Net Daily - Sept. 08, 2010

Weaver , Andrew J. & Barbara J. Wilson - The Role of Graphic and Sanitized Violence in the Enjoyment of Television Dramas © 2009 International Communication Association June 5, 2009

Kortchmar, Danny & Don Henley Don – "Dirty Laundry" Publisher Woody Creek Music/WB Music Corp. 1982

Crudup, Arthur "That's All Right Mama" Publisher unkown, written and originally performed by Crudup 1946.

Ballard, Hank "Work With Me Annie" 1954 "Published by Ft.Knox Music, BMI

Freedman, Max C. & James E. Myers, "Rock Around the Clock" 1952

Author Unknown "Yellow Rose of Texas" Original Publisher "Firth, Pond & Co" Center for American History has unpublished version dated 1836

Gibson, Walter B, Antonie Domino and Dave Bartholomew "Ain't That a Shame" released 1955

Street & Smith, "The Shadow" -Mutual Broadcast System 1937-1954 "evil that lurks in the minds of men."

Fuqua, Harvey & Alan Freed - "Sincerely" Universal Music Publishing 1954

Hammer, Jack & Otis Blackwell - "Great Balls of Fire" @1957 (renewed)Unichappell Music Inc., Mijac Music, Chappell & Co. and Mystical Light Music.

Young, Bill "Chocolate Pie @ The Elite Downtown" © 1999

Lee, Robert G. © (1886-1974) "Payday Someday" @1957 Zondervan Copyright 1957

Rousseau, Jean-Jacques (1820-1905) "Days of Absence" Familiar Quotations 10th Ed 1919 Alpha-1 Foundation http://www.alphaone.org/

Hall, C.R. This Business of Radio Programming "..a top 40 station where a very young Bill Young was programming.."

Berry, Charles Edward & Chuck Anderson - "Reelin' & Rockin" Isalee Music Publishing co./Arc Music Corp 1958

Whitney, Bob Radio Odyssey "a slice of bygone top forty" http://www.yubatube.com/ourradiosite/kbox-hotdamn/

Francisco, Ruth-The Secret Memoirs of Jacqueline Kennedy Onassis: a novel by Ruth Francisco "headed into nut country"

KLIF Radio, Dallas, Tx 11/22/1963 Gary Delaune "This KLIF bulletin from Dallas:Three shots fired at the motorcade"

Associated Press 11/22/63 "Dallas AP-President Kennedy was shot today as his motorcade..."

McLendon, Gordon, KLIF Radio, Dallas,Tx 11/22/1963 "The President is clearly--critically and perhaps fatally wounded"

Plutchik, Robert "The Nature of Emotions" "the relationship between opposites" American Scientist, July/August 2001

Weaver, Bill - "Triple Double Cross" Halcyon Press-the Radio Nord project" --

Baumgartner, Chris "Music Matters" quoted in "Music Biz Environmentalism: Greening or Preening?" LeMonde.fr 2008,

Keyes, Don "Gordon McLendon & Me" CD-2 *Ceilo was to Gordon what the corporate jet was to others*" ©2005

Exodus 20:15 *Thou shalt not steal*" The Ten Commandments (ancient Hebrew scripture) King James Version

Marsh, Dave "Louie Louie-New York: Hyperion, 1993 "Sex is Bad, and somebody singing about it would be really bad."

Martin, Linda & Kerry Segrave, "Anti-Rock: The Opposition to Rock n Roll" Da CapoPress, 1993 "..hippies know.."

Billboard Magazine, May 20, 1967 -- McLendon, Gordon "..we've had all we can stand of the record industry's glorifying marijuana, LSD and sexual activity"

Gore, Mary Elizabeth -Raising Pg Kids in X-Rated Society- "as parents and as consumers, we have the right and the power to pressure the entertainment industry.." Sept 1988– Bantom Pg 278

Flynt, Larry – Senate Commerce Comm--PMRC Hearings 9.19.1985 called r "cultural terrorist"

Zappa, Frank – Senate Commerce Committee-PMRC Hearings 9.19.1985 "bad facts make bad law"

Cockburn, Alexander, The Nation-Oct 2, 2000 "The Gores' Culture Wars" "industry has six months to clean up.."

Bellamy, David "If I Said You Had a Beautiful Body' Famous Music Corp./Bellamy Brothers Music

American Academy of Pediatrics "American Academy of Pediatrics (Vol.124 No.5 11 2009) Impact of Music, Lyrics and Music Videos on Children and Youth"

<http://pediatrics.aappublications.org/cgi/content/full/pediatrics;124/5/1488> (2009)

Barry, John & Don Black, "Born Free" 1966 (Winner Academy Award) Sony/ATV Music Publishing LLC

Laertius, Giogenes 3rd Century Greek philosopher-"nothing permanent except change'

McLean, Don –"day the music died" American Pie -- Don McLean United Artists UAS-5535 released October 1971

Dylan, Bob "The Times, They Are a-Changin" 10/24/63-Columbia Studios. Written by Bob Dylan, Prod Tom Wilson

Slick, Darby & Slick, Grace – Somebody To Love "When the truth is found..."

Fong-Torres, Ben – "The Hits Just Keep on Coming" "KLIF wishes to offer this apology..."

Perry , Nancy J. "How to Conquer Fear of Flying" Fortune Magazine "most creative types are neurotic" October 18, 1993

MacFarland, David T. – Future Radio Programming Strategies – Lawrence Erlbaum Inc 1997"

Fong-Torres, Ben – "The Hits Just Keep on Coming" "By the time the founders of Top 40..."

Broadcasting/Telecasting Magazine April, 1953 full-page ad for KOWH, Omaha "America's most listened to radio station" Hooper, Oct. 1951, thru Feb. 1955

Hall, Claude --Billboard Magazine interview of Bill Stewart, part 2, January 5, 1973.

Fisher, Marc "Something in the Air" Randon House @2007 "The lessons of top forty ... was beginning to seep in..."

Perry, Nancy J with associate Ricardo Sookdeo "How to Conquer Fear Of Flying" Fortune Magazine October 18, 1993

http://gocalipso.com/aircraft/boeing747/facts.php-"six million parts', 170 miles of wiring"

Connell, Bud – Interview with author - September, 2009 "...by this time, no one even knew where it came from"

Variety, March 10, 1922 "Radio Sweeping Country, 1 million sets in use"

Garay, Ronald "Gordon McLendon:The Maverick of Radio" "...intent to transfer the flagship.."

http://1650oldiesradio.com "Gordon set the earliest Top 40 arrival date as 1952 ..

http://1650oldiesradio.com/pgone.html "History of KLIF" "The real catalyst in the development of a true Top 40..."

Garay, Ronald "Gordon McLendon:The Maverick of Radio" *"plan your next vacation for.. Tanganyika"*.

Storz Station's Promotional Document--"Hooper Record of the Storz Stations", Document provided by Kent Burkhart

Time Magazine (author unknown) "SHOW BUSINESS: King of Giveaway" June 4, 1956 - http://www.time.com/time/magazine/ article/0,9171,866997,00.html

1650oldiesradio.com/pgone.html Don Keyes quote "...from his earler association with Todd Storz .."

Garay, Ronald "Gordon McLendon:The Maverick of Radio" "..transfer the flagship operations of Liberty.."

Fartherly, Richard "Radio's Revolution" *"the bar room is a mythology"*

Broadcasting-Telecasting magazine, April 13, 1953 "All It Took was Something Extra" KOWH full page ad

Chase, Sam, Billboard Magazine June 1, 1959 "rumors...of Stewart's departure to become VP.of the Metropolitan Broadcasting Company".

Encyclopedia of Radio (The Museum of Broadcast Communications)-Volume 3 O-Z – Editor Christopher H. Sterling, Consulting Editor Michael C. Keith "Variety *described the convention as a "drunken orgy"*

Brown, Dan (Miami Herald) June 5,1959 "an orgy of Booze, Broads and Bribes"

Fong-Torres, Ben "The Hits Just Keep on Coming' "Bill Stewart has been mentioned..he hasn't been mentioned enough"

Shannon, Bob "Legends" Ken Dowe interviews "Bill Stewart had his demons..but the man knew his business" Radio & Records" 8.17.01

Eberhart, Steve "History of KLIF Radio" http://1650oldiesradio.com"...the catalyst that made KLIF's initial success.."

Dallas Morning News Obituary - December 6, 1985 "Bill Stewart "

United Press International – December 6, 1985 "Gordon Mclendon...was in critical condition..."

Kennedy, Ray – Ft Worth Star Telegram 1988 *"..generally barge into your living room like a belligerent drunk!"*

http://en.wikipedia.org/wiki/Shock_jock "The shock jock movement was blossoming in markets around the country"

Cornell University Law School- TITLE 47 > CHAPTER 5 > SUBCHAPTER III > Part I > § 317 U.S. Code S317.Announcement of payment for broadcast

McShane, Larry – Associated Press 4.13.07 "economics often trumps emotion in an anything-goes business"

Thompson, Helen "Radio Foreplay" Texas Monthly - November 1992

Manzarek, Ray Robby Krieger, John Densmore, Spoken word lyrics by Jim Morrison, "The WASP"

Hoffman, Ken Hudson & Harrigan: Is their reign on the wane? Houston Chronicle, Aug 2, 1995

Karshner, Roger "The Music Machine" Nash Publishing (1st edition 1974)"..what really goes on in the music industry"

Anderson, Jack "Payola Returns to Record Industry" March 31, 1972

Kosar, Devin "Payola-Can Pay-For-Play Be Practically Enforced? Kosar Publication 1/25/2008 - http://www.stjohns.edu/media/3/42ed3f6559154193ad790c6a4f388562.pdf

R. Serge Denisonn – Solid gold: the popular record industry *"Let the Journalsts of CBS News cover the Story of CBS Records"*

Phillips, Chuck "Clear Channel Fined Just $8,000 for Payola Violation", Los Angeles Times, October 20, 2000

von Goeth, Johann Wolfgang (1749-1832) "Only a Creature as highly developed as man is capable of boredom"

Webb, Jimmy 1968 'MacArthur Park', "Someone left the cake out in the rain..." Canopy Music, Inc.1973

King, Larry & Peter Masterson, (Book)- "The Best Little Whorehouse in Texas", Story by Larry L. King, Music and Lyrics by Carole King, Directed by Peter Masterson and Tommy Tune.

UCLA Law & Columbia Law School - ZZ Top v. Chrysler Corp. -54 F. Supp. 2d 983 (W.D. Wa. 1999)

http://cip.law.ucla.edu/cases/case _zztopchryslercorp.html

Wheeler, Elmer 1937 Tested Sentences That Sell (pg 811) "don't sell the steak, sell the sizzle"

Porter, Cole 1937 "In the Still of The Night" CHAPPEL & CO. Publisher

Becker, Walter and Donald Fagen – FM (No Static at All) Steely Dan from –soundtrack of "FM" ©1978

Dunaway, Chuck "The Way I Saw it"

Bonfire, Mars 1968 ©MCA Music (BMI) "Born to be Wild"

Gordon, Lori Heyman & Jon Frandsen "Love is a feeling, Marriage is a contract..." Passage to Intimacy Publisher: Fireside; Revised edition (April 1, 2001)

Maltz, Dr Maxwell – "The Science of Psycho-Cybernetics"—"what we believe about our self-image'

Abrams, Lee 7.1.2007 (http://leeabrams.blogspot.com/2006_07_01_archive.html) "...

Kavanagh, Barry "hero's were not necessarily good" The Alan Moore Interview: Ideas, Entities and Aleister Crowly"

LaBarge, Scott 2 - 005 Santa Clara Univ. Markkula Center for Applied Ethics-http://www.scu.edu/ethics/publications/ethicsoutlook/ 2005/heroes.html

Crowley, Aleister --The Alan Moore Interview: Ideas, entities and Aleister Crowly —Oct.17, 2000 "If you're going to be doing something new.."

Thoreau, Henry David (1817-1862) "Our *Life is frittered away by detail*" Walden–Orignally published by Ticknor and Fields: Boston Publication date 1854

Made in the USA
Lexington, KY
27 April 2014